C-3508 CAREER EXAMINATION SERIES

This is your
PASSBOOK for...

Court Officer Sergeant

Test Preparation Study Guide
Questions & Answers

NATIONAL LEARNING CORPORATION®

COPYRIGHT NOTICE

This book is SOLELY intended for, is sold ONLY to, and its use is RESTRICTED to individual, bona fide applicants or candidates who qualify by virtue of having seriously filed applications for appropriate license, certificate, professional and/or promotional advancement, higher school matriculation, scholarship, or other legitimate requirements of education and/or governmental authorities.

This book is NOT intended for use, class instruction, tutoring, training, duplication, copying, reprinting, excerption, or adaptation, etc., by:

1) Other publishers
2) Proprietors and/or Instructors of "Coaching" and/or Preparatory Courses
3) Personnel and/or Training Divisions of commercial, industrial, and governmental organizations
4) Schools, colleges, or universities and/or their departments and staffs, including teachers and other personnel
5) Testing Agencies or Bureaus
6) Study groups which seek by the purchase of a single volume to copy and/or duplicate and/or adapt this material for use by the group as a whole without having purchased individual volumes for each of the members of the group
7) Et al.

Such persons would be in violation of appropriate Federal and State statutes.

PROVISION OF LICENSING AGREEMENTS – Recognized educational, commercial, industrial, and governmental institutions and organizations, and others legitimately engaged in educational pursuits, including training, testing, and measurement activities, may address request for a licensing agreement to the copyright owners, who will determine whether, and under what conditions, including fees and charges, the materials in this book may be used them. In other words, a licensing facility exists for the legitimate use of the material in this book on other than an individual basis. However, it is asseverated and affirmed here that the material in this book CANNOT be used without the receipt of the express permission of such a licensing agreement from the Publishers. Inquiries re licensing should be addressed to the company, attention rights and permissions department.

All rights reserved, including the right of reproduction in whole or in part, in any form or by any means, electronic or mechanical, including photocopying, recording, or by any information storage and retrieval system, without permission in writing from the Publisher.

Copyright © 2024 by
National Learning Corporation

212 Michael Drive, Syosset, NY 11791
(516) 921-8888 • www.passbooks.com
E-mail: info@passbooks.com

PUBLISHED IN THE UNITED STATES OF AMERICA

PASSBOOK® SERIES

THE *PASSBOOK® SERIES* has been created to prepare applicants and candidates for the ultimate academic battlefield – the examination room.

At some time in our lives, each and every one of us may be required to take an examination – for validation, matriculation, admission, qualification, registration, certification, or licensure.

Based on the assumption that every applicant or candidate has met the basic formal educational standards, has taken the required number of courses, and read the necessary texts, the *PASSBOOK® SERIES* furnishes the one special preparation which may assure passing with confidence, instead of failing with insecurity. Examination questions – together with answers – are furnished as the basic vehicle for study so that the mysteries of the examination and its compounding difficulties may be eliminated or diminished by a sure method.

This book is meant to help you pass your examination provided that you qualify and are serious in your objective.

The entire field is reviewed through the huge store of content information which is succinctly presented through a provocative and challenging approach – the question-and-answer method.

A climate of success is established by furnishing the correct answers at the end of each test.

You soon learn to recognize types of questions, forms of questions, and patterns of questioning. You may even begin to anticipate expected outcomes.

You perceive that many questions are repeated or adapted so that you can gain acute insights, which may enable you to score many sure points.

You learn how to confront new questions, or types of questions, and to attack them confidently and work out the correct answers.

You note objectives and emphases, and recognize pitfalls and dangers, so that you may make positive educational adjustments.

Moreover, you are kept fully informed in relation to new concepts, methods, practices, and directions in the field.

You discover that you are actually taking the examination all the time: you are preparing for the examination by "taking" an examination, not by reading extraneous and/or supererogatory textbooks.

In short, this PASSBOOK®, used directedly, should be an important factor in helping you to pass your test.

COURT OFFICER-SERGEANT

DUTIES

Under the direct supervision of a Court Officer-Lieutenant, or other security supervisory personnel, Court Officer-Sergeants are assigned to all trial courts and court agencies where they maintain order and provide security in courtrooms, court buildings, and grounds, and coordinate the activities of court security personnel in the area to which they are assigned. When assigned to a courtroom, Court Officer-Sergeants are responsible to the presiding judge and function as the courtroom security supervisor. Court Officer-Sergeants are responsible for on-the-job training of Court Officer-Trainees. Court Officer-Sergeants are responsible for the evaluation of Court Officer-Trainees and Court Officers. Court Officer-Sergeants are peace officers, required to wear uniforms and may be authorized to carry firearms. They execute bench warrants, make arrests and also perform administrative and other related duties.

EXAMPLES OF TYPICAL TASKS

Assigns and deploys security personnel to posts within area of responsibility to ensure adequate staffing and advises supervisory security personnel of a change in status of the area; provides training for Court Officer-Trainees and Court Officers; evaluates the performance of Court Officer-Trainees and Court Officers, correcting and improving job performance; instructs court officers by explaining specific duties and responsibilities, paperwork requirements, demonstrating physical techniques, and other aspects of performance; provides security in the courtroom and throughout court facilities and offices; assumes a post or patrols the courthouse and maintains order by removing or calming disruptive individuals; guards criminal defendants accused of both misdemeanors and felonies while in the courtroom and may escort them to and from detention pens; physically restrains, removes or arrests persons causing or attempting to cause disturbances; uses established search procedures to ensure that no electronic or photographic equipment, nor weapons, are brought into the courtroom or courthouse; conducts security screening procedures, including the use of electronic scanning devices and x-ray systems to detect concealed weapons; assumes lead role in securing arrangements for juror meals, lodging, and transportation; contacts jurors' families or place of employment when jury is sequestered overnight; supervises jurors' contact with family, public, media and other jurors; escorts and transports judges, jurors, witnesses, prisoners and others; accepts and safeguards exhibits that have been marked and stores them in accordance with established court procedures; guards evidence in jury possession; returns evidence to storage area; assigns calendar number on case jacket and places in file for part clerk; listens for case/calendar number and retrieves appropriate files; notes records; stamps and dates all papers received; checks bench to ensure that Judge has adequate supplies, proper forms, and other materials; checks prior to court sessions to ensure that all documents are organized according to established court procedures and available to the court; displays and safeguards exhibits in the courtroom; prepares and maintains records of current assignments; distributes and posts court calendars, court materials and other appropriate documents; provides assistance and assumes other appropriate responsibilities in emergency situations; administers first-aid and assistance to individuals during emergencies, accidents or illnesses; checks emergency or special equipment to ensure that the equipment is in working condition; reports inoperative equipment to supervisor; prepares and submits to supervisor written reports concerning incidents, unusual occurrences, requests for time or leave, hazardous situations, workers' compensation and injuries; provides general information to visitors on court premises; checks with presiding Judge about courtroom procedures; opens court by making opening statement and calls parties into courtrooms according to established procedures; sets up stations, microphones, flip charts, etc. in appropriate locations of courtroom; photocopies documents when needed; and performs clerical functions as directed.

SCOPE OF THE EXAMINATION
The written test will cover knowledge, skills and abilities in such areas as: Criminal Procedure Law, Penal Law, and Court Officer Rules and Procedures Manual; preparation and review of incident reports; rights of visitors, prisoners, defendants, attorneys, and police officers; search, arrest, and "use of force" guidelines and procedures; job functions, responsibilities, and standards of Court Officers and Court Officer-Trainees; procedures for communicating with court-related agencies; proper operation/use of radio communications, security equipment, and security screening operations (e.g., handcuffs, batons, magnetometer, and hand scanners); general courtroom terminology, trial procedures, and procedures for handling prisoners; rules and procedures for the possession, control, use, registration, inspection, and safeguarding of firearms; basic first aid, Cardiopulmonary Resuscitation (CPR) and Automated External Defibrillator (AED) procedures, including using and reporting requirements; prescribed uniform and equipment regulations; procedures for handling emergency responses in situations such as fires, aided cases (including, but not limited to, a sick or injured person, a mentally ill or emotionally disturbed person, a lost person, a neglected, abandoned, destitute or abused child, or a maternity case), bomb threats, hostage situations, crowd control, and hazardous materials; facility lock-down and building evacuation procedures; procedures for receiving, handling, storing, retrieving and disposing evidence in the courtroom; the Incident Command System (ICS); strength, muscular endurance, and stamina; arm-hand steadiness; observing one's surroundings using near and far vision; planning and coordinating the proper assignment of personnel and the appropriate allocation of resources for specific parts of the court; expressing ideas clearly both orally and in written format; recognizing and evaluating situations, events, and conditions related to observable ongoing activities; observing subordinates' job performance and addressing concerns through training and feedback; exercising judgment and developing alternative courses of action based on logical assumptions and factual information; handling conflict situations; demonstrating the operation of new equipment and participating in the training of subordinates.

HOW TO TAKE A TEST

I. YOU MUST PASS AN EXAMINATION

A. WHAT EVERY CANDIDATE SHOULD KNOW

Examination applicants often ask us for help in preparing for the written test. What can I study in advance? What kinds of questions will be asked? How will the test be given? How will the papers be graded?

As an applicant for a civil service examination, you may be wondering about some of these things. Our purpose here is to suggest effective methods of advance study and to describe civil service examinations.

Your chances for success on this examination can be increased if you know how to prepare. Those "pre-examination jitters" can be reduced if you know what to expect. You can even experience an adventure in good citizenship if you know why civil service exams are given.

B. WHY ARE CIVIL SERVICE EXAMINATIONS GIVEN?

Civil service examinations are important to you in two ways. As a citizen, you want public jobs filled by employees who know how to do their work. As a job seeker, you want a fair chance to compete for that job on an equal footing with other candidates. The best-known means of accomplishing this two-fold goal is the competitive examination.

Exams are widely publicized throughout the nation. They may be administered for jobs in federal, state, city, municipal, town or village governments or agencies.

Any citizen may apply, with some limitations, such as the age or residence of applicants. Your experience and education may be reviewed to see whether you meet the requirements for the particular examination. When these requirements exist, they are reasonable and applied consistently to all applicants. Thus, a competitive examination may cause you some uneasiness now, but it is your privilege and safeguard.

C. HOW ARE CIVIL SERVICE EXAMS DEVELOPED?

Examinations are carefully written by trained technicians who are specialists in the field known as "psychological measurement," in consultation with recognized authorities in the field of work that the test will cover. These experts recommend the subject matter areas or skills to be tested; only those knowledges or skills important to your success on the job are included. The most reliable books and source materials available are used as references. Together, the experts and technicians judge the difficulty level of the questions.

Test technicians know how to phrase questions so that the problem is clearly stated. Their ethics do not permit "trick" or "catch" questions. Questions may have been tried out on sample groups, or subjected to statistical analysis, to determine their usefulness.

Written tests are often used in combination with performance tests, ratings of training and experience, and oral interviews. All of these measures combine to form the best-known means of finding the right person for the right job.

II. HOW TO PASS THE WRITTEN TEST

A. NATURE OF THE EXAMINATION

To prepare intelligently for civil service examinations, you should know how they differ from school examinations you have taken. In school you were assigned certain definite pages to read or subjects to cover. The examination questions were quite detailed and usually emphasized memory. Civil service exams, on the other hand, try to discover your present ability to perform the duties of a position, plus your potentiality to learn these duties. In other words, a civil service exam attempts to predict how successful you will be. Questions cover such a broad area that they cannot be as minute and detailed as school exam questions.

In the public service similar kinds of work, or positions, are grouped together in one "class." This process is known as *position-classification*. All the positions in a class are paid according to the salary range for that class. One class title covers all of these positions, and they are all tested by the same examination.

B. FOUR BASIC STEPS

1) Study the announcement

How, then, can you know what subjects to study? Our best answer is: "Learn as much as possible about the class of positions for which you've applied." The exam will test the knowledge, skills and abilities needed to do the work.

Your most valuable source of information about the position you want is the official exam announcement. This announcement lists the training and experience qualifications. Check these standards and apply only if you come reasonably close to meeting them.

The brief description of the position in the examination announcement offers some clues to the subjects which will be tested. Think about the job itself. Review the duties in your mind. Can you perform them, or are there some in which you are rusty? Fill in the blank spots in your preparation.

Many jurisdictions preview the written test in the exam announcement by including a section called "Knowledge and Abilities Required," "Scope of the Examination," or some similar heading. Here you will find out specifically what fields will be tested.

2) Review your own background

Once you learn in general what the position is all about, and what you need to know to do the work, ask yourself which subjects you already know fairly well and which need improvement. You may wonder whether to concentrate on improving your strong areas or on building some background in your fields of weakness. When the announcement has specified "some knowledge" or "considerable knowledge," or has used adjectives like "beginning principles of..." or "advanced ... methods," you can get a clue as to the number and difficulty of questions to be asked in any given field. More questions, and hence broader coverage, would be included for those subjects which are more important in the work. Now weigh your strengths and weaknesses against the job requirements and prepare accordingly.

3) Determine the level of the position

Another way to tell how intensively you should prepare is to understand the level of the job for which you are applying. Is it the entering level? In other words, is this the position in which beginners in a field of work are hired? Or is it an intermediate or advanced level? Sometimes this is indicated by such words as "Junior" or "Senior" in the class title. Other jurisdictions use Roman numerals to designate the level – Clerk I, Clerk II, for example. The word "Supervisor" sometimes appears in the title. If the level is not indicated by the title, check the description of duties. Will you be working under very close supervision, or will you have responsibility for independent decisions in this work?

4) Choose appropriate study materials

Now that you know the subjects to be examined and the relative amount of each subject to be covered, you can choose suitable study materials. For beginning level jobs, or even advanced ones, if you have a pronounced weakness in some aspect of your training, read a modern, standard textbook in that field. Be sure it is up to date and has general coverage. Such books are normally available at your library, and the librarian will be glad to help you locate one. For entry-level positions, questions of appropriate difficulty are chosen -- neither highly advanced questions, nor those too simple. Such questions require careful thought but not advanced training.

If the position for which you are applying is technical or advanced, you will read more advanced, specialized material. If you are already familiar with the basic principles of your field, elementary textbooks would waste your time. Concentrate on advanced textbooks and technical periodicals. Think through the concepts and review difficult problems in your field.

These are all general sources. You can get more ideas on your own initiative, following these leads. For example, training manuals and publications of the government agency which employs workers in your field can be useful, particularly for technical and professional positions. A letter or visit to the government department involved may result in more specific study suggestions, and certainly will provide you with a more definite idea of the exact nature of the position you are seeking.

III. KINDS OF TESTS

Tests are used for purposes other than measuring knowledge and ability to perform specified duties. For some positions, it is equally important to test ability to make adjustments to new situations or to profit from training. In others, basic mental abilities not dependent on information are essential. Questions which test these things may not appear as pertinent to the duties of the position as those which test for knowledge and information. Yet they are often highly important parts of a fair examination. For very general questions, it is almost impossible to help you direct your study efforts. What we can do is to point out some of the more common of these general abilities needed in public service positions and describe some typical questions.

1) General information

Broad, general information has been found useful for predicting job success in some kinds of work. This is tested in a variety of ways, from vocabulary lists to questions about current events. Basic background in some field of work, such as sociology or economics, may be sampled in a group of questions. Often these are principles which have become familiar to most persons through exposure rather than through formal training. It is difficult to advise you how to study for these questions; being alert to the world around you is our best suggestion.

2) Verbal ability

An example of an ability needed in many positions is verbal or language ability. Verbal ability is, in brief, the ability to use and understand words. Vocabulary and grammar tests are typical measures of this ability. Reading comprehension or paragraph interpretation questions are common in many kinds of civil service tests. You are given a paragraph of written material and asked to find its central meaning.

3) Numerical ability

Number skills can be tested by the familiar arithmetic problem, by checking paired lists of numbers to see which are alike and which are different, or by interpreting charts and graphs. In the latter test, a graph may be printed in the test booklet which you are asked to use as the basis for answering questions.

4) Observation

A popular test for law-enforcement positions is the observation test. A picture is shown to you for several minutes, then taken away. Questions about the picture test your ability to observe both details and larger elements.

5) Following directions

In many positions in the public service, the employee must be able to carry out written instructions dependably and accurately. You may be given a chart with several columns, each column listing a variety of information. The questions require you to carry out directions involving the information given in the chart.

6) Skills and aptitudes

Performance tests effectively measure some manual skills and aptitudes. When the skill is one in which you are trained, such as typing or shorthand, you can practice. These tests are often very much like those given in business school or high school courses. For many of the other skills and aptitudes, however, no short-time preparation can be made. Skills and abilities natural to you or that you have developed throughout your lifetime are being tested.

Many of the general questions just described provide all the data needed to answer the questions and ask you to use your reasoning ability to find the answers. Your best preparation for these tests, as well as for tests of facts and ideas, is to be at your physical and mental best. You, no doubt, have your own methods of getting into an exam-taking mood and keeping "in shape." The next section lists some ideas on this subject.

IV. KINDS OF QUESTIONS

Only rarely is the "essay" question, which you answer in narrative form, used in civil service tests. Civil service tests are usually of the short-answer type. Full instructions for answering these questions will be given to you at the examination. But in case this is your first experience with short-answer questions and separate answer sheets, here is what you need to know:

1) Multiple-choice Questions

Most popular of the short-answer questions is the "multiple choice" or "best answer" question. It can be used, for example, to test for factual knowledge, ability to solve problems or judgment in meeting situations found at work.

A multiple-choice question is normally one of three types—
- It can begin with an incomplete statement followed by several possible endings. You are to find the one ending which *best* completes the statement, although some of the others may not be entirely wrong.
- It can also be a complete statement in the form of a question which is answered by choosing one of the statements listed.

- It can be in the form of a problem – again you select the best answer.

Here is an example of a multiple-choice question with a discussion which should give you some clues as to the method for choosing the right answer:

When an employee has a complaint about his assignment, the action which will *best* help him overcome his difficulty is to
- A. discuss his difficulty with his coworkers
- B. take the problem to the head of the organization
- C. take the problem to the person who gave him the assignment
- D. say nothing to anyone about his complaint

In answering this question, you should study each of the choices to find which is best. Consider choice "A" – Certainly an employee may discuss his complaint with fellow employees, but no change or improvement can result, and the complaint remains unresolved. Choice "B" is a poor choice since the head of the organization probably does not know what assignment you have been given, and taking your problem to him is known as "going over the head" of the supervisor. The supervisor, or person who made the assignment, is the person who can clarify it or correct any injustice. Choice "C" is, therefore, correct. To say nothing, as in choice "D," is unwise. Supervisors have and interest in knowing the problems employees are facing, and the employee is seeking a solution to his problem.

2) True/False Questions

The "true/false" or "right/wrong" form of question is sometimes used. Here a complete statement is given. Your job is to decide whether the statement is right or wrong.

SAMPLE: A roaming cell-phone call to a nearby city costs less than a non-roaming call to a distant city.

This statement is wrong, or false, since roaming calls are more expensive.

This is not a complete list of all possible question forms, although most of the others are variations of these common types. You will always get complete directions for answering questions. Be sure you understand *how* to mark your answers – ask questions until you do.

V. RECORDING YOUR ANSWERS

Computer terminals are used more and more today for many different kinds of exams. For an examination with very few applicants, you may be told to record your answers in the test booklet itself. Separate answer sheets are much more common. If this separate answer sheet is to be scored by machine – and this is often the case – it is highly important that you mark your answers correctly in order to get credit.

An electronic scoring machine is often used in civil service offices because of the speed with which papers can be scored. Machine-scored answer sheets must be marked with a pencil, which will be given to you. This pencil has a high graphite content which responds to the electronic scoring machine. As a matter of fact, stray dots may register as answers, so do not let your pencil rest on the answer sheet while you are pondering the correct answer. Also, if your pencil lead breaks or is otherwise defective, ask for another.

Since the answer sheet will be dropped in a slot in the scoring machine, be careful not to bend the corners or get the paper crumpled.

The answer sheet normally has five vertical columns of numbers, with 30 numbers to a column. These numbers correspond to the question numbers in your test booklet. After each number, going across the page are four or five pairs of dotted lines. These short dotted lines have small letters or numbers above them. The first two pairs may also have a "T" or "F" above the letters. This indicates that the first two pairs only are to be used if the questions are of the true-false type. If the questions are multiple choice, disregard the "T" and "F" and pay attention only to the small letters or numbers.

Answer your questions in the manner of the sample that follows:

32. The largest city in the United States is
    A. Washington, D.C.
    B. New York City
    C. Chicago
    D. Detroit
    E. San Francisco

1) Choose the answer you think is best. (New York City is the largest, so "B" is correct.)
2) Find the row of dotted lines numbered the same as the question you are answering. (Find row number 32)
3) Find the pair of dotted lines corresponding to the answer. (Find the pair of lines under the mark "B.")
4) Make a solid black mark between the dotted lines.

VI. BEFORE THE TEST

Common sense will help you find procedures to follow to get ready for an examination. Too many of us, however, overlook these sensible measures. Indeed, nervousness and fatigue have been found to be the most serious reasons why applicants fail to do their best on civil service tests. Here is a list of reminders:

- Begin your preparation early – Don't wait until the last minute to go scurrying around for books and materials or to find out what the position is all about.
- Prepare continuously – An hour a night for a week is better than an all-night cram session. This has been definitely established. What is more, a night a week for a month will return better dividends than crowding your study into a shorter period of time.
- Locate the place of the exam – You have been sent a notice telling you when and where to report for the examination. If the location is in a different town or otherwise unfamiliar to you, it would be well to inquire the best route and learn something about the building.
- Relax the night before the test – Allow your mind to rest. Do not study at all that night. Plan some mild recreation or diversion; then go to bed early and get a good night's sleep.
- Get up early enough to make a leisurely trip to the place for the test – This way unforeseen events, traffic snarls, unfamiliar buildings, etc. will not upset you.
- Dress comfortably – A written test is not a fashion show. You will be known by number and not by name, so wear something comfortable.

- Leave excess paraphernalia at home – Shopping bags and odd bundles will get in your way. You need bring only the items mentioned in the official notice you received; usually everything you need is provided. Do not bring reference books to the exam. They will only confuse those last minutes and be taken away from you when in the test room.
- Arrive somewhat ahead of time – If because of transportation schedules you must get there very early, bring a newspaper or magazine to take your mind off yourself while waiting.
- Locate the examination room – When you have found the proper room, you will be directed to the seat or part of the room where you will sit. Sometimes you are given a sheet of instructions to read while you are waiting. Do not fill out any forms until you are told to do so; just read them and be prepared.
- Relax and prepare to listen to the instructions
- If you have any physical problem that may keep you from doing your best, be sure to tell the test administrator. If you are sick or in poor health, you really cannot do your best on the exam. You can come back and take the test some other time.

VII. AT THE TEST

The day of the test is here and you have the test booklet in your hand. The temptation to get going is very strong. Caution! There is more to success than knowing the right answers. You must know how to identify your papers and understand variations in the type of short-answer question used in this particular examination. Follow these suggestions for maximum results from your efforts:

1) Cooperate with the monitor

The test administrator has a duty to create a situation in which you can be as much at ease as possible. He will give instructions, tell you when to begin, check to see that you are marking your answer sheet correctly, and so on. He is not there to guard you, although he will see that your competitors do not take unfair advantage. He wants to help you do your best.

2) Listen to all instructions

Don't jump the gun! Wait until you understand all directions. In most civil service tests you get more time than you need to answer the questions. So don't be in a hurry. Read each word of instructions until you clearly understand the meaning. Study the examples, listen to all announcements and follow directions. Ask questions if you do not understand what to do.

3) Identify your papers

Civil service exams are usually identified by number only. You will be assigned a number; you must not put your name on your test papers. Be sure to copy your number correctly. Since more than one exam may be given, copy your exact examination title.

4) Plan your time

Unless you are told that a test is a "speed" or "rate of work" test, speed itself is usually not important. Time enough to answer all the questions will be provided, but this does not mean that you have all day. An overall time limit has been set. Divide the total time (in minutes) by the number of questions to determine the approximate time you have for each question.

5) Do not linger over difficult questions

If you come across a difficult question, mark it with a paper clip (useful to have along) and come back to it when you have been through the booklet. One caution if you do this – be sure to skip a number on your answer sheet as well. Check often to be sure that you have not lost your place and that you are marking in the row numbered the same as the question you are answering.

6) Read the questions

Be sure you know what the question asks! Many capable people are unsuccessful because they failed to *read* the questions correctly.

7) Answer all questions

Unless you have been instructed that a penalty will be deducted for incorrect answers, it is better to guess than to omit a question.

8) Speed tests

It is often better NOT to guess on speed tests. It has been found that on timed tests people are tempted to spend the last few seconds before time is called in marking answers at random – without even reading them – in the hope of picking up a few extra points. To discourage this practice, the instructions may warn you that your score will be "corrected" for guessing. That is, a penalty will be applied. The incorrect answers will be deducted from the correct ones, or some other penalty formula will be used.

9) Review your answers

If you finish before time is called, go back to the questions you guessed or omitted to give them further thought. Review other answers if you have time.

10) Return your test materials

If you are ready to leave before others have finished or time is called, take ALL your materials to the monitor and leave quietly. Never take any test material with you. The monitor can discover whose papers are not complete, and taking a test booklet may be grounds for disqualification.

VIII. EXAMINATION TECHNIQUES

1) Read the general instructions carefully. These are usually printed on the first page of the exam booklet. As a rule, these instructions refer to the timing of the examination; the fact that you should not start work until the signal and must stop work at a signal, etc. If there are any *special* instructions, such as a choice of questions to be answered, make sure that you note this instruction carefully.

2) When you are ready to start work on the examination, that is as soon as the signal has been given, read the instructions to each question booklet, underline any key words or phrases, such as *least, best, outline, describe* and the like. In this way you will tend to answer as requested rather than discover on reviewing your paper that you *listed without describing*, that you selected the *worst* choice rather than the *best* choice, etc.

3) If the examination is of the objective or multiple-choice type – that is, each question will also give a series of possible answers: A, B, C or D, and you are called upon to select the best answer and write the letter next to that answer on your answer paper – it is advisable to start answering each question in turn. There may be anywhere from 50 to 100 such questions in the three or four hours allotted and you can see how much time would be taken if you read through all the questions before beginning to answer any. Furthermore, if you come across a question or group of questions which you know would be difficult to answer, it would undoubtedly affect your handling of all the other questions.

4) If the examination is of the essay type and contains but a few questions, it is a moot point as to whether you should read all the questions before starting to answer any one. Of course, if you are given a choice – say five out of seven and the like – then it is essential to read all the questions so you can eliminate the two that are most difficult. If, however, you are asked to answer all the questions, there may be danger in trying to answer the easiest one first because you may find that you will spend too much time on it. The best technique is to answer the first question, then proceed to the second, etc.

5) Time your answers. Before the exam begins, write down the time it started, then add the time allowed for the examination and write down the time it must be completed, then divide the time available somewhat as follows:
    - If 3-1/2 hours are allowed, that would be 210 minutes. If you have 80 objective-type questions, that would be an average of 2-1/2 minutes per question. Allow yourself no more than 2 minutes per question, or a total of 160 minutes, which will permit about 50 minutes to review.
    - If for the time allotment of 210 minutes there are 7 essay questions to answer, that would average about 30 minutes a question. Give yourself only 25 minutes per question so that you have about 35 minutes to review.

6) The most important instruction is to *read each question* and make sure you know what is wanted. The second most important instruction is to *time yourself properly* so that you answer every question. The third most important instruction is to *answer every question*. Guess if you have to but include something for each question. Remember that you will receive no credit for a blank and will probably receive some credit if you write something in answer to an essay question. If you guess a letter – say "B" for a multiple-choice question – you may have guessed right. If you leave a blank as an answer to a multiple-choice question, the examiners may respect your feelings but it will not add a point to your score. Some exams may penalize you for wrong answers, so in such cases *only*, you may not want to guess unless you have some basis for your answer.

7) Suggestions
    a. Objective-type questions
        1. Examine the question booklet for proper sequence of pages and questions
        2. Read all instructions carefully
        3. Skip any question which seems too difficult; return to it after all other questions have been answered
        4. Apportion your time properly; do not spend too much time on any single question or group of questions

5. Note and underline key words – *all, most, fewest, least, best, worst, same, opposite,* etc.
6. Pay particular attention to negatives
7. Note unusual option, e.g., unduly long, short, complex, different or similar in content to the body of the question
8. Observe the use of "hedging" words – *probably, may, most likely,* etc.
9. Make sure that your answer is put next to the same number as the question
10. Do not second-guess unless you have good reason to believe the second answer is definitely more correct
11. Cross out original answer if you decide another answer is more accurate; do not erase until you are ready to hand your paper in
12. Answer all questions; guess unless instructed otherwise
13. Leave time for review

   b. Essay questions
1. Read each question carefully
2. Determine exactly what is wanted. Underline key words or phrases.
3. Decide on outline or paragraph answer
4. Include many different points and elements unless asked to develop any one or two points or elements
5. Show impartiality by giving pros and cons unless directed to select one side only
6. Make and write down any assumptions you find necessary to answer the questions
7. Watch your English, grammar, punctuation and choice of words
8. Time your answers; don't crowd material

8) Answering the essay question

Most essay questions can be answered by framing the specific response around several key words or ideas. Here are a few such key words or ideas:

M's: manpower, materials, methods, money, management
P's: purpose, program, policy, plan, procedure, practice, problems, pitfalls, personnel, public relations

   a. Six basic steps in handling problems:
1. Preliminary plan and background development
2. Collect information, data and facts
3. Analyze and interpret information, data and facts
4. Analyze and develop solutions as well as make recommendations
5. Prepare report and sell recommendations
6. Install recommendations and follow up effectiveness

   b. Pitfalls to avoid
1. *Taking things for granted* – A statement of the situation does not necessarily imply that each of the elements is necessarily true; for example, a complaint may be invalid and biased so that all that can be taken for granted is that a complaint has been registered

2. *Considering only one side of a situation* – Wherever possible, indicate several alternatives and then point out the reasons you selected the best one
3. *Failing to indicate follow up* – Whenever your answer indicates action on your part, make certain that you will take proper follow-up action to see how successful your recommendations, procedures or actions turn out to be
4. *Taking too long in answering any single question* – Remember to time your answers properly

IX. AFTER THE TEST

Scoring procedures differ in detail among civil service jurisdictions although the general principles are the same. Whether the papers are hand-scored or graded by machine we have described, they are nearly always graded by number. That is, the person who marks the paper knows only the number – never the name – of the applicant. Not until all the papers have been graded will they be matched with names. If other tests, such as training and experience or oral interview ratings have been given, scores will be combined. Different parts of the examination usually have different weights. For example, the written test might count 60 percent of the final grade, and a rating of training and experience 40 percent. In many jurisdictions, veterans will have a certain number of points added to their grades.

After the final grade has been determined, the names are placed in grade order and an eligible list is established. There are various methods for resolving ties between those who get the same final grade – probably the most common is to place first the name of the person whose application was received first. Job offers are made from the eligible list in the order the names appear on it. You will be notified of your grade and your rank as soon as all these computations have been made. This will be done as rapidly as possible.

People who are found to meet the requirements in the announcement are called "eligibles." Their names are put on a list of eligible candidates. An eligible's chances of getting a job depend on how high he stands on this list and how fast agencies are filling jobs from the list.

When a job is to be filled from a list of eligibles, the agency asks for the names of people on the list of eligibles for that job. When the civil service commission receives this request, it sends to the agency the names of the three people highest on this list. Or, if the job to be filled has specialized requirements, the office sends the agency the names of the top three persons who meet these requirements from the general list.

The appointing officer makes a choice from among the three people whose names were sent to him. If the selected person accepts the appointment, the names of the others are put back on the list to be considered for future openings.

That is the rule in hiring from all kinds of eligible lists, whether they are for typist, carpenter, chemist, or something else. For every vacancy, the appointing officer has his choice of any one of the top three eligibles on the list. This explains why the person whose name is on top of the list sometimes does not get an appointment when some of the persons lower on the list do. If the appointing officer chooses the second or third eligible, the No. 1 eligible does not get a job at once, but stays on the list until he is appointed or the list is terminated.

X. HOW TO PASS THE INTERVIEW TEST

The examination for which you applied requires an oral interview test. You have already taken the written test and you are now being called for the interview test – the final part of the formal examination.

You may think that it is not possible to prepare for an interview test and that there are no procedures to follow during an interview. Our purpose is to point out some things you can do in advance that will help you and some good rules to follow and pitfalls to avoid while you are being interviewed.

What is an interview supposed to test?

The written examination is designed to test the technical knowledge and competence of the candidate; the oral is designed to evaluate intangible qualities, not readily measured otherwise, and to establish a list showing the relative fitness of each candidate – as measured against his competitors – for the position sought. Scoring is not on the basis of "right" and "wrong," but on a sliding scale of values ranging from "not passable" to "outstanding." As a matter of fact, it is possible to achieve a relatively low score without a single "incorrect" answer because of evident weakness in the qualities being measured.

Occasionally, an examination may consist entirely of an oral test – either an individual or a group oral. In such cases, information is sought concerning the technical knowledges and abilities of the candidate, since there has been no written examination for this purpose. More commonly, however, an oral test is used to supplement a written examination.

Who conducts interviews?

The composition of oral boards varies among different jurisdictions. In nearly all, a representative of the personnel department serves as chairman. One of the members of the board may be a representative of the department in which the candidate would work. In some cases, "outside experts" are used, and, frequently, a businessman or some other representative of the general public is asked to serve. Labor and management or other special groups may be represented. The aim is to secure the services of experts in the appropriate field.

However the board is composed, it is a good idea (and not at all improper or unethical) to ascertain in advance of the interview who the members are and what groups they represent. When you are introduced to them, you will have some idea of their backgrounds and interests, and at least you will not stutter and stammer over their names.

What should be done before the interview?

While knowledge about the board members is useful and takes some of the surprise element out of the interview, there is other preparation which is more substantive. It *is* possible to prepare for an oral interview – in several ways:

1) Keep a copy of your application and review it carefully before the interview

This may be the only document before the oral board, and the starting point of the interview. Know what education and experience you have listed there, and the sequence and dates of all of it. Sometimes the board will ask you to review the highlights of your experience for them; you should not have to hem and haw doing it.

2) Study the class specification and the examination announcement

Usually, the oral board has one or both of these to guide them. The qualities, characteristics or knowledges required by the position sought are stated in these documents. They offer valuable clues as to the nature of the oral interview. For example, if the job involves supervisory responsibilities, the announcement will usually indicate that knowledge of modern supervisory methods and the qualifications of the candidate as a supervisor will be tested. If so, you can expect such questions, frequently in the form of a hypothetical situation which you are expected to solve. NEVER go into an oral without knowledge of the duties and responsibilities of the job you seek.

3) Think through each qualification required

Try to visualize the kind of questions you would ask if you were a board member. How well could you answer them? Try especially to appraise your own knowledge and background in each area, *measured against the job sought*, and identify any areas in which you are weak. Be critical and realistic – do not flatter yourself.

4) Do some general reading in areas in which you feel you may be weak

For example, if the job involves supervision and your past experience has NOT, some general reading in supervisory methods and practices, particularly in the field of human relations, might be useful. Do NOT study agency procedures or detailed manuals. The oral board will be testing your understanding and capacity, not your memory.

5) Get a good night's sleep and watch your general health and mental attitude

You will want a clear head at the interview. Take care of a cold or any other minor ailment, and of course, no hangovers.

What should be done on the day of the interview?

Now comes the day of the interview itself. Give yourself plenty of time to get there. Plan to arrive somewhat ahead of the scheduled time, particularly if your appointment is in the fore part of the day. If a previous candidate fails to appear, the board might be ready for you a bit early. By early afternoon an oral board is almost invariably behind schedule if there are many candidates, and you may have to wait. Take along a book or magazine to read, or your application to review, but leave any extraneous material in the waiting room when you go in for your interview. In any event, relax and compose yourself.

The matter of dress is important. The board is forming impressions about you – from your experience, your manners, your attitude, and your appearance. Give your personal appearance careful attention. Dress your best, but not your flashiest. Choose conservative, appropriate clothing, and be sure it is immaculate. This is a business interview, and your appearance should indicate that you regard it as such. Besides, being well groomed and properly dressed will help boost your confidence.

Sooner or later, someone will call your name and escort you into the interview room. *This is it.* From here on you are on your own. It is too late for any more preparation. But remember, you asked for this opportunity to prove your fitness and you are here because your request was granted.

What happens when you go in?

The usual sequence of events will be as follows: The clerk (who is often the board stenographer) will introduce you to the chairman of the oral board, who will introduce you to the other members of the board. Acknowledge the introductions before you sit down. Do not be surprised if you find a microphone facing you or a stenotypist sitting by. Oral interviews are usually recorded in the event of an appeal or other review.

Usually the chairman of the board will open the interview by reviewing the highlights of your education and work experience from your application – primarily for the benefit of the other members of the board, as well as to get the material into the record. Do not interrupt or comment unless there is an error or significant misinterpretation; if that is the case, do not hesitate. But do not quibble about insignificant matters. Also, he will usually ask you some question about your education, experience or your present job – partly to get you to start talking and to establish the interviewing "rapport." He may start the actual questioning, or turn it over to one of the other members. Frequently, each member undertakes the questioning on a particular area, one in which he is perhaps most competent, so you can expect each member to participate in the examination. Because time is limited, you may also expect some rather abrupt switches in the direction the questioning takes, so do not be upset by it. Normally, a board member will not pursue a single line of questioning unless he discovers a particular strength or weakness.

After each member has participated, the chairman will usually ask whether any member has any further questions, then will ask you if you have anything you wish to add. Unless you are expecting this question, it may floor you. Worse, it may start you off on an extended, extemporaneous speech. The board is not usually seeking more information. The question is principally to offer you a last opportunity to present further qualifications or to indicate that you have nothing to add. So, if you feel that a significant qualification or characteristic has been overlooked, it is proper to point it out in a sentence or so. Do not compliment the board on the thoroughness of their examination – they have been sketchy, and you know it. If you wish, merely say, "No thank you, I have nothing further to add." This is a point where you can "talk yourself out" of a good impression or fail to present an important bit of information. Remember, *you close the interview yourself*.

The chairman will then say, "That is all, Mr. _____, thank you." Do not be startled; the interview is over, and quicker than you think. Thank him, gather your belongings and take your leave. Save your sigh of relief for the other side of the door.

How to put your best foot forward

Throughout this entire process, you may feel that the board individually and collectively is trying to pierce your defenses, seek out your hidden weaknesses and embarrass and confuse you. Actually, this is not true. They are obliged to make an appraisal of your qualifications for the job you are seeking, and they want to see you in your best light. Remember, they must interview all candidates and a non-cooperative candidate may become a failure in spite of their best efforts to bring out his qualifications. Here are 15 suggestions that will help you:

1) Be natural – Keep your attitude confident, not cocky

If you are not confident that you can do the job, do not expect the board to be. Do not apologize for your weaknesses, try to bring out your strong points. The board is interested in a positive, not negative, presentation. Cockiness will antagonize any board member and make him wonder if you are covering up a weakness by a false show of strength.

2) Get comfortable, but don't lounge or sprawl

Sit erectly but not stiffly. A careless posture may lead the board to conclude that you are careless in other things, or at least that you are not impressed by the importance of the occasion. Either conclusion is natural, even if incorrect. Do not fuss with your clothing, a pencil or an ashtray. Your hands may occasionally be useful to emphasize a point; do not let them become a point of distraction.

3) Do not wisecrack or make small talk

This is a serious situation, and your attitude should show that you consider it as such. Further, the time of the board is limited – they do not want to waste it, and neither should you.

4) Do not exaggerate your experience or abilities

In the first place, from information in the application or other interviews and sources, the board may know more about you than you think. Secondly, you probably will not get away with it. An experienced board is rather adept at spotting such a situation, so do not take the chance.

5) If you know a board member, do not make a point of it, yet do not hide it

Certainly you are not fooling him, and probably not the other members of the board. Do not try to take advantage of your acquaintanceship – it will probably do you little good.

6) Do not dominate the interview

Let the board do that. They will give you the clues – do not assume that you have to do all the talking. Realize that the board has a number of questions to ask you, and do not try to take up all the interview time by showing off your extensive knowledge of the answer to the first one.

7) Be attentive

You only have 20 minutes or so, and you should keep your attention at its sharpest throughout. When a member is addressing a problem or question to you, give him your undivided attention. Address your reply principally to him, but do not exclude the other board members.

8) Do not interrupt

A board member may be stating a problem for you to analyze. He will ask you a question when the time comes. Let him state the problem, and wait for the question.

9) Make sure you understand the question

Do not try to answer until you are sure what the question is. If it is not clear, restate it in your own words or ask the board member to clarify it for you. However, do not haggle about minor elements.

10) Reply promptly but not hastily

A common entry on oral board rating sheets is "candidate responded readily," or "candidate hesitated in replies." Respond as promptly and quickly as you can, but do not jump to a hasty, ill-considered answer.

11) Do not be peremptory in your answers

A brief answer is proper – but do not fire your answer back. That is a losing game from your point of view. The board member can probably ask questions much faster than you can answer them.

12) Do not try to create the answer you think the board member wants

He is interested in what kind of mind you have and how it works – not in playing games. Furthermore, he can usually spot this practice and will actually grade you down on it.

13) Do not switch sides in your reply merely to agree with a board member

Frequently, a member will take a contrary position merely to draw you out and to see if you are willing and able to defend your point of view. Do not start a debate, yet do not surrender a good position. If a position is worth taking, it is worth defending.

14) Do not be afraid to admit an error in judgment if you are shown to be wrong

The board knows that you are forced to reply without any opportunity for careful consideration. Your answer may be demonstrably wrong. If so, admit it and get on with the interview.

15) Do not dwell at length on your present job

The opening question may relate to your present assignment. Answer the question but do not go into an extended discussion. You are being examined for a *new* job, not your present one. As a matter of fact, try to phrase ALL your answers in terms of the job for which you are being examined.

Basis of Rating

Probably you will forget most of these "do's" and "don'ts" when you walk into the oral interview room. Even remembering them all will not ensure you a passing grade. Perhaps you did not have the qualifications in the first place. But remembering them will help you to put your best foot forward, without treading on the toes of the board members.

Rumor and popular opinion to the contrary notwithstanding, an oral board wants you to make the best appearance possible. They know you are under pressure – but they also want to see how you respond to it as a guide to what your reaction would be under the pressures of the job you seek. They will be influenced by the degree of poise you display, the personal traits you show and the manner in which you respond.

ABOUT THIS BOOK

This book contains tests divided into Examination Sections. Go through each test, answering every question in the margin. We have also attached a sample answer sheet at the back of the book that can be removed and used. At the end of each test look at the answer key and check your answers. On the ones you got wrong, look at the right answer choice and learn. Do not fill in the answers first. Do not memorize the questions and answers, but understand the answer and principles involved. On your test, the questions will likely be different from the samples. Questions are changed and new ones added. If you understand these past questions you should have success with any changes that arise. Tests may consist of several types of questions. We have additional books on each subject should more study be advisable or necessary for you. Finally, the more you study, the better prepared you will be. This book is intended to be the last thing you study before you walk into the examination room. Prior study of relevant texts is also recommended. NLC publishes some of these in our Fundamental Series. Knowledge and good sense are important factors in passing your exam. Good luck also helps. So now study this Passbook, absorb the material contained within and take that knowledge into the examination. Then do your best to pass that exam.

EXAMINATION SECTION

EXAMINATION SECTION

TEST 1

DIRECTIONS: Each question or incomplete statement is followed by several suggested answers or completions. Select the one that BEST answers the question or completes the statement. *PRINT THE LETTER OF THE CORRECT ANSWER IN THE SPACE AT THE RIGHT.*

Questions 1-5.

DIRECTIONS: Questions 1 through 5 are to be answered on the basis of the following fact pattern.

A restless crowd has gathered on the lower level of the Supreme Courthouse. The judge has not yet descended from chambers and the law clerk is also missing. The forty to fifty person crowd is a mix of jurors, attorneys, and parties.

1. As an initial order of business, what should the court officer be concerned with?
   A. Taming the crowd
   B. Locating the judge
   C. Locating the law clerk
   D. Sending prospective jurors upstairs to the jury pool room

2. Two attorneys' voices have risen above all the rest. It is unclear whether they are shouting at one another in anger or catching up on old times. They are attracting onlookers as their conversation grows more animated.
   What is the MOST appropriate action for the court officer to take?
   A. Separate the two attorneys
   B. Ask that they lower their voices or speak privately in another area of the courthouse
   C. Sequester the jurors
   D. Ask that the two attorneys step into the courtroom to resolve their dispute

3. Some of the members of the crowd seem to be holding a single white sheet of paper which appears to be a summons.
   What is the MOST reasonable next step?
   The court officer should
   A. ask those a summons holders to head upstairs to check in with the clerk
   B. sequester summons holders to the side to confer with one another
   C. ask that those people sued stay put for now
   D. ask the law clerk announce herself to the possible defendants in the room

4. How should the court officer categorize and separate the crowd?
   A. Separate by the time each person arrived
   B. Separate by those with counsel present
   C. Separate by the reason he or she is at the courthouse
   D. Separate by age, gender, then race

5. In determining where each individual rightfully belongs, the court officer should be MOST familiar with which of the following?
   A. The location of each judge's chamber
   B. The times when each law clerk is scheduled to arrive at the courthouse
   C. The location of the clerk's desk, courtrooms, and preliminary hearing conference area
   D. The security desk and exits of the courtroom

5.____

Questions 6-10.

DIRECTIONS: Questions 6 through 10 are to be answered on the basis of the following fact pattern.

Jury selection has begun. Prospective jurors are gathered in the far courtroom and, after signing in, take their seats and wait to be called for sequestration.

6. During jury pool selection, two prospective jurors start to argue about a recent murder trial that made the New York Post. You should immediately
   A. shout at them to calm down or else they will be chosen for jury as punishment
   B. intervene to de-escalate the situation
   C. get the attention of the law clerk
   D. inform the judge of the jurors' behavior

6.____

7. Three women in the back of the courtroom are overhead chatting. They are being relatively quiet and not disrupting anyone around them. However, one of the women says that she knows who may be on trial today. Her nephew was arrested last night for drinking. If she is picked to serve on the jury, she says she will absolutely try to ensure he is acquitted.
   You should
   A. interrupt their conversation to inform them they are being inappropriate
   B. interrupt their conversation to inform them that what they plan on doing is illegal
   C. allow them to finish their conversation in peace
   D. allow them to finish their conversation but, if selected, inform the judge of what was overheard

7.____

8. Once the jury is selected, which of the following responsibilities will MOST likely be your role?
   A. Reciting the applicable law of the case
   B. Providing the jury with opening statements
   C. Swearing in the jury
   D. Coordinating the jurors' lunch order

8.____

9. One of the jurors asks you how long the trial is scheduled to take. 9.____
What is the MOST appropriate response?
   A. Trials can be extremely lengthy and take several months or take a few hours.
   B. You should pay attention to every aspect of the trial and not worry about how long you'll be here.
   C. Not respond at all as it may create bias in the courtroom.
   D. Civil trials are typically three to five days, while criminal trials are generally five to ten days.

10. After the jury is selected, one of the jurors recognizes the defendant's 10.____
attorney and begins to scream at him from the jury box.
You immediately start to
   A. remove the individual from the courtroom
   B. ask him to calm down and reserve his opinion about attorneys for later
   C. physically restrain the juror using force
   D. inform the judge that the juror may be biased in this matter

Questions 111-15.

DIRECTIONS: Questions 11 through 15 are to be answered on the basis of the following fact pattern.

During a civil litigation trial, multiple pieces of evidence must be presented to the jury, the witnesses, and the judge.

11. During opening statements, the plaintiff's attorney mentions that the jury will 11.____
see and hear over 1,000 pieces of evidence during the trial that will convince
them the plaintiff should prevail. Nearing the end of the trial, however, the
plaintiff has not produced one piece of physical evidence.
You should
   A. raise the issue with the judge
   B. remind the attorney during a break that they have not delivered their promise
   C. stay silent
   D. suggest the attorney produce something into evidence

12. During examination of one of the defendant's witnesses, Attorney Bob 12.____
referred to a piece of evidence as the "receipt from the gas station, marked as
#34." When you pick it up from the defendant, you notice the evidence is
actually marked as #36.
Should you intervene to correct the attorney's mistake?
   A. Absolutely not
   B. Yes, but point out to the attorney that it is marked as a different number to give him an opportunity to correct himself
   C. Yes but point out to the jury that the evidence is marked differently so that they are not confused
   D. Yes, but only to the judge in his or her chambers after the trial is complete

13. The two attorneys begin to argue with one another during the trial. 13.____
    How do you intervene?
    A. Stand between them to signal their behavior will not be tolerated
    B. Issue each of them a stern warning that they will be removed if they do not cease immediately
    C. Allow the judge to intervene first, then follow his or her instructions on how to intervene
    D. Ask the jury to remove themselves from the courtroom

14. As the two attorneys start to become more aggressive, the judge slams his 14.____
    gavel. The attorneys ignore the warning from the court.
    How would you intervene at this point?
    A. Physically restrain the plaintiff's attorney
    B. Physically restrain the defendant's attorney
    C. Stand between the two of them, hold out your arms to both sides, and order them to stop speaking directly to one another
    D. Ask the jury to remove themselves from the courtroom

15. During the trial, the defendant mutters an expletive under his breath while 15.____
    the judge gives an order as a show of blatant disrespect for the court.
    What is the MOST appropriate action to take?
    A. Allow the judge to sanction the defendant, then escort him or her out of the courtroom
    B. Physically restrain the defendant
    C. Await instruction from the judge on how to intervene
    D. Arrest the individual and remove him or her from the courtroom

16. One of the jurors appears faint and starts to wobble while seated in the jury 16.____
    box. How should you handle the situation?
    A. Let one of the jurors come to the ailing juror's aid first
    B. Alert the clerk of what you see and ask that the trial be held indefinitely
    C. Politely interject the trial proceedings and ask the juror if he or she is feeling well
    D. Quietly remove the juror from his or her seat, trying not to disrupt the trial proceedings

17. During trial, you believe that you see the defendant winking at one of the 17.____
    jurors. No one else seems to notice their interaction, including the judge and the attorneys.
    What action would you take?
    A. Alert the judge in chambers
    B. Tell the law clerk during a break in trial
    C. Interrupt the trial to make all parties aware of the behavior
    D. Confirm with the juror in question that the defendant is winking at her to determine if the feeling is mutual

18. During a sentencing hearing, the convicted defendant seems to be fiddling more than usual.
    Where would you place yourself during the remainder of the hearing?
    A. As close to the judge as possible in the event you may need to protect him or her
    B. As close to the defendant's attorney as possible in the event you may need to protect him or her
    C. As close to the defendant as possible in the event you will need to restrain them
    D. At the back of the courtroom

19. In the trial of a serial killer, many prospective jurors have indicated they feel unsafe. During jury deliberations, you overhear at least two different jurors say that they want to convict the defendant simply because he has seen their faces during the trial.
    What are your next steps?
    A. Interject into the jury room and inform them that their decision on that premise alone is unethical
    B. Interject into the jury room and inform them that their decision on that premise alone is unconstitutional
    C. Alert the judge immediately
    D. Instruct the jury that they do not need to look directly at the defendant in the courtroom

20. During a recess in the trial, the defendant's expert witness is seen chatting with one of the alternate jurors outside the courthouse. While it is unclear what they are talking about, it seems to be a friendly exchange of information.
    What should you do before the court is called back to order?
    A. Tell the juror she must disclose her conversation with the expert witness in open court
    B. Tell the expert witness he must disclose the conversation with the juror in open court
    C. Inform the plaintiff's attorney about the conversation
    D. Inform the judge about the conversation

Questions 21-25.

DIRECTIONS: Questions 21 through 25 are to be answered on the basis of the following fact pattern.

After a TRO is issued to the plaintiff, the ex-wife of the defendant, both parties are free to go. The defendant appeared in court and rigorously opposed his ex-wife's request. His ex-wife already has sole custody of their three children, and he seems incredibly distraught by the judge's grant of her request.

21. How should you allow the parties to exit the courtroom? 21.____
    A. It is permissible and more efficient if everyone exited together.
    B. The defendant should be escorted out of the courtroom through judge's chambers.
    C. The plaintiff and her attorney should be escorted out of the courtroom first.
    D. People are free to choose how they enter and exit a building.

22. After the hearing, you see the plaintiff and the defendant's attorney chatting outside of the courtroom. Should you intervene? 22.____
    A. No, unless the conversation grows heated and someone may need to be restrained
    B. No, but you should make your presence known by moving closer to the two as they converse with one another
    C. No, because the plaintiff is not speaking directly with the defendant
    D. No

23. After the hearing, you see the defendant speaking directly with the law clerk who was present during the hearing. How should you intervene? 23.____
    A. There is no need to intervene since the hearing is over.
    B. There is no need to intervene since the law clerk is not the judge.
    C. You should inform the judge of the conversation, but not intervene in the conversation itself.
    D. You should stop the conversation immediately by announcing that it is inappropriate.

24. In a follow-up hearing, where the plaintiff is requested to extend the TRO, the defendant does not show up. Instead, the defendant's brother appears at the hearing on his behalf. 24.____
    Is the defendant's brother permitted to voice his concerns about extending the TRO?
    The defendant's brother
    A. is not a party to the action and must wait outside of the courtroom during proceedings
    B. is welcome to testify on his brother's behalf
    C. can testify on his brother's behalf as long as he remains calm while doing so
    D. can testify on his brother's behalf so long as the plaintiff's sister can testify on her behalf

25. In judge's chambers, the judge's law clerk indicates that she believes the plaintiff is lying about the defendant's alleged dangerous behavior. The judge does not agree or disagree with the clerk's statement. During proceedings, however, the clerk rolls her eyes and is not taking notes. 25.____
    The MOST appropriate step is to
    A. inform the judge after the hearing and allow the judge to handle the clerk's behavior
    B. ask that the clerk excuse herself if she cannot behave in a professional manner during hearings

C. pause the hearings and demand that the clerk leave the courtroom
D. pause the hearings and allow the clerk to correct her own behavior before the hearings can resume

KEY (CORRECT ANSWERS)

1.	A		11.	C
2.	B		12.	B
3.	A		13.	C
4.	C		14.	C
5.	C		15.	A
6.	B		16.	C
7.	D		17.	A
8.	C		18.	C
9.	D		19.	C
10.	A		20.	D

21. C
22. B
23. C
24. A
25. A

TEST 2

DIRECTIONS: Each question or incomplete statement is followed by several suggested answers or completions. Select the one that BEST answers the question or completes the statement. *PRINT THE LETTER OF THE CORRECT ANSWER IN THE SPACE AT THE RIGHT.*

Questions 1-5.

DIRECTIONS: Questions 1 through 5 are to be answered on the basis of the following fact pattern.

A trial is set to start at 9:30 A.M. At 9:45 A.M., the judge and the judge's clerk have yet to arrive. At 9:50 A.M., the law clerk enters the courtroom and takes her assigned seat beneath the judge. The judge, however, has still not appeared.

1. Should you leave the courtroom to locate the judge? 1.____
   A. Yes, but only if there is another court officer there to maintain the order of the courtroom
   B. Yes, but only if the law clerk is comfortable maintaining the order of the courtroom on her own
   C. Yes, but only if the jury has not filed into the courtroom yet
   D. No

2. At half past 10 A.M., you try to locate the judge. You see that she has entered her chambers but does not look well. 2.____
   What information do you need to ascertain your next steps?
   Whether the judge
   A. is judicially fit to hear the case
   B. is intoxicated
   C. is feeling well and needs you to adjourn the case for the day
   C. needs physical assistance by way of wheelchair or other device

3. The judge has indicated she is well enough to hear the cases for the day, but needs another few moments to collect herself. She enters her chambers and summons only one of the attorneys from the first trial. 3.____
   What is the LEAST appropriate response?
   A. Collect the attorney as requested
   B. Inform the judge that she will be commencing ex parte communications if you were to do
   C. Refuse and demand the judge recuse herself from proceedings for the day
   D. Confirm the instruction and politely inform the judge this would be inappropriate

4. When you re-enter the courtroom which is still occupied with spectators, attorneys, the parties and the law clerk, who are you MOST likely to inform that the judge does not seem to be feeling well?
   A. The clerk
   B. The attorneys
   C. The entire courtroom
   D. No one

5. During the swearing-in ceremony of attorneys who passed the Bar exam, one of the attorneys stops you after going through the security check to indicate that her boyfriend is parking the car. Because she is not allowed to have her cellphone on, she cannot inform him to leave his firearm in the car. Which question would be MOST helpful in determining your next step?
   A. Does your boyfriend have a license to carry a firearm?
   B. Is the weapon loaded?
   C. Is your boyfriend dangerous?
   D. How far away is he?

6. How many alternate jurors are typically sworn in for trial?
   A. Up to 12   B. Up to 14   C. Up to 10   D. Up to 6

7. A TRO is a _____, while a QDRO is a _____.
   A. temporary restraining order; qualified domicile relations order
   B. territorial restraining order; qualified domicile relations order
   C. temporary restraining order; qualified domestic revision order
   D. temporary restraining order; qualified domestic relations order

8. There is a shortage of court officer personnel this morning, and two trials are set to start at the District Court. The first trial is a bench trial and involves a no-fault reimbursement claim. The second trial is a jury trial of a twice-convicted child rapist. Your presence is requested at both trials.
   Which should you cover?
   A. The bench trial should last a few hours, so you should cover that trial first.
   B. The jury trial has a more pressing need for law enforcement presence, so you should cover that trial in its entirety.
   C. The jury trial has a more pressing need for law enforcement presence, so you should cover the trial at least until the first recess.
   D. You are required to swear in the judge, so you must cover the bench trial.

9. The crowd of people outside the preliminary conference desk is becoming unwieldy. Attorneys are piling out of the small room in droves and seem to be overpowering the sole clerk at the front.
   What is your role in taming the crowd as it relates to the clerk?
   A. The clerk should handle the crowd, especially since they are mostly attorneys.
   B. You are responsible for calming the crowd and de-escalating any issues that arise; the clerk deserves an orderly and respectful line.
   C. You are responsible for taming the crowd by yourself and can ask for the clerk's assistance if needed.
   D. You do not need to be in or around the preliminary conference desk at all.

10. As you read the counts of the indictment, one of the jurors begins to cough uncontrollably. Should you continue reading or pause while the juror gathers herself?
    You should
    A. pause and allow the juror to gather herself but not repeat the counts
    B. continue reading the indictment without pause
    C. pause and politely ask the juror if she is okay, then repeat the counts of the indictment from the beginning
    D. remove the juror

10.____

11. A twice-convicted felon is being charged with attempted rape of a minor. During a brief recess, one of the jurors returns to the courtroom to quickly grab her purse and makes eye contact with the defendant.
    How do you intervene?
    A. The juror is allowed to make eye contact with the defendant, therefore no intervention is necessary.
    B. You stand in the middle of the two of them to protect the juror.
    C. You report the eye contact to the judge immediately, since bias was clearly created.
    D. You ask the judge to excuse the juror because of her impropriety.

11.____

12. Which of the following is MOST deserving of court officer intervention?
    A. A raucous crowd starting to gather a half mile outside the courthouse
    B. A disorderly jury
    C. An ex parte communication between the judge and one of the attorneys
    D. A motion hearing where one party requests an expedited trial date

12.____

13. Which of the following procedures is MOST deserving of a court officer's attention?
    A. Discovery procedures
    B. Prison handling and escort procedures
    C. Evidentiary exchange procedures
    D. Development of character witness procedures

13.____

14. One of Judge Diamond's recent decisions has sparked an outrage in the local community. Approximately one week after the decision, a peaceful and planned protest has begun outside of the courthouse.
    Which of the following is MOST important during the protest?
    A. Securing the safety of Judge Diamond
    B. Controlling the media
    C. Identifying any and all aggressors in the protest
    D. Securing the safety of Judge Diamond's law clerk, Judy

14.____

15. Judge Ross is seen discussing Judge Diamond's decision with one of the media outlets covering the protest.
    Which of the following actions should you be the MOST mindful of during Judge Ross's comments?
    A. Any inflammatory words against Judge Diamond
    B. The behavior of the protestors, including any persons who may charge the judge
    C. The behavior of the interviewer who may attack Judge Diamond personally
    D. The behavior of the media more generally who may try to access the courthouse while Judge Ross is speaking to the interviewer

15.____

Questions 16-18.

DIRECTIONS: Questions 16 through 18 are to be answered on the basis of the following fact pattern.

While those waiting for the court to open file into the hallway, an argument breaks out between two women and one man. When you intervene between the parties, you discover the two women are arguing over custody of a child – who is standing nearby – and the man is one of their attorneys. Barbara is the biological mother of the child. Tina raised the child from birth. Tina and her attorney, Bill, came with the child to court today.

16. Which party should stay with the child?
    A. The biological mother, Barbara, of the child should stay with the child while they await for court to begin.
    B. Tina and Bill should stay with the child since she raised the child from birth.
    C. The parties should separate and the child should come with you to a sequestered part of the courthouse.
    D. Tina and Bill should stay with the child as petitioners of the court; Barbara should wait in a separate area away from all three and refrain from contact.

16.____

17. Which of the following are Barbara and her attorney MOST likely to request in court?
    A. A No-Contact Order
    B. Order to Expunge
    C. Order to Impeach
    D. Deposition

17.____

18. Should you tell the judge about the behavior of the parties during the hearing?
    A. You can inform the judge if asked, but not during the hearing itself.
    B. You can inform the judge if asked, but should wait until the hearing is not in session.
    C. Before the hearing is set to begin, you should inform the judge of your encounter with the parties and let the judge decide how to best confront the situation between all involved.
    D. No.

18.____

19. Before the start of a trial, which is the court officer MOST likely to administer? 19.____
    Swearing in of the
    A. judge
    B. judge's clerk
    C. attorneys
    D. jury

Questions 20-25.

DIRECTIONS: Questions 20 through 25 are to be answered on the basis of the following fact pattern.

At Kings County Supreme Court, a trial of a group of alleged rapists has drawn a huge crowd of spectators at each day of the hearings. Two of the defendants are locals of Kings County while the other is a local of Bronx County. The trial date has been set and moved multiple times.

20. In determining which spectators should be allowed into the courthouse to watch the trial, which should be secured FIRST? 20.____
    A. Judge's permission
    B. Clerk's permission
    C. Jury's permission
    D. The mayor's permission

21. Which should NOT be employed in determining which spectators are allowed into the courthouse to watch the trial? 21.____
    A. The age of the spectator
    B. The spectator's affiliation with local media outlets
    C. Gender or race of the spectator
    D. The length of time the spectator has waited for the courthouse to open

22. Which of the following will the defendants MOST likely be charged with? 22.____
    A. An information
    B. A felony
    C. A misdemeanor
    D. An indictment

23. In reading the charge, which of the following is LEAST likely to appear? 23.____
    A. The name of the attorneys of record
    B. The names of the victims
    C. The number of counts of each crime
    D. The name of the judge hearing the case

24. There are likely to be multiples of which during this trial? 24.____
    A. Multiple court officers
    B. Multiple attorneys
    C. Multiple charges
    D. All of the above

25. The venue of the trial is MOST likely to be 25.____
    A. Kings County
    B. Bronx County
    C. Determined by the jury
    D. Determined by the judge

KEY (CORRECT ANSWERS)

1.	D		11	A
2.	C		12	B
3.	A		13	B
4.	D		14	A
5.	A		15	C
6.	D		16	D
7.	D		17	A
8.	B		18	C
9.	B		19	D
10.	C		20	A

21. C
22. B
23. B
24. D
25. D

TEST 3

DIRECTIONS: Each question or incomplete statement is followed by several suggested answers or completions. Select the one that BEST answers the question or completes the statement. *PRINT THE LETTER OF THE CORRECT ANSWER IN THE SPACE AT THE RIGHT.*

1. What is one of the MOST effective ways to disperse a large crowd in a courthouse?
    A. Start yelling that a trial is about to start
    B. Ask the crowd to form one or multiple lines
    C. Inform the crowd that they are being disruptive and should keep the volume of their voices low
    D. There aren't any effective ways to manage a crowd

1.____

2. Which of the following is a court officer MOST likely to be volunteered for?
    A. Domestic violence awareness training
    B. Prisoner escort services
    C. Jury monitoring
    D. All of the above

2.____

3. One of the jurors starts to strike up a conversation with you outside of the courtroom. How should you respond?
Politely decline to
    A. engage, unless he or she is asking for directions
    B. engage, unless he or she would like to talk about the case
    C. engage, unless he or she knows you personally
    D. engage

3.____

4. After a prisoner is escorted into the courtroom, he attempts to kick his attorney. He should
    A. be removed from the courtroom
    B. be restrained with leg restraints
    C. apologize to his attorney
    D. be forced to stand during the remainder of the proceedings

4.____

5. A charge of attempted murder is LEAST likely to accompany a charge of
    A. murder   B. burglary   C. robbery   D. assault

5.____

6. You begin to notice that jurors are growing sleepy and irritable towards the end of a six-week trial. Many jurors have stopped taking notes.
Should you inform the law clerk or judge of their behavior?
    A. The jurors' behavior in this instance does not warrant concern.
    B. You should inform the judge's clerk so he or she can warn the jurors they may miss a critical piece of information.
    C. You should inform the judge so he or she can warn the jurors they may miss a critical piece of evidence.
    D. You should request that the jury remain alert at all times during proceedings.

6.____

7. In an attempt to diffuse a heated argument between two attorneys at the New York County Civil Court, which factor should the court officer be MOST mindful of?
   A. The respective law firms of each attorney
   B. The volume of their voices as t carries throughout the building
   C. The likelihood these attorneys will see one another again on another case
   D. The ability for either attorney to recognize he or she is being warned about their behavior inside a court of law

8. A woman, Leslie, approaches you inside the Supreme Court and says that she has been served with a lawsuit.
   Which of the following is the MOST appropriate response you can provide to Leslie?
   She should have a copy of the _____ with her and refer to it, which will tell her where she would report within the courthouse.
   A. answer   B. complaint   C. summons   D. information

9. Mary produces the document, but does not know where exactly in the courthouse she should report. What is your NEXT direction?
   She should
   A. check in at Courtroom A
   B. check in with the clerk's office
   C. check in at the Preliminary Conference desk
   D. wait to be called and have a seat on a nearby bench

10. Who decides whether the jurors are allowed to take notes during the trial?
    A. The judge
    B. The plaintiff's attorney, since they are bringing the case to court
    C. Jurors are always allowed to take notes during trials
    D. Jurors are never allowed to take notes during trials

11. During a trial, one of the jurors writes a question for one of the witnesses on a piece of paper and hands it to you.
    What is your NEXT step?
    A. Keep it to yourself; jurors are not allowed to ask a witness questions
    B. Pass the written question to the judge, who may or may not ask the witness the question posed
    C. Decline to receive the written message
    D. Read the question to the witness on the witness stand after cross examination

12. If questions arise during the jury deliberation process, what is the role of the court officer?
    A. To deliver the written question from the jury foreperson to the judge
    B. To repeat the question orally as told to the court officer by the jury foreperson to the judge
    C. To read the written question in open court with all parties present other than the defendant
    D. To record the written question in the docket

13. In maintaining the security of the courtroom itself, what should the court officer be mindful of as it relates to non-parties to a lawsuit?
    A. Their interest level in the case
    B. How close they are sitting to the defendant and/or plaintiff
    C. Their demeanor, including a sudden change in demeanor
    D. Their note taking of court proceedings

14. A juror has informed you that she accidentally read information about the case she is serving on while she was at the supermarket last night.
    How should you respond to her?
    A. Berate her for not being more diligent in seeking out information about the case
    B. Inform the clerk that the juror should be replaced
    C. Remove the juror from the jury box and replace him or her with an alternate juror yourself
    D. Inform the judge immediately

15. The court officer is MOST likely to participate in which of the following duties?
    A. Collection of evidence at the scene of the crime
    B. Record court proceedings in the docket
    C. Schedule witnesses for trial, categorized alphabetically by their last name
    D. Assist the judge as necessary with extraneous tasks

16. One of the State's expert witnesses has failed to appear at trial when scheduled.
    Which document will the judge execute to compel his or her appearance?
    A. An indictment
    B. An information
    C. An execution
    D. A warrant

17. Which court proceeding takes place closest in time to an arrest?
    A. Arraignment
    B. Sentencing
    C. Trial
    D. Jury selection

18. Which of the following is LEAST likely to occur at the conclusion of a trial?
    A. Sentencing
    B. Appeal
    C. Reversal
    D. Plea bargaining

19. It has come to your attention that two of the jurors are related to one another. They are overheard talking about the case outside of the courtroom and in the court hallway.
    Should you intervene?
    A. Yes, because someone could overhear their conversation
    B. Yes, because the other jurors should be aware of how they plan on voting
    C. No, because they are siblings
    D. No, because they are outside of the courtroom and talking amongst themselves

20. How many jurors typically serve on a trial?
    A. 12   B. 18   C. 16   D. 6

21. During jury selection, the judge has already excused 25 prospective jurors for cause.
    How many more jurors can be excused for cause before reaching the excusal limit?
    A. 5
    B. 10
    C. The judge has reached the limit
    D. There is no excusal limit for "cause"

22. Which of the following is the jury prohibited from doing during a trial on which they are serving?
    A. Visiting the scene of the alleged crime
    B. Read or listen to news about the trial from outside sources
    C. Research case law that applies to the trial
    D. All of the above

23. Are court officers needed during bench trials?
    A. No, because heinous offenses are not tried by bench
    B. No, because bench trials are relatively quick
    C. Yes, because bench trials require extra security
    D. Yes, because court officers are needed for a variety of tasks during each trial

24. In New York City, jury trials are conducted at which of the following courts?
    A. Supreme Court   B. New York City Civil Court
    C. New York City Criminal Court   D. All of the above

25. A trial involving an alleged assault and battery is MOST likely to occur at which New York City court?
    A. Town and Village Court   B. New York City Civil Court
    C. New York City Criminal Court   D. County Court

KEY (CORRECT ANSWERS)

1.	B		11.	B
2.	D		12.	A
3.	D		13.	C
4.	A		14.	D
5.	A		15.	D
6.	A		16.	D
7.	D		17.	A
8.	C		18.	D
9.	B		19.	A
10.	A		20.	A

21. D
22. D
23. D
24. D
25. C

TEST 4

DIRECTIONS: Each question or incomplete statement is followed by several suggested answers or completions Select the one that BEST answers the question or completes the statement. PRINT THE LETTER OF THE CORRECT ANSWER IN THE SPACE AT THE RIGHT.

1. One device that court officers can employ that others in the court cannot, including the clerks or judges, include
   A. power to detail
   B. use of force
   C. defensive strategy
   D. all of the above

   1._____

2. Which of the following parties is LEAST likely to be in the courtroom during every trial?
   A. Defendant
   B. Court reporter
   C. Attorneys
   D. Translator

   2._____

3. The order of the steps of a typical trial from first to last is:
   I. Opening statements
   II. Jury selection
   III. Deliberations
   IV. Oath and preliminary instructions
   The CORRECT answer is:
   A. I, II, III, IV   B. IV, III, II, I   C. I, II, IV, III   D. II, IV, I, III

   3._____

Questions 4-8.

DIRECTIONS: Questions 4 through 8 are to be answered on the basis of the following fact pattern.

Pre-trial conferences are scheduled for the entire day in courtroom A with Judge Dredd presiding. Each pre-trial conference is scheduled to last 30-45 minutes.

4. During the first pre-trial conference, attorneys Bill and April become agitated with one another. Bill has accused April of ignoring the judge's order and April accuses Bill of hiding key information about the case.
   How would you diffuse the situation?
   A. The situation most likely does not require diffusing, but if they become more animated you will require they each calm down.
   B. Step between the two parties and demand respect for the court.
   C. Ask the plaintiff's attorney to step into the hallway to cool off for 5-10 minutes.
   D. Ask the defendant's attorney to step into the hallway to cool off for 5-10 minutes.

   4._____

5. During the second pre-trial hearing, the plaintiff's attorney, John, has called an expert witness to come in and testify. Your role in this process is to
   A. swear in the witness
   B. Escort the witness to the stand
   C. Record the witness testimony into the docket
   D. Relay the importance of the witnesses' testimony to him or her before they take the stand

   5._____

6. The second pre-trial conference took longer than the time allotted. The attorneys for the third pre-trial hearing have also seemed to disappear and cannot be located.
   Your NEXT step is to
   A. attempt to locate the attorneys for the hearing
   B. skip the third pre-trial hearing and hear the next conference
   C. issue a warrant for the attorneys' appearance
   D. record the lack of appearance in the docket

7. All of the following are required parties to the pre-trial hearing EXCEPT
   A. judge   B. attorneys   C. jury   D. court officer

8. The pre-trial hearing is MOST likely to take place after _____, but before _____.
   A. arraignment; jury selection
   B. deliberations; closing statements
   C. assignment; adjudication
   D. plea bargain; opening statement

9. During a court recess, you see one of the jurors walking into the judge's chambers.
   You immediately
   A. halt the juror and demand he or she return to the deliberation room
   B. allow the juror to proceed, but ask the judge about the incident later
   C. allow the juror to proceed and assume they know one another personally
   D. allow the juror to proceed but inform the law clerk of the incident

10. When reading an indictment in court, each charge represents a(n)
    A. allegation of a crime
    B. proven criminal act
    C. evidentiary plea
    D. legal certainty

11. After a defendant has been acquitted, he or she will likely be
    A. free to leave the courthouse
    B. remanded to federal prison
    C. detained until further notice
    D. formally sentenced

12. Highway Patrol Officer Rowan requests to bring his firearm into the Nassau County Supreme Court as he will be testifying in a case before Judge Pirro.
    Will he be able to?
    A. Yes, as he is licensed to carry the weapon
    B. Yes, as long as he provides proper identification
    C. Yes, if he is willing to discharge it in an emergency
    D. No, he must check his weapon before entering the courtroom

13. Dominic, a defense attorney, has approached you in the hallways of the New York City Civil Court. He is concerned that his client, Don, may become violent during court proceedings.
    How do you handle Dominic's request to closely supervise Don while court is in session?
    A. Inform the judge of Dominic's request and allow proceedings to continue as normal
    B. Ask that another court officer be present during court proceedings

C. Request the judge to sequester the jury while Don is present
D. Ignore Dominic's request for now, until you see how Don behaves yourself

14. Jury sequestration is
    A. extremely common given the complex nature of most criminal trials
    B. becoming increasingly common
    C. more common in civil cases than in criminal trials
    D. rare

15. The judge confides in you that she believes the defendant in an ongoing trial is guilty.
    You have a duty to
    A. report the judge to the local authorities
    B. inform the clerk's office that the judge is biased
    C. there is no duty to report as the judge is free to reserve their opinion of the case
    D. there is no duty to report the judge's comment in this instance

16. It is critical after use of force to
    A. document it as well as the circumstance that provided for it
    B. recording the reactions of witnesses
    C. presenting the judge for reasoning as to why you applied it
    D. destroying any contrary evidence

17. During a witness' testimony, which may take place that will likely require your intervention?
    A. Outburst by one of the parties
    B. Disruption by the spectators in the courtroom
    C. Disagreement by the clerk and stenographer
    D. Objection by the judge

18. At arraignment, the defendant is MOST likely to
    A. state his case
    B. convince the judge of his or her innocence
    C. enter a plea
    D. gather information on his or her case from the State's attorney

19. A warrant can be issued for an individual's arrest or for
    A. search of premises outlined in the warrant itself
    B. testimony
    C. deposition of the arrested individual
    D. evidence found at the scene

20. The responsibility to record notes for the judge and listen to issues of law that may need to be researched later are reserved for the
    A. court officer   B. stenographer
    C. judge's clerk   D. jury

21. Information about the charges against the defendant, as well as the parties involved in the case, can MOST likely be found in the
    A. judge's notes
    B. docket
    C. information
    D. discovery report

Questions 22-23.

DIRECTIONS: Questions 22 and 23 are to be answered on the basis of the following fact pattern.

The clerk's office has a line out of the door, with at least eighteen people waiting to be seen. Many of the attorneys are waiting to file documents while some others are waiting for their clients.

22. How would you move the crowd out of the clerk's office?
    A. Ask that anyone who is waiting for another party to step outside
    B. Ask that anyone who is able to use the automatic filer do so
    C. Ask that only those with a question specifically for the clerk remain in the office
    D. All of the above

23. An example of a question that can only be answered by the court clerk is:
    A. When the trial is scheduled to start
    B. Where courtroom B is located
    C. The name of the attorney representing the defendant
    D. The name of the judge who hears no-fault cases

24. The opening statements in a trial are delivered by the
    A. defendant
    B. plaintiff
    C. attorneys
    D. judge

25. The court officer is the MOST likely party to
    A. dissolve a dispute between two jurors
    B. dissolve a dispute between the judge and the attorneys
    C. dissolve a dispute between spectators
    D. all of the above

KEY (CORRECT ANSWERS)

1.	D	11.	A
2.	D	12.	D
3.	D	13.	B
4.	A	14.	D
5.	B	15.	D
6.	A	16.	A
7.	C	17.	B
8.	A	18.	C
9.	A	19.	A
10.	A	20.	C

21. B
22. D
23. D
24. C
25. D

EXAMINATION SECTION
TEST 1

DIRECTIONS: Each question or incomplete statement is followed by several suggested answers or completions. Select the one that BEST answers the question or completes the statement. *PRINT THE LETTER OF THE CORRECT ANSWER IN THE SPACE AT THE RIGHT.*

1. Physical and mental health are essential to the officer. According to this statement, the officer MUST be

    A. as wise as he is strong
    B. smarter than most people
    C. sound in mind and body
    D. stronger than the average criminal

2. Teamwork is the basis of successful law enforcement. The factor stressed by this statement is

    A. cooperation B. determination
    C. initiative   D. pride

3. Legal procedure is a means, not an end. Its function is merely to accomplish the enforcement of legal rights.
    A litigant has no vested interest in the observance of the rules of procedure as such. All that he should be entitled to demand is that he be given an opportunity for a fair and impartial trial of his case. He should not be permitted to invoke the aid of technical rules merely to embarrass his adversary.
    According to this paragraph, it is MOST correct to state that

    A. observance of the rules of procedure guarantees a fair trial
    B. embarrassment of an adversary through technical rules does not make a fair trial
    C. a litigant is not interested in the observance of rules of procedure
    D. technical rules must not be used in a trial

4. One theory states that all criminal behavior is taught by a process of communication within small intimate groups. An individual engages in criminal behavior if the number of criminal patterns which he has acquired exceed the number of non-criminal patterns. This statement indicates that criminal behavior is

    A. learned   B. instinctive
    C. hereditary   D. reprehensible

5. The law enforcement staff of today requires training and mental qualities of a high order. The poorly or partially prepared staff member lowers the standard of work, retards his own earning power, and fails in a career meant to provide a livelihood and social improvement.
    According to this statement,

    A. an inefficient member of a law enforcement staff will still earn a good livelihood
    B. law enforcement officers move in good social circles
    C. many people fail in law enforcement careers
    D. persons of training and ability are essential to a law enforcement staff

6. In any state, no crime can occur unless there is a written law forbidding the act or the omission in question; and even though an act may not be exactly in harmony with public policy, such act is not a crime unless it is expressly forbidden by legislative statement. According to the above statement,

   A. a crime is committed with reference to a particular law
   B. acts not in harmony with public policy should be forbidden by law
   C. non-criminal activity will promote public welfare
   D. legislative enactments frequently forbid actions in harmony with public policy

7. The unrestricted sale of firearms is one of the main causes of our shameful crime record. According to this statement, one of the causes of our crime record is

   A. development of firepower
   B. ease of securing weapons
   C. increased skill in using guns
   D. scientific perfection of firearms

8. Every person must be informed of the reason for his arrest unless he is arrested in the actual commission of a crime. Sufficient force to effect the arrest may be used, but the courts frown on brutal methods.
   According to this statement, a person does not have to be informed of the reason for his arrest if

   A. brutal force was not used in effecting it
   B. the courts will later turn the defendant loose
   C. the person arrested knows force will be used if necessary
   D. the reason for it is clearly evident from the circumstances

9. An important duty of an officer is to keep order in the court.
   On the basis of this statement, it is PROBABLY true that

   A. it is more important for an officer to be strong than it is for him to be smart
   B. people involved in court trials are noisy if not kept in check
   C. not every duty of an officer is important
   D. the maintenance of order is important for the proper conduct of court business

10. Ideally, a correctional system should include several types of institutions to provide different degrees of custody.
    On the basis of this statement, one could MOST reasonably say that

    A. as the number of institutions in a correctional system increases, the efficiency of the system increases
    B. the difference in degree of custody for the inmate depends on the types of institutions in a correctional system
    C. the greater the variety of institutions, the stricter the degree of custody that can be maintained
    D. the same type of correctional institution is not desirable for the custody of all prisoners

11. The enforced idleness of a large percentage of adult men and women in our prisons is one of the direct causes of the tensions which burst forth in riot and disorder.
    On the basis of this statement, a good reason why inmates should perform daily work of some kind is that

    A. better morale and discipline can be maintained when inmates are kept busy
    B. daily work is an effective way of punishing inmates for the crimes they have committed
    C. law-abiding citizens must work, therefore labor should also be required of inmates
    D. products of inmates' labor will in part pay the cost of their maintenance

12. With industry invading rural areas, the use of the automobile, and the speed of modern communications and transportation, the problems of neglect and delinquency are no longer peculiar to cities but an established feature of everyday life.
    This statement implies MOST directly that

    A. delinquents are moving from cities to rural areas
    B. delinquency and neglect are found in rural areas
    C. delinquency is not as much of a problem in rural areas as in cities
    D. rural areas now surpass cities in industry

13. Young men from minority groups, if unable to find employment, become discouraged and hopeless because of their economic position and may finally resort to any means of supplying their wants.
    The MOST reasonable of the following conclusions that may be drawn from this statement only is that

    A. discouragement sometimes leads to crime
    B. in general, young men from minority groups are criminals
    C. unemployment turns young men from crime
    D. young men from minority groups are seldom employed

14. To prevent crime, we must deal with the possible criminal long before he reaches the prison. Our aim should be not merely to reform the law breakers but to strike at the roots of crime: neglectful parents, bad companions, unsatisfactory homes, selfishness, disregard for the rights of others, and bad social conditions.
    The above statement recommends

    A. abolition of prisons   B. better reformatories
    C. compulsory education   D. general social reform

15. There is evidence which shows that comic books which glorify the criminal and criminal acts have a distinct influence in producing young criminals.
    According to this statement,

    A. comic books affect the development of criminal careers
    B. comic books specialize in reporting criminal acts
    C. young criminals read comic books exclusively
    D. young criminals should not be permitted to read comic books

16. Suppose a study shows that juvenile delinquents are equal in intelligence but three school grades behind juvenile non-delinquents.
On the basis of this information only, it is MOST reasonable to say that

    A. a delinquent usually progresses to the educational limit set by his intelligence
    B. educational achievement depends on intelligence only
    C. educational achievement is closely associated with delinquency
    D. lack of intelligence is closely associated with delinquency

17. There is no proof today that the experience of a prison sentence makes a better citizen of an adult. On the contrary, there seems some evidence that the experience is an unwholesome one that frequently confirms the criminality of the inmate.
From the above paragraph only, it may be BEST concluded that

    A. prison sentences tend to punish rather than rehabilitate
    B. all criminals should be given prison sentences
    C. we should abandon our penal institutions
    D. penal institutions are effective in rehabilitating criminals

18. Some courts are referred to as *criminal* courts while others are known as *civil* courts.
This distinction in name is MOST probably based on the

    A. historical origin of the court
    B. link between the court and the police
    C. manner in which the judges are chosen
    D. type of cases tried there

19. Many children who are exposed to contacts and experiences of a delinquent nature become educated and trained in crime in the course of participating in the daily life of the neighborhood.
From this statement only, we may reasonably conclude that

    A. delinquency passes from parent to child
    B. neighborhood influences are usually bad
    C. schools are training grounds for delinquents
    D. none of the above conclusions is reasonable

20. Old age insurance, for whose benefits a quarter of a million city employees may elect to become eligible, is one feature of the Social Security Act that is wholly administered by the Federal government.
On the basis of this paragraph only, it may MOST reasonably be inferred that

    A. a quarter of a million city employees are drawing old age insurance
    B. a quarter of a million city employees have elected to become eligible for old age insurance
    C. the city has no part in administering Social Security old age insurance
    D. only the Federal government administers the Social Security Act

21. An officer's revolver is a defensive, and not offensive, weapon.
On the basis of this statement only, an officer should BEST draw his revolver to

    A. fire at an unarmed burglar
    B. force a suspect to confess
    C. frighten a juvenile delinquent
    D. protect his own life

22. Prevention of crime is of greater value to the community than the punishment of crime. 22._____
    If this statement is accepted as true, GREATEST emphasis should be placed on

    A. malingering   B. medication
    C. imprisonment   D. rehabilitation

23. The criminal is rarely or never reformed. Acceptance of this statement as true would 23._____
    mean that GREATEST emphasis should be placed on

    A. imprisonment   B. parole
    C. probation   D. malingering

24. The MOST accurate of the following statements about persons convicted of crimes is 24._____
    that

    A. their criminal behavior is almost invariably the result of low intelligence
    B. they are almost invariably legally insane
    C. they are more likely to come from underprivileged groups than from other groups
    D. they have certain facial characteristics which distinguish them from non-criminals

25. Suppose a study shows that the I.Q. (Intelligence Quotient) of prison inmates is 95 as 25._____
    opposed to an I.Q. of 100 for a numerically equivalent civilian group.
    A claim, on the basis of this study, that criminals have a lower I.Q. than non-criminals
    would be

    A. *improper;* prison inmates are criminals who have been caught
    B. *proper;* the study was numerically well done
    C. *improper;* the sample was inadequate
    D. *proper;* even misdemeanors are sometimes penalized by prison sentences

Questions 26-45.

DIRECTIONS: Select the number of the word or expression that MOST NEARLY expresses the meaning of the capitalized word in the group.

26. ABDUCT 26._____

    A. lead   B. kidnap   C. sudden   D. worthless

27. BIAS 27._____

    A. ability   B. envy   C. prejudice   D. privilege

28. COERCE 28._____

    A. cancel   B. force   C. rescind   D. rugged

29. CONDONE 29._____

    A. combine   B. pardon   C. revive   D. spice

30. CONSISTENCY 30._____

    A. bravery   B. readiness
    C. strain   D. uniformity

31. CREDENCE
    A. belief   B. devotion
    C. resemblance   D. tempo

32. CURRENT
    A. backward   B. brave
    C. prevailing   D. wary

33. CUSTODY
    A. advisement   B. belligerence
    C. guardianship   D. suspicion

34. DEBILITY
    A. deceitfulness   B. decency
    C. strength   D. weakness

35. DEPLETE
    A. beg   B. empty   C. excuse   D. fold

36. ENUMERATE
    A. name one by one   B. disappear
    C. get rid of   D. pretend

37. FEIGN
    A. allow   B. incur   C. pretend   D. weaken

38. INSTIGATE
    A. analyze   B. coordinate
    C. oppose   D. provoke

39. LIABLE
    A. careless   B. growing
    C. mistaken   D. responsible

40. PONDER
    A. attack   B. heavy   C. meditate   D. solicit

41. PUGILIST
    A. farmer   B. politician
    C. prize fighter   D. stage actor

42. QUELL
    A. explode   B. inform   C. shake   D. suppress

43. RECIPROCAL
    A. mutual   B. organized
    C. redundant   D. thoughtful

44. RUSE
    A. burn   B. impolite   C. rot   D. trick

45. STEALTHY
    A. crazed   B. flowing   C. sly   D. wicked

Questions 46-50.

DIRECTIONS: Each of the sentences in Questions 46 through 50 may be classified under one of the following four categories:
A. faulty because of incorrect grammar
B. faulty because of incorrect punctuation
C. faulty because of incorrect capitalization or incorrect spelling
D. correct

Examine each sentence carefully to determine under which of the above four options it is best classified. Then, in the space at the right, print the capital letter preceding the option which is the BEST of the four suggested above. Each faulty sentence contains but one type of error. Consider a sentence to be correct if it contains none of the types of errors mentioned, even though there may be other correct ways of expressing the same thought.

46. They told both he and I that the prisoner had escaped.

47. Any superior officer, who, disregards the just complaints of his subordinates, is remiss in the performance of his duty.

48. Only those members of the national organization who resided in the Middle west attended the conference in Chicago.

49. We told him to give the investigation assignment to whoever was available.

50. Please do not disappoint and embarass us by not appearing in court.

KEY (CORRECT ANSWERS)

1. C	11. A	21. D	31. A	41. C
2. A	12. B	22. D	32. C	42. D
3. B	13. A	23. A	33. C	43. A
4. A	14. D	24. C	34. D	44. D
5. D	15. A	25. A	35. B	45. C
6. A	16. C	26. B	36. A	46. A
7. B	17. A	27. C	37. C	47. B
8. D	18. D	28. B	38. D	48. C
9. D	19. D	29. B	39. D	49. D
10. D	20. C	30. D	40. C	50. C

TEST 2

DIRECTIONS: Each question or incomplete statement is followed by several suggested answers or completions. Select the one that BEST answers the question or completes the statement. *PRINT THE LETTER OF THE CORRECT ANSWER IN THE SPACE AT THE RIGHT.*

1. Suppose a man falls from a two-story high scaffold and is unconscious. You should   1.___

   A. call for medical assistance and avoid moving the man
   B. get someone to help you move him indoors to a bed
   C. have someone help you walk him around until he revives
   D. hold his head up and pour a stimulant down his throat

2. For proper first aid treatment, a person who has fainted should be   2.___

   A. doused with cold water and then warmly covered
   B. given artificial respiration until he is revived
   C. laid down with his head lower than the rest of his body
   D. slapped on the face until he is revived

3. If you are called on to give first aid to a person who is suffering from shock, you should   3.___

   A. apply cold towels   B. give him a stimulant
   C. keep him awake   D. wrap him warmly

4. Artificial respiration would NOT be proper first aid for a person suffering from   4.___

   A. drowning   B. electric shock
   C. external bleeding   D. suffocation

5. Suppose you are called on to give first aid to several victims of an accident. First attention should be given to the one who is   5.___

   A. bleeding severely   B. groaning loudly
   C. unconscious   D. vomiting

6. If an officer's weekly salary is increased from $480 to $540, then the percent of increase is _____ percent.   6.___

   A. 10   B. 11 1/9   C. 12 1/2   D. 20

7. Suppose that one-half the officers in a department have served for more than ten years and one-third have served for more than 15 years.
Then, the fraction of officers who have served between ten and fifteen years is   7.___

   A. 1/3   B. 1/5   C. 1/6   D. 1/12

8. In a city prison there are four floors on which prisoners are housed. The top floor houses one-quarter of the inmates, the bottom floor houses one-sixth of the inmates, one-third are housed on the second floor. The rest of the inmates are housed on the third floor. If there are 90 inmates housed on the third floor, the TOTAL number of inmates housed on all four floors together is   8.___

   A. 270   B. 360   C. 450   D. 540

32

9. Suppose that ten percent of those who commit serious crimes are convicted and that fifteen percent of those convicted are sentenced for more than 3 years.
   The percentage of those committing serious crimes who are sentenced for more than 3 years is _____ percent.

   A. 15   B. 1.5   C. .15   D. .015

10. Assume that there are 1,100 employees in a city agency. Of these, 15 percent are officers, 80 percent of whom are attorneys; of the attorneys, two-fifths have been with the agency over five years.
    Then, the number of officers who are attorneys and have over five years experience with the agency is MOST NEARLY

    A. 45   B. 53   C. 132   D. 165

11. An employee who has 500 cartons of supplies to pack can pack them at the rate of 50 an hour. After this employee has worked for 1/2 hour, he is joined by another employee who can pack 45 cartons an hour.
    Assuming that both employees can maintain their respective rates of speed, then the TOTAL number of hours required to pack all the cartons is

    A. 4 1/2   B. 5   C. 5 1/2   D. 6 1/2

12. Thirty-six officers can complete an assignment in 22 days. Assuming that all officers work at the same rate of speed, the number of officers that would be needed to complete this assignment in 12 days is

    A. 42   B. 54   C. 66   D. 72

Questions 13-15.

DIRECTIONS: Questions 13 through 15 are to be answered on the basis of the table below. Data for certain categories have been omitted from the table. You are to calculate the missing numbers if needed to answer the questions.

	2007	2008	Numerical Increase
Correction Officers	1,226	1,347	
Court Officers		529	34
Deputy Sheriffs	38	40	
Supervisors			
	2,180	2,414	

13. The number in the *Supervisors* group in 2007 was MOST NEARLY

    A. 500   B. 475   C. 450   D. 425

14. The LARGEST percentage increase from 2007 to 2008 was in the group of

    A. Correction Officers   B. Court Officers
    C. Deputy Sheriffs   D. Supervisors

15. In 2008, the ratio of the number of Correction Officers to the total of the other three categories of employees was MOST NEARLY

    A. 1:1   B. 2:1   C. 3:1   D. 4:1

16. A directed verdict is made by a court when

    A. the facts are not disputed
    B. the defendant's motion for a directed verdict has been denied
    C. there is no question of law involved
    D. neither party has moved for a directed verdict

17. Papers on appeal of a criminal case do NOT include one of the following:

    A. Summons
    B. Minutes of trial
    C. Complaint
    D. Intermediate motion papers

18. A pleading titled *Smith vs. Jones, et al* indicates

    A. two plaintiffs
    B. two defendants
    C. more than two defendants
    D. unknown defendants

19. A District Attorney makes a *prima facie* case when

    A. there is proof of guilt beyond a reasonable doubt
    B. the evidence is sufficient to convict in the absence of rebutting evidence
    C. the prosecution presents more evidence than the defense
    D. the defendant fails to take the stand

20. A person is NOT qualified to act as a trial juror in a criminal action if he or she

    A. has been convicted previously of a misdemeanor
    B. is under 18 years of age
    C. has scruples against the death penalty
    D. does not own property of a value at least $500

21. A court clerk who falsifies a court record commits a(n)

    A. misdemeanor
    B. offense
    C. felony
    D. no crime, but automatically forfeits his tenure

22. Insolent and contemptuous behavior to a judge during a court of record proceeding is punishable as

    A. civil contempt
    B. criminal contempt
    C. disorderly conduct
    D. a disorderly person

23. Offering a bribe to a court clerk would not constitute a crime UNLESS the

    A. court clerk accepted the bribe
    B. bribe consisted of money
    C. bribe was given with intent to influence the court clerk in his official functions
    D. court was actually in session

24. A defendant comes to trial in the same court in which he had previously been defendant in a similar case.
    The court officer should

    A. tell him, *Knew we'd be seeing you again*
    B. tell newspaper reporters what he knows of the previous action
    C. treat him the same as he would any other defendant
    D. warn the judge that the man had previously been a defendant

25. Suppose in conversation with you, an attorney strongly criticizes a ruling of the judge and you believe the attorney to be correct.
    You should

    A. assure him you feel the same way
    B. tell him the judge knows the law
    C. tell him to ask for an exception
    D. refuse to discuss the matter

26. Assume that you are a court officer. A woman sees you in the hall and attempts to register a complaint that her husband raped her two hours earlier.
    Which one of the following is the MOST appropriate action for you to take FIRST in this case?

    A. Refer her to Family Court.
    B. Advise her that her husband has not committed any crime.
    C. Ask her for additional information about the circumstances surrounding her allegation so that you may refer her to the proper office or agency.
    D. Have her sign a criminal information in the court.

27. Which one of the following is the BEST example of a privileged communication which is NOT admissible as evidence in a court of law without the consent of the communicator?

    A. Client to his accountant
    B. Informant to a law enforcement officer
    C. Parent to his child
    D. Defendant to his spouse

28. A court officer has many contacts with the public. In these contacts, it is MOST important that he

    A. be brief and complete in his answers
    B. be courteous and helpful
    C. go along with what they ask
    D. know the law

29. Suppose a witness becomes engaged in a very heated argument with an attorney who is cross-examining him. The court officer should

    A. ask the attorney to avoid exciting the witness
    B. ask the judge if he wishes any action to be taken
    C. await the judge's order before interceding
    D. caution the witness to be more respectful

30. Suppose that you are a court officer stationed at the door of the courtroom to prevent anyone from entering while the judge is charging the jury. A man whom you recognize as a City Councilman, accompanied by a woman, attempts to enter the courtroom.
The BEST action for you to take is to

    A. apologize and explain why they cannot be permitted to enter
    B. permit the man to enter since he is a Councilman but exclude the woman
    C. permit them to enter since the judge would surely make an exception for them
    D. send a note in to the judge to find if they may be permitted to enter

31. It is desirable that a court officer acquire a knowledge of the procedures of the court to which he is assigned MAINLY because such knowledge will help him

    A. become familiar with anti-social behavior
    B. discharge his duties properly
    C. gain insight into causes of crime
    D. in any personal legal proceeding

32. Since he is a city employee, a court officer who refuses to waive immunity from prosecution when called on to testify in court automatically terminates his employment. From this statement ONLY, it may be BEST inferred that

    A. a court officer is a city employee
    B. all city employees are court officers
    C. city employees may be fired only for malfeasance
    D. court attendants who waive immunity may not be prosecuted

33. Referees of the Civil Court are former judges of this court who have served at least ten years and whose term of office terminated at the age of 55 or over, or any judge who has served in a court of record and has retired.
According to this statement, a person can be a referee of the Civil Court ONLY if he

    A. has been a judge
    B. has retired
    C. has served at least 10 years in the court
    D. meets certain age requirements

34. Assume that you are assigned to a jury room where you are to guard the jury until 4 P.M. Your relief does not arrive and the jury is still deliberating.
Of the following, the BEST action for you to take is to

    A. ask the foreman of the jury to assume responsibility until your relief arrives
    B. find out what the jurors may need, get it, and then lock them in for the night
    C. inform your supervisor but remain on duty until you are relieved
    D. wait until 5 P.M., your usual closing time, and then leave if the relief has not arrived by then

35. When, at a trial, a piece of evidence is tagged as *Exhibit A*, the CHIEF purpose is to

    A. assure its return to the owner
    B. make it possible to examine it for fingerprints without chance of error
    C. make it possible to identify and refer to it easily
    D. prevent the defendant from denying he had it

36. In one case, a mistrial was declared because the indictment used the pronoun he instead of she.
The MOST useful information a court attendant can derive from this statement is that

   A. accuracy is important
   B. mistrial is a legal term
   C. one must always use good grammar
   D. to misrepresent is criminal

37. Suppose a newspaper reporter asks you for information about what happened at a trial where the judge had ordered the courtroom cleared of reporters and spectators.
You should

   A. give him the information he wants
   B. refer him to the judge for information
   C. refuse to talk to him unless reporters from other papers are present
   D. give him misleading information

38. Assume that you are the court officer on duty outside the judge's chambers in the court house. One day, one of the judges informs you that he will be too busy that day to see any visitors, and he tells you to refer them to his secretary for new appointments. Later in the day, an important visitor comes in and asks to see the judge about urgent business.
Of the following, the BEST course of action for you to take in this situation is to

   A. ask the visitor to come back another day when the judge may be able to see him
   B. call the judge on the phone and tell him that the visitor has urgent business to discuss with him
   C. refer the visitor to one of the other judges who may be present in chambers
   D. tell the visitor that the judge is not available, but his secretary may be able to help him or make a new appointment

39. To gain a verdict against X in a trial, it was necessary to show that he could have been at Y Street at 5 P.M.
It was proven that he was seen at Z Street at 4:45 P.M. The question that MUST be answered to show whether the verdict should be against X is:

   A. How long does it take to get from Z Street to Y Street?
   B. In what sort of neighborhood is Y Street located?
   C. Was X acting suspiciously on the day in question?
   D. Who was with X when he was seen at Z Street at 4:45 P.M.?

40. If, at the instructions of the judge, a court officer calls the name of a defendant in a lawsuit and the person does not answer, the court officer should FIRST

   A. ask the judge if he called the person's name correctly
   B. call the person's name again
   C. look outside the doors of the courtroom for the defendant
   D. tell the judge the person doesn't answer

41. When X is accused of having cheated Y of a sum of money and Y is proven to have been deprived of the money, there is an additional requirement for a verdict against X.
The additional requirement is to prove that

   A. the money was stolen from Y
   B. X had the money after Y had it
   C. X had the money before Y had it
   D. X cheated Y of the money

42. Assume that you are on duty in a courtroom and during the judge's absence one of the witnesses for a pending case becomes very angry about the delay.
Of the following, the BEST action for you to take is to

   A. listen to him until he calms down and then explain the reason for the delay
   B. tell him your court is no different from any other court
   C. walk away from him so that you will not get involved in a dispute
   D. warn him that the judge may be back at any minute and will hold him in contempt

43. Assume that you are assigned to the post outside judge's chambers in the court house. A visitor tells you he has an appointment with Judge Jones who is expected to arrive shortly. He asks for permission to wait in the judge's office which is unoccupied at the present time.
For you to permit him to wait there would be

   A. *wise;* the judge would no doubt wish to speak to the man privately
   B. *wise;* it would keep the anteroom where you are stationed clear, allowing other employees to work without any disturbance
   C. *unwise;* it is rude to allow a visitor to sit alone in an office
   D. *unwise;* there may be confidential material on the judge's desk or bookcases

44. A court officer shall not receive a gift from any defendant or other person on the defendant's behalf.
The BEST explanation for this rule is that

   A. acceptance of a gift has no significance
   B. defendants cannot usually afford gifts
   C. favors may be expected in return
   D. gifts are only an expression of good will

45. When a jury is selected, the attorney for each side has a right to refuse to accept a certain number of prospective jurors without giving any reason therefor.
The reason for this is MAINLY that

   A. attorneys can exclude persons likely to be biased even though no prejudice is admitted
   B. persons who will suffer economically by being summoned for jury duty can be excused forthwith
   C. relatives of the litigants can be excused thus insuring a fair trial for each side
   D. there will be a greater number of people from which the jury can be selected

46. Where the defendant in a criminal case is too poor to afford counsel, the court will assign one and he will be paid by the government.
The principle BEST established by this statement is that

   A. it is improper for the government to provide both prosecuting and defending counsel in a trial
   B. laws are usually violated because of poverty and defendants are too poor to employ counsel
   C. only wealthy law violators may hope to be represented by competent counsel
   D. the government is obligated to shield the innocent as well as punish the guilty

47. If a visitor to the court asks foolish questions, the BEST action for the court officer to take is to

    A. answer in a brusque manner to discourage further foolish questions
    B. refer the questioner to his supervisor
    C. answer them the same way as he would any other questions
    D. ignore them since the person doesn't really expect an answer

48. A man plus a uniform makes a good court officer. This statement is FALSE because

    A. a court officer is also required to wear a badge
    B. a good court officer is not made merely by putting on a uniform
    C. it makes no mention of the fact that the uniform must be neat
    D. patrolmen as well as court officers wear uniforms

49. It is a frequent misconception that court officers can be recruited from those registers established for the recruitment of city police or firemen. While it is true that many common qualifications are found in all of these, specific standards for court work are indicated, varying with the size, geographical location, and policies of the court.
    According to this paragraph ONLY, it may BEST be inferred that

    A. a successful court officer must have some qualifications not required of a policeman or fireman
    B. qualifications which make a successful patrolman will also make a successful fireman
    C. the same qualifications are required of a court officer regardless of the court to which he is assigned
    D. the successful court officer is required to be both more intelligent and stronger than a fireman

50. One of the duties of a court officer is to assist the public with their problems.
    A PROPER exercise of this duty by a court officer would be for the officer to

    A. advise members of the public to settle their differences out of court
    B. advise a member of the public how to fill out forms required by the court
    C. lend money to a member of the public to pay the required court fees
    D. recommend a lawyer to a member of the public who does not have one

KEY (CORRECT ANSWERS)

1. A	11. C	21. C	31. B	41. D
2. C	12. C	22. B	32. A	42. A
3. D	13. D	23. C	33. A	43. D
4. C	14. D	24. C	34. C	44. C
5. A	15. A	25. D	35. C	45. A
6. C	16. A	26. C	36. A	46. D
7. C	17. D	27. D	37. B	47. C
8. B	18. C	28. B	38. D	48. B
9. B	19. B	29. C	39. A	49. A
10. B	20. B	30. A	40. B	50. B

EXAMINATION SECTION

TEST 1

DIRECTIONS: Each question or incomplete statement is followed by several suggested answers or completions. Select the one that BEST answers the question or completes the statement. *PRINT THE LETTER OF THE CORRECT ANSWER IN THE SPACE AT THE RIGHT.*

Questions 1-4 are based solely on the information in the paragraph below:

> A Court Officer shall give reasonable aid to a sick or injured person. He or she shall summon an ambulance, if necessary, by telephoning the Police Department, which shall notify the hospital. He or she shall wait in a place where the arriving ambulance can see him or her, if possible, so as to direct the ambulance attendant to the patient. If the ambulance does not arrive within a half-hour, the Court Officer should call a second time, telling the department that this is a second call. However, if the injured person is conscious, the Court Officer should ask whether such person is willing to go to a hospital before calling for an ambulance.

1. The Court Officer who wishes to summon an ambulance should telephone the
    - A. nearest hospital
    - B. Health and Hospitals Corporation
    - C. Police Department
    - D. nearest police precinct

2. If an ambulance does not arrive within half an hour, the Court Officer should
    - A. ask the person injured if he/she wants to go to the hospital in a cab
    - B. call the Police Department
    - C. call the nearest police precinct
    - D. call the nearest hospital

3. A Court Officer who is called to help a person who has fallen on the courthouse steps and apparently has a broken leg should
    - A. put the leg in traction so the doctor will have no difficulty setting it
    - B. ask the person, if he/she is conscious, whether he/she wishes to go to the hospital
    - C. attempt to get the story behind the injury
    - D. put in a call for an ambulance at once

4. A Court Officer who is present when a witness becomes ill while waiting to testify should
    - A. wait in front of the room until the ambulance arrives
    - B. send a bystander to the courtroom to page a doctor
    - C. ask the withness if he/she wishes to go to a hospital
    - D. call the Court Clerk for instructions

5. "Physical and mental health are essential to the Court Officer."
According to this statement, a peace officer must be
   A. wise as well as strong
   B. smarter than most people
   C. sound in mind and body
   D. smarter than the average criminal

6. "Teamwork is the basis of successful law enforcement."
The factor stressed by this statement is
   A. cooperation
   B. determination
   C. initiative
   D. pride

7. "A sufficient quantity of material supplied as evidence enables the laboratory expert to determine the true nature of the substance, whereas an extremely limited specimen may be an abnormal sample containing foreign matter not indicative of the true nature of the material."
On the basis of this statement alone, it may be concluded that a reason for giving an adequate sample of material for evidence to a laboratory expert is that
   A. a limited specimen spoils more quickly than a larger sample
   B. a small sample may not truly represent the evidence
   C. he or she cannot analyze a small sample correctly
   D. he or she must have enough material to keep a part of it untouched to show in court

8. "The Housing Authority not only faces every problem of the private developer, it must also assume responsibilities of which a private building is free. The authority must account to the community; it must conform to Federal regulations and it must overcome the prejudices of contractors, bankers and prospective tenants against public operations. These authorities are being watched for the first error of judgment or the first evidence of high costs that can be torn to bits before a congressional committee."
On the basis of this selection, which statement would be most correct?
   A. Private builders do not have the opposition of contractors, bankers and prospective tenants
   B. Congressional committees impede the progress of public housing by petty investigations
   C. A housing authority must deal with all the difficulties encountered by the private builder
   D. Housing authorities are not more immune to errors in judgment than private developers

9. Accident proneness is a subject that deserves much more objective and competent study than it has received to date. In discussing accident proneness, it is important to differentiate between the employee who is a "repeater" and one who is truly accident-prone. It is obvious that any person assigned to work without thorough training is liable to injury until he or she does learn the "how" of it. Few workers left to their own devices develop adequate safe practices, and therefore they must be trained. Only those who fail to respond to proper training should be regarded as accident-prone. The repeater whose accident record can be explained by a correctable physical defect, correctable plant or machine hazards, or by assignment to work for which he or she is not suited because of physical deficiencies or special abilities cannot be fairly called accident-prone.

   According to the passage, people are considered accident-prone if
   - A. they have accidents regardless of the fact that they have been properly trained
   - B. they have many accidents
   - C. it is possible for them to have accidents
   - D. they work at a job where accidents are possible

Questions 10 through 12 are based on the following paragraph:

Discontent of some citizens with the practices and policies of local government leads to the creation of local civic associations. Completely outside of government, manned by a few devoted volunteers, understaffed, and with pitifully few dues-paying members, they attempt to arouse widespread public opinion on selected issues by presenting facts and ideas. The findings of these civic associations are widely trusted by the press and public, and amidst the records of rebuffs received are found more than enough achievements to justify what little their activities cost. Civic associations are politically non-partisan. Hence their vitality is drawn from true political independents who in most communities are a trifling minority. Except in a few large cities, civic associations are seldom affluent enough to maintain an office or to afford even a small paid staff.

10. The main reason for the formation of civic associations is to
    - A. provide independent candidates for local public office with an opportunity to be heard
    - B. bring about changes in the activities of local government
    - C. allow persons who are politically non-partisan to express themselves on local public issues
    - D. permit the small minority of true political independents to supply leadership for non-partisan causes

11. The statements that civic associations make on issues of general interest are
    - A. accepted by large segments of the public
    - B. taken at face value only by the few people who are true political independents
    - C. questioned as to their accuracy by most newspapers
    - D. expressed as a result of aroused widespread public opinion

12. It is most accurate to conclude that since
    A. they deal with many public issues, the cost of their efforts on each issue is small
    B. their attempts to attain their objectives often fail, little money is contributed to civic associations
    C. they spend little money in their efforts, they are ineffective when they become involved in major issues
    D. their achievements outweigh the small cost of their efforts, civic associations are considered worthwhile

13. "If you are in doubt as to whether any matter is properly mailable, you should ask the postmaster. Even though the post office has not expressly declared any matter to be nonmailable, the sender of such matter may be held fully liable for violation of law if he does actually send nonmailable matter through the mails."
    Of the following, the most accurate statement made concerning this selection is
    A. nonmailable matter is not always clearly defined
    B. ignorance of what constitutes nonmailable matter relieves the sender of all responsibility
    C. though doubt may exist about the mailability of any matter, the sender is fully liable for any law violation if such matter should be nonmailable
    D. the post office is not explicit in its position on the violation of the nonmailable matter law

Questions 14 through 16 are based on the following paragraph:

What is required is a program that will protect our citizens and their property from criminal and anti-social acts, will effectively restrain and reform juvenile delinquents, and will prevent the further development of anti-social behavior. Discipline and punishment of offenders must necessarily play an important part in any such program. Serious offenders cannot be mollycoddled merely because they are under 21. Restraint and punishment necessarily follow serious anti-social acts. But punishment, if it is to be effective, must be a planned part of a more comprehensive program of treating delinquency.

14. The one goal not included among those listed in the paragraph is to
    A. stop young people from defacing public property
    B. keep homes from being broken into
    C. develop an intra-city boys baseball league
    D. change juvenile delinquents into useful citizens

15. Punishment is
    A. not satisfactory in any program dealing with juvenile delinquents
    B. the most effective means by which young vandals and hooligans can be reformed
    C. not used sufficiently when dealing with serious offenders who are under 21
    D. of value in reducing juvenile delinquency only if it is part of a complete program

16. With respect to serious offenders who are under 21 years of age, the paragraph suggests that they
    A. be mollycoddled
    B. be dealt with as part of a comprehensive program to punish mature criminals
    C. should be punished
    D. be prevented, by brute force if necessary, from performing anti-social acts

    16._____

17. Statistics tell us that heart disease kills more people than any other illness, and the death rate continues to rise. People over 30 have a 50-50 chance of escaping, for heart disease is chiefly an illness of people in late middle age and advanced years. Since more people in this age group are living today than were some years ago, heart disease is able to find more victims.
    On the basis of this selection, the statement which is most nearly correct is that
    A. half the people over 30 years of age have heart disease today
    B. more people die of heart disease than of all other diseases combined
    C. older people are the chief victims of heart disease
    D. the rising birth rate has increased the possibility that the average person will die of heart disease

    17._____

18. Assume that a Court Officer is allowed 25 cents a mile for the use of her automobile for the purpose of conducting defendants to and from court sessions. The first month she drove 416 miles; the second month 328 miles; the third month 2,012 miles; the fourth month 187 miles; the fifth month 713 miles; the sixth month 1,608 miles. Her expenditures for gasoline averaged $2.70 a gallon and her general average of miles per gallon was 16; she used 32 quarts of oil at $1.25 per quart and spent $351.20 on care and general upkeep of her car for the six months. Without considering the depreciation in value of her car, she would have received above her expenditures:
    A. $36.50
    B. $40
    C. $96.10
    D. $263.20

    18._____

19. Assume that you borrowed $2,000 on Nov. 1, 1999, for the use of which you were required to pay simple interest semi-annually at seven percent a year. By May 1, 2005, you would have paid interest amounting to
    A. $140
    B. $280
    C. $700
    D. $770

    19._____

20. A courtroom contains 72 persons, which is two-fifths of its capacity. The number of persons that the courtroom can hold is
    A. 28   B. 129   C. 180   D. 200-300

    20._____

21. The total cost of 30 pencils at 18 cents a dozen, 12 paper pads at 27-1/2 cents each and eight boxes of paper clips at 5-1/4 cents a box is
    A. more than $10
    B. $1.50
    C. $4.17
    D. $1.52

    21._____

22. "A" worked five days on overhauling an old car. Then "B" worked four days to finish the job. After the sale of the car, the net profit was $243. They wanted to divide the profit on the basis of time spent by each. A's share of the profit was
    A. $108
    B. $135
    C. $127
    D. $143

    22._____

Questions 23-26

DIRECTIONS: Each of the following questions contains four sentences. Select the sentence in each question that is best with respect to grammar and good usage.

23. A. One of us have to make the reply before tomorrow.
    B. Making the reply before tomorrow will have to be done by one of us.
    C. One of us has to reply before tomorrow.
    D. Anyone has to reply before tomorrow.

    23._____

24. A. There is several ways to organize a good report.
    B. Several ways exist in organizing a good report.
    C. To organize a good report, several ways exist.
    D. There are several ways to organize a good report.

    24._____

25. A. All employees whose record of service ranged between 51 down to 40 years were retired.
    B. All employees who had served from 40 to 51 years were retired.
    C. All employees serving 40 to 51 years were retired.
    D. Those retired were employees serving 40 to 51 years.

    25._____

26. A. Of all the employees, he spends the most time at the office.
    B. He spends more time at the office than that of his employees.
    C. His working hours are longer than or equal to those of other employees.
    D. He devotes as much, if not more, time to his work than the rest of the employees.

    26._____

Question 27 is based on the following paragraph:

Certain inmate types are generally found in prisons. These types are called gorillas, toughs, hipsters and merchants. Gorillas deliberately use violence to intimidate fearful inmates into providing favors. Toughs are swift to explode into violence against prisoners, because of real or imagined insults. Exploitation of others is not their major goal. Hipsters are bullies who choose victims with caution in order to win acceptance among inmates by demonstrating physical bravery. Their bravery, however, is false. Merchants exploit other inmates through manipulation in sharp trading of goods stolen from prison supplies or in trickery in gambling.

27. Martins frequently beats up Smith and Brooks. Smith and Brooks provide Martins with extra cigarettes and coffee. Martins is a
    A. tough
    B. gorilla
    C. merchant
    D. hipster

Questions 28 through 30 are based on the following description of the duties of the Court Officer:

Throughout the session of the court, the officer must see that proper order and decorum are maintained in the courtroom. Above all else, silence must be constantly observed, and every possible distraction must be eliminated so as not to delay the most efficient functioning of the court.
The officer must carry out such duties as may be required by the court and clerk. Examples of such duties are directing witnesses to the witness stand and assisting the Court Clerk and counsel in the handling of exhibits. At times, the officer must act as a messenger in procuring any books from the court library that are required by the attorneys and ordered by the Court Clerk.
The enforcement of the rules of the court requires courteous behavior on the part of the Court Officer, although firmness and strictness are necessary when the occasion requires such an attitude.

28. Testimony has been given, the witnesses have been cross-examined and the attorneys have given their summations. Now the judge is charging the jury. A Court Officer has been stationed outside the courtroom door to prevent anyone from entering during the charge. The City Council President arrives, accompanied by a woman, and attempts to enter the courtroom. The Court Officer should
    A. apologize and explain why they cannot be permitted to enter
    B. permit the man to enter, since he is the City Council President, but exclude the woman
    C. permit them to enter because surely the judge would make an exception for such important people
    D. send a note to the judge to ask whether they may be permitted to enter

29. A witness who is waiting to be called to the stand appears to be very nervous. He wiggles and squirms, stands and stretches, looks over his shoulder at the courtroom door and waves to spectators. The officer should
    A. tell the witness to leave the courtroom at once
    B. handcuff the witness
    C. ask the witness to please sit still and try to restrain himself
    D. suggest to the judge that he call this witness next

30. During the course of cross-examination, a defendant frequently refers to a book that she claims has had a great influence on her life and that she claims justifies her behavior in the crime for which she is charged. In the jury box, two jurors begin a lively discussion of whether the defendant is quoting accurately. The best action for the Court Officer is to
    A. ask the Court Clerk for permission to go to the library to get the book
    B. send a messenger to get the book
    C. assure the jurors that the book is being accurately quoted and that only the interpretation is in question
    D. remind the jurors that they are not to converse in the courtroom

31. "Ideally, a correctional system should include several types of institutions to provide different degrees of custody."
    On the basis of this statement, one could most reasonably say that
    A. as the number of institutions in a correctional system increases, the efficiency of the system increases
    B. the difference in degree of custody for the inmate depends on the types of institutions in a correctional system
    C. the greater the variety of institutions, the stricter the degree of custody that can be maintained
    D. the same type of correctional institution is not desirable for the custody of all prisoners

32. "The enforced idleness of a large percentage of adult men and women in our prisons is one of the direct causes of the tensions that burst forth in riot and disorder."
    On the basis of this statement, a good reason why inmates should perform daily work of some kind is that
    A. better morale and discipline can be maintained when inmates are kept busy
    B. daily work is an effective way of punishing inmates for the crimes they have committed
    C. law-abiding citizens must work therefore labor should also be required of inmates
    D. products of inmates' labor will in part pay the cost of their maintenance

33. "With industry invading rural areas, the use of the automobile, and the speed of modern communications and transportation, the problems of neglect and delinquency are no longer peculiar to cities but are an established feature of everyday life."
    This statement implies most directly that
    A. delinquents are moving from cities to rural areas
    B. delinquency and neglect are found in rural areas
    C. delinquency is not as much of a problem in rural areas as in cities
    D. rural areas now surpass cities in industry

33._____

34. "Young men from minority groups, if unable to find employment, become discouraged and hopeless because of their economic position and may finally resort to any means of supplying their wants."
    The most reasonable of the following conclusions that may be drawn from this statement only is that
    A. discouragement sometimes leads to crime
    B. in general, young men from minority groups are criminals
    C. unemployment turns young men from crime
    D. young men from minority groups are seldom employed

34._____

35. "To prevent crime, we must deal with the possible criminals long before they reach the prison. Our aim should be not merely to reform the lawbreakers but to strike at the roots of crime: neglectful parents, bad companions, unsatisfactory homes, selfishness, disregard for the rights of others and bad social conditions."
    The above statement recommends
    A. abolition of prisons
    B. better reformatories
    C. compulsory education
    D. general social reform

35._____

36. "There is evidence that shows that comic books which glorify the criminal and criminal acts have a distinct influence in producing young criminals."
    According to this statement
    A. comic books affect the development of criminal careers
    B. comic books specialize in reporting criminal acts
    C. young criminals read comic books exclusively
    D. young criminals should not be permitted to read comic books

36._____

37. A study shows that juvenile delinquents are equal in intelligence to but three school grades behind juvenile nondelinquents. On the basis of this information only, it is most reasonable to say that
    A. a delinquent usually progresses to the educational limit set by intelligence
    B. educational achievement depends on intelligence only
    C. educational achievement is closely associated with delinquency
    D. lack of intelligence is closely associated with delinquency

37._____

38. "Prevention of crime is of greater value to the community than the punishment of crime."
If this statement is accepted as true, greatest emphasis should be placed on
   A. execution
   B. medication
   C. imprisonment
   D. rehabilitation

39. A Court Assistant being instructed in his duties was told by the Court Clerk, "experience is the best teacher."
The one of the following that most nearly expresses the meaning of this quotation is:
   A. A good teacher will make a hard job look easy
   B. Bad experience does more harm than good
   C. Lack of experience will make an easy job hard
   D. The best way to learn to do a thing is by doing it

40. "Once the purposes or goals of an organization have been determined, they must be communicated to subordinate levels of supervisory staff."
On the basis of this quotation, the most accurate statement is that
   A. supervisory personnel should participate in the formulation of the goals of an organization
   B. the structure of an organization should be considered in determining the organization's goals
   C. the goals that have been established for the different levels of an organization should be reviewed regularly
   D. information about the goals of an organization should be distributed to supervisory personnel

41. "Close examination of traffic accident statistics reveals that traffic accidents are frequently the result of violations of traffic laws—and usually the violations are the result of illegal and dangerous driving behavior, rather than the result of mechanical defects or poor road conditions."
According to this statement, the majority of dangerous traffic violations are cause by
   A. poor driving
   B. bad roads
   C. unsafe cars
   D. unwise traffic laws

Questions 42 through 44 are based on the following paragraph:

The supervisor gains the respect of his staff members and increases his influence over them by controlling his temper and avoiding criticizing anyone publicly. When a mistake is made, the good supervisor will talk it over with the employee quietly and privately. The supervisor listens to the employee's story, suggests a better way to do the job, and offers help so the mistake won't happen again. Before closing the discussion, the supervisor should try to find something good to say about other aspects of the employee's work. Some praise and appreciation, along with instruction, is likely to encourage an employee to improve in those areas where he is weakest.

42. A good title that would show the meaning of this entire paragraph would be:
    A. How to Correct Employee Errors
    B. How to Praise Employees
    C. Mistakes are Preventable
    D. The Weak Employee

43. According to the preceding paragraph, the work of an employee who has made a mistake is more likely to improve if the supervisor
    A. avoids criticizing him
    B. gives him a chance to suggest a better way of doing the work
    C. listens to the employee's excuses to see if he's right
    D. praises good work at the same time he corrects the mistake

44. When a supervisor needs to correct an employee's mistake, it is important that he
    A. allow some time to go by after the mistake has been made
    B. do so when other employees are not present
    C. show his influence by his tone of voice
    D. tell other employees to avoid the same mistake

45. "Determination of total, or even partial, guilt and responsibility as viewed by law cannot be made solely on the basis of a consideration of the external factors of the case, but rather should be made mainly in the light of the individual defendant's history and development."
    The above statement reflects a philosophy of law that requires that
    A. the punishment fit the crime
    B. the individual, rather than the crime, be considered first
    C. motivations behind a crime are relatively unimportant
    D. the individual's knowledge of right and wrong be the sole determinant of guilt

46. A traffic regulation says, "No driver shall enter an intersection unless there is sufficient unobstructed space beyond the intersection to accommodate the vehicle he or she is operating, not withstanding any traffic-control signal indication to the contrary."
This regulation means that:
   A. a driver should not go through an intersection if there are no parking spaces available on the next block
   B. a driver should not enter an intersection when the traffic light is red
   C. a driver should not enter an intersection if traffic ahead is so badly backed up that he or she would not be able to go ahead and would block the intersection
   D. a driver should ignore traffic signals completely whenever there are obstructions in the road ahead

Questions 47 through 51 are based on the following passage:

A large proportion of people behind bars are not convicted criminals, but people who have been arrested and are being held until their trial in court. Experts have often pointed out that this detention system does not operate fairly. For instance, a person who can afford to pay bail usually will not get locked up.

The theory of the bail system is that the person will make sure to show up in court when he or she is supposed to; otherwise, bail will be forfeited—the person will lose the money that was put up. Sometimes a person who can show that he or she is a stable citizen with a job and a family will be released on "personal recognizance" (without bail). The result is that the well-to-do, the employed and the family men can often avoid the detention system. The people who do wind up in detention tend to be the poor, the unemployed, the single and the young.

47. People who are put behind bars
   A. are almost always dangerous criminals
   B. include many innocent people who have been arrested by mistake
   C. are often people who have been arrested but have not yet come to trial
   D. are all poor people who tend to be young and single

48. The passage says that the detention system works unfairly against people who are
   A. rich
   B. old
   C. married
   D. unemployed

49. The passage uses the expression "bail will be forfeited." Even if you had not seen the word *forfeit* before, you could figure out from the way it is used that forfeiting probably means _____ something.
   A. losing track of
   B. finding
   C. giving up
   D. avoiding

13 (#1)

50. When someone is released on personal recognizance, this means that 50.____
    A. the judge knows that the person is innocent
    B. he or she does not have to show up for a trial
    C. he or she has a record of previous convictions
    D. he or she does not have to pay bail

51. Suppose that two men were booked on the same charge at the same 51.____
    time and that the same bail was set for both of them. One man was able
    to put up bail and was released. The second man was not able to put up
    bail and was held in detention. The writer of the passage would most
    likely feel that this result is
    A. unfair, because it does not have any relationship to guilt or
       innocence
    B. unfair, because the first man deserves severe punishment
    C. fair, because the first man is obviously innocent
    D. fair, because the law should be tougher on the poor people than
       on the rich

Questions 52 through 55 are based on the following passage:

The Court Officer has important functions in connection with control of the jury. He or she must confirm that every juror has the proper place in the box and must be constantly on watch to prevent any juror from leaving the jury box while the trial is in progress. Should a juror decide to leave the box while the case is going on, the Court Officer must first inform the judge of the juror's desire to determine whether the judge will grant or refuse the juror's wish. If the judge approves, the trial is stopped and the Court Officer is instructed to accompany the juror while he or she is out of the jury box.

In order to prevent any stoppage or mistrial, the Court Officer must not allow the juror to get out of the range of sight or hearing. The officer must always bear in mind that the juror should be returned as quickly as possible, without any unnecessary delay. The juror must not enter into any conversation with anybody or read any matter that he or she may have or that may be given by another person.

The Court Officer must be particularly careful when placed in charge of a jury that has retired to deliberate. The Court Officer must conduct the jury to the jury room and see to it that no juror talks with anyone on the way. If a juror does talk with someone, the event may afford grounds for a mistrial.

52. A juror has requested and received permission to go to the men's room. 52.____
    As he approaches the door, he takes out a sports magazine he has
    brought from home as "bathroom literature." The Court Officer should
    A. permit the juror to read the magazine
    B. check the magazine for papers that might be hidden between the
       pages, then let the juror read it
    C. offer the juror something of his own to read, something that he
       knows will not influence the juror in any way
    D. tell the juror that reading in the men's room is not permitted

53. While leading a jury from the courtroom to the jury room, a Court Officer notices a person leaning against a corridor wall making active hand motions as a juror stares intently. The *first* thing for a Court Officer to do is
    A. tell the juror to look straight ahead and keep walking
    B. step between the juror and the person so as to interrupt the juror's line of vision
    C. ask the juror what he is looking at
    D. call a police officer to arrest the person with the active hands

54. If the Court Officer ascertains that a message has been transmitted by an outside person to a juror, it would be best for the Court Officer to
    A. keep this information secret
    B. ask the juror what the message was about
    C. deliver the juror to the jury room, then discuss the matter with the Court Clerk
    D. accompany the juror to the judge and tell the judge exactly what the Court Officer observed

55. During the course of testimony, a juror begins to cough uncontrollably. The coughing is loud and distressing. The Court Officer should
    A. summon a doctor at once
    B. lead the juror from the courtroom as quickly and quietly as possible
    C. bring the juror a glass of water
    D. ask the judge what to do

KEY (CORRECT ANSWERS)

1. C	11. A	21. C	31. D	41. A	51. A
2. B	12. D	22. B	32. A	42. A	52. D
3. B	13. C	23. C	33. B	43. D	53. A
4. C	14. C	24. D	34. A	44. B	54. B
5. C	15. D	25. B	35. D	45. B	55. B
6. A	16. C	26. A	36. A	46. C	
7. B	17. C	27. B	37. C	47. C	
8. C	18. A	28. A	38. D	48. D	
9. A	19. D	29. C	39. D	49. C	
10. A	20. C	30. D	40. D	50. D	

EXAMINATION SECTION
TEST 1

DIRECTIONS: Each question or incomplete statement is followed by several suggested answers or completions. Select the one that BEST answers the question or completes the statement. *PRINT THE LETTER OF THE CORRECT ANSWER IN THE SPACE AT THE RIGHT.*

Questions 1-3.

DIRECTIONS: Questions 1 through 3 are to be answered on the basis of the following paragraph.

The Jingle-Dress dance is a popular competitive dance performed at intertribal powwows. The costume of the Jingle-Dress dancer is adorned with small metal cones. The cones are made from chewing tobacco lids, which are rolled into cylinders and sewn onto the dress. During the dance, these tin cones strike one another to produce a soft, rhythmic sound. The dancer blends complicated footwork with a series of gentle hops, causing the cones to jingle in time to the drumbeat.

1. The purpose of the cones in the Jingle-Dress dance is to

   A. shine and sparkle during the dance
   B. produce a soft, rhythmic sound
   C. aid the dancer with the complicated footwork required by the dance
   D. make use of recycled tobacco can lids

2. The dancer causes the cones to make sounds by

   A. making large cones to sew onto the dress
   B. sewing the cones as close to another as possible
   C. jumping up and down as quickly as possible
   D. combining footwork with gentle hops

3. The Jingle-Dress dance is performed as a

   A. ceremonial dance at semi-annual powwows
   B. healing dance at intertribal powwows
   C. competitive dance at intertribal powwows
   D. costume dance at annual powwows

Questions 4-6.

DIRECTIONS: Questions 4 through 6 are to be answered on the basis of the following paragraph.

Although volleyball is a unique sport, it shares one important similarity with other well-known sports. Like most sports, the ability to win doesn't just depend on a team's ability to score the most points, but on its ability to make the fewest number of errors. In volleyball, a team cannot score unless it is serving. Serving errors, therefore, are extremely costly since losing the serve also means granting your opponent a scoring opportunity.

4. To win a volleyball game, it is MOST important to make sure your team 4.___

    A. makes the fewest number of errors
    B. plays good defense
    C. grants scoring opportunities to your opponents
    D. serves first

5. What important similarity does volleyball share with other sports? 5.___

    A. It's exciting to watch.
    B. Winning depends on a powerful serve.
    C. A volleyball team cannot score unless it is serving.
    D. The winning team usually commits the fewest errors.

6. Serving errors are costly in a volleyball game because they 6.___

    A. count as an error against your team
    B. provide your opponent with a scoring opportunity
    C. place your team in a receiving position
    D. can result in a delay-of-game penalty

Questions 7-8.

DIRECTIONS: Questions 7 and 8 are to be answered on the basis of the following paragraph.

Throughout history, solar eclipses have sometimes caused great fear and anxiety. Some cultures believed eclipses predicted the end of the world. Many older cultures believed a dragon was swallowing the sun and, in order to save the sun, people made as much noise as possible to frighten the dragon away. When the sun returned, whole and bright, the noise-makers celebrated their success.

7. Why have eclipses caused such anxiety throughout history? 7.___

    A. People believed they signaled the end of the world
    B. No one knows what causes them
    C. Because people make so much noise when they appear
    D. Because watching one can harm the eyes

8. Why did ancient cultures often make noise during an eclipse? 8.___

    A. People were frightened in the darkness
    B. To celebrate the arrival of the eclipse
    C. To summon the dragon who would swallow the sun
    D. To chase away the dragon they thought had swallowed the sun

Questions 9-11.

DIRECTIONS: Questions 9 through 11 are to be answered on the basis of the following paragraph.

In the films of the 1940s, most American Indians appeared as enemies. They spoke broken English and blocked civilization's progress. During this same time, however, a group of Navajo Indians used their unique language to develop a code for the U.S. military which would become one of the most successful codes in military history. During World War II, this group, known as the Navajo Code Talkers, played a key role in many of the most crucial victories fought by the U.S. military in the Pacific.

9. What role did the Navajo Code Talkers play in World War II?
They

    A. appeared as enemies in many films
    B. spoke broken English and blocked civilization's progress
    C. developed a military code which helped win the war in the Pacific
    D. used their unique language to block civilization's progress

10. In films from the 1940s, American Indians were most often depicted as enemies by

    A. speaking broken English and blocking civilization's progress
    B. speaking only in their native Navajo tongue
    C. using their language to develop secret codes
    D. trying to block crucial American victories in the Pacific

11. The Navajo Code Talkers used their language to

    A. block civilization's progress
    B. fight Hollywood stereotypes
    C. defeat their enemies in other tribes
    D. develop one of the most effective U.S. military codes in history

Questions 12-13.

DIRECTIONS: Questions 12 and 13 are to be answered on the basis of the following paragraph.

In the last several years, judges throughout the country have attracted controversy by practicing *creative sentencing*. The term refers to the judges tendency for offering defendants what they consider valid alternatives to jail sentences. For example, to qualify for probation, one defendant had to wear a tee shirt that announced his status as a criminal on probation. An abusive husband had to donate his car to a shelter for battered women. In one case, a judge gave a woman found guilty of child abuse a chance to avoid jail if she would voluntarily allow Norplant, a form of birth control, to be implanted in her arm.

12. What does the term *creative sentencing* refer to?

    A. Various judicial controversies
    B. Judges who offer defendants alternatives to jail sentences

C. Defendants who are forced to undergo humiliating punishments in addition to jail sentences
D. Judges who have the power to determine how much time a defendant spends in jail

13. Creative sentencing is considered controversial because the   13.___

    A. judges are overstepping the bounds of their power by forcing defendants to submit to these punishments
    B. defendants have no opportunity to defend themselves
    C. alternatives offered to defendants are often surprising and odd
    D. judges have been forced to these extreme measures because of prison overcrowding

Questions 14-16.

DIRECTIONS: Questions 14 through 16 are to be answered on the basis of the following paragraph.

When examined closely, Earth's position in the solar system is something of a miracle. If it were closer to the sun, the heat would be so intense that water would be vaporized. If it were farther away, water would be frozen. Of all the planets in the solar system, only Earth and Mars share the temperature band which allows water to exist in the three states which are necessary to produce and sustain life. But only Earth is surrounded by a protective ozone layer which aids water in making the transition between these three states.

14. Why is Earth's position in the solar system something of a miracle?   14.___

    A. If it were closer to the sun, water would vaporize.
    B. If it were farther from the sun, water would freeze.
    C. It exists in the narrow temperature band which allows water to exist in the three states necessary to sustain life.
    D. It exists in the narrow temperature band which allows a protective ozone layer to form around the planet.

15. What is the difference between Earth and Mars?   15.___

    A. Mars is surrounded by a protective ozone layer.
    B. Earth is surrounded by a protective ozone layer.
    C. Only Earth exists within the narrow temperature band which allows water to exist in the three states necessary to sustain life.
    D. Only Mars exists within the narrow temperature band which allows water to exist in the three states necessary to sustain life.

16. The ozone layer is important to the production and sustenance of life because it   16.___

    A. helps water make the transition between the three forms necessary to sustain life
    B. keeps water from being vaporized by the sun's harmful rays
    C. keeps water from being frozen when the sun sets
    D. keeps water from leaving the atmosphere

Questions 17-19.

DIRECTIONS: Questions 17 through 19 are to be answered on the basis of the following paragraph.

During the seventeenth century, sailors at sea often suffered from muscle weakness and unexplained bleeding. This disease often proved fatal until the discovery that sailors who ate oranges and lines either didn't get sick, or suffered a much milder form of the illness. As a result, the British navy required every ship to provide lemons and limes for the entire crew. By accident, it had discovered that the vitamin C contained in the citrus fruits prevented scurvy.

17. What disease did sailors at sea often suffer from? 17._____

 A. Malnourishment
 B. Overdoses of vitamin C
 C. Muscle weakness and unexplained bleeding
 D. Scurvy

18. How is the disease prevented? 18._____

 A. Consumption of vitamin C   B. Consumption of fresh water
 C. Hard work   D. Bed rest

19. The cure for scurvy was discovered 19._____

 A. as a result of careful testing in laboratories
 B. through the accidental discovery that sailors who consumed vitamin C didn't grow ill
 C. through the accidental discovery that sailors who consumed vitamin C often grew ill
 D. as a result of years of study and experimentation

Questions 20-22.

DIRECTIONS: Questions 20 through 22 are to be answered on the basis of the following paragraph.

 Unlike dogs, cats are typically a solitary animal species who avoid social interaction, but they do display specific social responses to each other upon meeting. When two cats meet who are strangers, their first actions and gestures determine who the *dominant* cat will be. If a cat desires dominance or sees the other cat as a threat to its territory, it will stare directly at the intruder with a lowered tail. If the other cat responds with a similar gesture, or with the strong defensive posture of an arched back, laid-back ears, and raised tail, a fight or chase is likely if neither cat gives in. This is unlikely, however; before such a point of open hostility is reached, one of the cats will usually take the *submissive* position of crouching down while looking away from the other cat.

20. A cat signals its dominance over another cat by 20._____

 A. crouching down and looking away from the other cat
 B. arching its back and raising its tail
 C. staring directly at the other cat and lowering its tail
 D. chasing the other cat

21. Cats usually greet each other by

    A. displaying specific social responses
    B. staring directly at one another
    C. raising their tails
    D. arching their backs

22. Why is it unlikely for cats who are strangers to reach a point of open hostility with one another?

    A. Cats are solitary animals.
    B. One of the cats usually runs away.
    C. One of the cats usually takes a submissive position before they reach the point of open hostility.
    D. The two cats generally stare at each other with lowered tails until the hostility passes.

Questions 23-25.

DIRECTIONS: Questions 23 through 25 are to be answered on the basis of the following paragraph.

Between the nineteenth and twentieth centuries, the area in America known as the Great Plains underwent startling changes. At the beginning of the nineteenth century, there were few settlements. One could walk for miles without seeing a house. By the end of the century, settlements had sprung up all over. More and more people began to seek their fortunes in this area. In 1800, the Plains were covered by herds of buffalo. These huge animals were the natural cattle of the Plains. By 1900 the buffalo had almost disappeared, however, and the tribes who had roamed the Plains in pursuit of the buffalo had been forced to live on reservations.

23. When did these changes occur on the Great Plains?

    A. Between the 1700s and the 1800s
    B. Between the 1800s and the 1900s
    C. During the 1900s
    D. Between 1850 and 1950

24. What caused the sudden increase in the number of settlements on the Great Plains?

    A. The disappearance of the buffalo
    B. The disappearance of the Plains tribes
    C. An increased desire to hunt buffalo for sport
    D. An increased number of people seeking their fortunes in the area

25. What happened to the Plains tribes after the buffalo disappeared?
They

    A. were forced to live on reservations
    B. were all killed
    C. died of starvation
    D. moved farther west, away from the settlers

Questions 26-28.

DIRECTIONS: Questions 26 through 28 are to be answered on the basis of the following paragraph.

One important line of thinking about stress focuses on the differences between Type A and Type B personalities. Type A individuals are extremely competitive, are very devoted to work, and have a strong sense of time urgency. They are likely to be aggressive, impatient, and very work-oriented. Type B individuals are less competitive, less devoted to work, and have a weaker sense of time urgency. These individuals are less likely to experience conflict with other people and more likely to have a balanced, relaxed approach to life.

26. Type B individuals are likely to display which of the following characteristics? 26.____

    A. A strong sense of time urgency
    B. Devotion to work
    C. A balanced approach to life
    D. Aggressiveness

27. Type A individuals are likely to display which of the following characteristics? 27.____

    A. A balanced approach to life
    B. Passivity
    C. Contentment
    D. A strong sense of time urgency

28. These personality types help researchers study which of the following problems? 28.____

    A. Stress   B. Apathy
    C. Criminal behavior   D. Underachievement

Questions 29-36.

The paragraphs which follow contain blank spaces with numbers corresponding to the questions. Each of the corresponding questions contains one lettered choice whose meaning fits in the space. Place the letter of the correct choice in the answer space to the right of the question.

Most successful job interviews (29) three basic steps. Step 1 lasts about three minutes and (30) when you first introduce yourself. Those people who have a firm handshake, who maintain eye contact, smile, and seem friendly, are the (31) successful during this phase. Step 2 is the (32) phase. This is the point at which interviewees (33) their skills and work to *sell* themselves. Step 3 comes at the (34) of the interview and, like Step 1, lasts only a few minutes. After the employer says, *We'll call you,* successful interviewees are quick (35) respond. *I'll get in touch with you if I don't hear from you in a few days.* This final gesture conveys (36).

| 29. | A. | lack | | | B. | mimic | | | 29.__ |
| | C. | follow | | | D. | end with | | | |

| 30. | A. | begins | B. | ends | C. | stalls | D. | fails | 30.__ |

| 31. | A. | least | B. | mostly | C. | more | D. | most | 31.__ |

| 32. | A. | least challenging | | | B. | most boring | | | 32.__ |
| | C. | longest | | | D. | shortest | | | |

| 33. | A. | brag about | B. | explain | C. | enunciate | D. | lie about | 33.__ |

| 34. | A. | middle | B. | outset | C. | beginning | D. | end | 34.__ |

| 35. | A. | to | B. | at | C. | with | D. | for | 35.__ |

| 36. | A. | insistence | | | B. | impatience | | | 36.__ |
| | C. | enthusiasm | | | D. | hope | | | |

Questions 37-40.

The idea of duty is important to the followers of Hinduism, the major (37) in India. In fact, the many duties prescribed by Hinduism make it a way of life that (38) each day. From an early age, children learn that nothing is more important (39) doing one's duty. In fact doing (40) duty is, in itself, a form of worship.

| 37. | A. | belief | | | B. | religion | | | 37.__ |
| | C. | system | | | D. | political institution | | | |

| 38. | A. | organizes | | | B. | disrupts | | | 38.__ |
| | C. | produces | | | D. | destabilizes | | | |

| 39. | A. | if | B. | with | C. | of | D. | than | 39.__ |

| 40. | A. | your | B. | his | C. | one's | D. | its | 40.__ |

Questions 41-46.

Strong emotions are accompanied (41) physiological changes. When we are extremely fearful or angry, for example, (42) heartbeat speeds up, our pulse races, and our breathing rate tends to increase. The body's metabolism (43), burning up sugar in the bloodstream and fats in the tissues at a faster rate. The salivary glands become less active, making the mouth feel (44). The sweat glands may overreact, (45) a dripping forehead, clammy hands, and cold sweat. Finally, the pupils may (46), producing the wide-eyed look that is characteristic of both terror and rage.

| 41. | A. | with | B. | to | C. | beside | D. | by | 41.__ |

| 42. | A. | your | B. | our | C. | the | D. | a | 42.__ |

43.	A. accelerates	B. slows down	43._____
	C. works	D. stays the same	

44.	A. hot	B. cold	C. wet	D. dry	44._____

45.	A. with	B. showing	C. producing	D. fearing	45._____

46.	A. dilate	B. enlarge	C. blacken	D. disappear	46._____

Questions 47-52.

Increased numbers of women are (47) going to college and graduating with degrees in law and medicine. More women than ever before are (48) careers and earning as much as men. Many career women who are married have also achieved economic equality (49) their husbands. The number of women in elected office has also increased, and a large majority of Americans are now willing to vote for a qualified (50) for president. A growing number of women are entering the military, with the U.S. now having more female soldiers than any other (51). These are all signs that women have made significant headway toward (52) equality.

47.	A. now	B. then	C. yet	D. not	47._____
48.	A. leaving	B. changing	C. avoiding	D. pursuing	48._____
49.	A. to	B. with	C. at	D. for	49._____
50.	A. Republican	B. candidate	C. woman	D. man	50._____
51.	A. woman	B. country	C. man	D. branch	51._____
52.	A. racial	B. economic	C. religious	D. gender	52._____

Questions 53-56.

Understanding does not mean manipulating someone to agree (53) your point of view. Although a manipulative person views understanding as having someone else come around to his or her opinion, an understanding person conveys a sense of open-mindedness and (54). A communicator who is understanding does (55) insist upon agreement. He or she understands that, in order to be understood, you must also (56) others.

53.	A. to	B. at	C. with	D. for	53._____
54.	A. acceptance	B. exclusion	C. anger	D. elation	54._____
55.	A. always	B. not	C. sometimes	D. generally	55._____

56.	A. disagree with	B. judge	56._____
	C. love	D. understand	

Questions 57-62.

DIRECTIONS: Questions 57 through 62 are to be answered on the basis of the following facts.

Apollo Elementary School serves students in grades kindergarten through fifth. The school library is located in the center of the school. Classrooms surround the library, forming a large circle. Throughout the school day, teachers bring their classes into the library to conduct research and reading activities. There are usually several classes using the library at any one time.

The school librarian is Mrs. Samuels. She is a tall, middle-aged woman with brown hair and green eyes. Her part-time assistant is Velma Thomas. Velma is a student at the local community college, where she studies library science.

On the afternoon of Wednesday, April 11, Mrs. Simon brought her fourth-grade class to the library at approximately 1:50 P.M. Mrs. Samuels was already working with a third-grade class, so Velma began assisting the fourth grade students. A young girl from Mrs. Simon's class asked Velma how to find her book in the card catalog. As Velma guided the girl through the procedure, she noticed that one of the third graders had drifted away from his class and was attempting to reach a book by standing on one of the bookshelves.

Just as Velma called to the boy, he lost his footing and fell. Mrs. Samuels rushed to his side and checked him for injuries. The boy had a slight bruise on his wrist, but was otherwise uninjured.

57. Who checked the boy for injuries after his fall?

    A. Mrs. Samuels
    B. Velma Thomas
    C. Mrs. Simon
    D. The third grade teacher

58. Who is the school librarian?

    A. Mrs. Samuels
    B. Velma Thomas
    C. Mrs. Simon
    D. She is not named in this passage

59. On what day of the week did the incident occur?

    A. Monday   B. Tuesday   C. Wednesday   D. Friday

60. In what grade was the boy who fell from the shelf?

    A. Fifth   B. Fourth   C. Third   D. Second

61. What grade does Mrs. Simon teach?

    A. Fifth   B. Fourth   C. Third   D. Second

62. What grades does Apollo Elementary serve?   62._____

    A. First through fifth
    B. First through sixth
    C. Kindergarten through fourth
    D. Kindergarten through fifth

Questions 63-68.

DIRECTIONS: Questions 63 through 68 are to be answered on the basis of the following facts.

There is a small hot dog cart located in the outdoor plaza of the Smith County Courthouse. The cart sells Polish hot dogs, sausages, bratwurst, soft pretzels, and soda. In the mornings between 7:00 and 9:30, fresh coffee and danishes are also sold. Employees of the court and other nearby businesses often purchase their lunch there, and eat on the plaza benches and tables.

The cart opens at 7:00 A.M. and closes at 3:00 P.M. during weekdays. It does not operate on weekends. It is owned and operated by Luisa Gonzalez, who is a 21-year-old college student with brown hair and brown eyes. Her father is Martin Gonzalez, a retired police officer, and he often works with her. At approximately 12:00 P.M. on October 3, Court Officer Laura Innes stopped at the cart to buy her lunch. After paying Luisa, Laura moved to the condiment table, located just to the right of the cart. She noticed Martin Gonzalez struggling to pour a large tub of boiling water into the hot dog steamer. Before she could move to help him, however, Martin lost his grip and dropped the tub of water, splashing himself.

The Court Officer administered first aid, and Martin was taken to St. Luke's hospital. He had received second degree burns on his arms and feet and was not able to return to the hot dog cart for three weeks.

63. What hospital was Martin taken to?   63._____

    A. St. Mark's   B. St. Peter's
    C. St. Mary's   D. St. Luke's

64. What part of his body did Martin burn?   64._____
    His

    A. arms and feet   B. arms
    C. feet and ankles   D. arms and face

65. Who owns the hot dog cart?   65._____

    A. Martin Gonzalez   B. Luisa Gonzalez
    C. Laura Innes   D. Luke Martin

66. During what hours does the cart operate on weekends?   66._____

    A. 7:00 A.M. to 3:00 P.M.
    B. 9:30 A.M. to 3:00 P.M.
    C. 7:00 A.M. to 9:30 A.M.
    D. The cart does not operate on weekends

67. Where is the hot dog cart located?
    On the _____ of the courthouse.

    A. first floor
    B. roof
    C. outdoor plaza
    D. third floor

68. Who was first to administer first aid to Martin?

    A. Laura Innes
    B. Luisa Gonzalez
    C. Luke Martin
    D. Paramedics

Questions 69-74.

DIRECTIONS: Questions 69 through 74 are to be answered on the basis of the following facts.

The offices of Judge Anjelica Chen are located on the third floor of the Peak County Courthouse. The offices of Judge Benjamin Laurence are also located on the third floor of the courthouse, across a courtyard. The windows of these offices face one another.

Judge Chen keeps her pet parrot, Mabel, in her offices. Although Mabel has a cage, Judge Chen keeps the door open, allowing Mabel to perch on bookshelves and lamps while the Judge finishes paperwork late in the evenings. Judge Laurence has no pets, but he often feeds pigeons from his window, sprinkling breadcrumbs along his sill.

On the evening of Tuesday, May 2, Court Officer Roger Crawford heard a scream from Judge Chen's office. He arrived to find the judge searching frantically through her office for Mabel, who had apparently disappeared. The window to the judge's office was open. The court officer assisted the judge in her search. At approximately 7:30, nearly 45 minutes after he had arrived in Judge Chen's office, the court officer heard someone hollering from the other side of the building.

Officer Crawford rushed toward the noise and found Judge Laurence in his office, trying to fend off the bright parrot flying back and forth across his office. The court officer summoned Judge Chen, who calmed Mabel and led her back to her cage.

69. Where was Mabel found?

    A. In Judge Chen's office
    B. In Judge Laurence's office
    C. In the courtyard
    D. In her cage

70. What kind of bird is Mabel?

    A. Pigeon
    B. Canary
    C. Chickadee
    D. Parrot

71. Where is Judge Chen's office located?
    _____ Judge Laurence's office.

    A. Below
    B. Next to
    C. Across from
    D. Above

13 (#1)

72. Why does Judge Laurence leave breadcrumbs on his window-sill? 72._____
    A. To feed pigeons
    B. To feed Mabel
    C. To feed squirrels
    D. To keep food litter out of his office

73. How long did Judge Chen and Officer Crawford look for Mabel before they heard Judge 73._____
    Laurence yelling in his office?
    _____ minutes.
    A. 30   B. 45   C. 60   D. 15

74. Why does Judge Chen leave Mabel's cage door open? 74._____
    A. To allow Mabel to escape
    B. To allow Mabel a clearer view of Judge Laurence's windowsill
    C. Judge Chen does not leave Mabel's cage door open
    D. To allow Mabel to perch on bookshelves and lamps while the Judge finishes her paperwork

Questions 75-80.

DIRECTIONS: Questions 75 through 80 are to be answered on the basis of the following facts.

The Hickory Ridge Courthouse is located just across the street from the Hickory Ridge Public Library. Employees begin arriving at the courthouse at approximately 7:00 A.M. each weekday morning. The library opens at 9:00 A.M. and closes at 5:00 P.M. each weekday. Both the courthouse and the library have bicycle stands in front of them. Bicyclists lock their bikes to the stands while they run their errands and conduct their business.

Court Officer Melinda Thompson eats her lunch each day at a small cafe next to the library. The cafe caters mainly to employees of the library and courthouse. It operates from 11:00 A.M. to 3:00 P.M. each day.

On the afternoon of August 11, the court officer observed a young man with a backpack lock his bike to a stand in front of the library. The young man had blond hair, green eyes, and long sideburns. Approximately 30 minutes after the young man entered the library, a dark-haired man emerged from the cafe where the court officer was eating her lunch. The man had a beard, and was of medium build. He walked to the bicycle stand and began jiggling a lock on one of the bikes.

The court officer recognized the bicycle as the same one the blond-haired young man had locked to the stand. By the time the court officer reached the bicycle stand, the second man had already broken the lock. Although she called for him to stop, he rode away on the young man's bicycle. Her excellent description, however, helped police locate the bicycle thief and the bicycle a short time later.

75. What time does the library open? 75._____
    A. 7:00 A.M.   B. 9:00 A.M.   C. 11:00 A.M.   D. 3:00 P.M.

76. Where is the cafe located?

    A. Next to the courthouse
    B. Across from the library
    C. Next to the library
    D. Between the library and the courthouse

77. Who stole the bicycle?

    A. The blond-haired man
    B. The dark-haired man
    C. The man with the backpack
    D. The man with the long sideburns

78. What hours is the cafe open?

    A. 11:00 A.M. to 3:00 P.M.
    B. 9:00 A.M. to 5:00 P.M.
    C. 7:00 A.M. to 5:00 P.M.
    D. 7:00 A.M. to 3:00 P.M.

79. When do employees begin arriving at the courthouse each day?

    A. 7:00 A.M.   B. 9:00 A.M.   C. 10:00 A.M.   D. 11:00 A.M.

80. What did the bicycle thief do when the court officer ordered him to stop?

    A. He stopped.
    B. He rode away.
    C. He threw down the bicycle and ran.
    D. He insisted the bicycle was his.

Questions 81-87.

DIRECTIONS: Questions 81 through 87 are to be answered on the basis of the following facts.

The Jade Market is located on the first floor of the Angel County Courthouse. The courthouse is located across the street from San Gabriel High School. Jade Market sells newspapers, magazines, sandwiches, beverages, and sodas. In the mornings, between 7:00 A.M. and 9:00 A.M., the market is frequented mostly by employees of the courthouse. In the afternoons, between 1:45 and 2:45, the small market is crowded with teenagers wearing cumbersome backpacks. Classes at San Gabriel High School end at 1:30 P.M.

Jade Market is operated by James Chang, who is 55 years old, with graying black hair and brown eyes. His wife, Lola, also helps at the market during the afternoon and evening hours.

On the afternoon of Thursday, September 1, Court Officer Mason Stewart stopped at Jade Market to buy a newspaper and some coffee. While he was talking with Lola Chang, twelve to fifteen high school students walked into the market. They moved noisily up and down the narrow aisles. They each carried a heavy backpack. As they walked through the store, their packs often knocked items from the shelves.

As the court officer watched the students, he noticed one young woman knock several magazines from the magazine stand located at the back of the store. Several other students walked past the magazine stand before the young woman was able to turn around and pick the magazines up. The young woman had blond hair and brown eyes, and she carried a red backpack. When she returned to the stand, Officer Stewart saw that she only replaced one magazine.

When the court officer approached the girl about the missing magazines, she insisted that she had not seen them. He asked her to wait at the front counter, which she did. Officer Stewart studied the magazine stand for a brief moment, and then bent down to peer beneath it. He saw the magazines lying there, where they had been accidentally kicked by the other passing students. The young woman helped gather the magazines, and then left the store after apologizing to Mr. and Mrs. Chang.

81. What hours is the market open?

    A. 7:00 A.M. to 2:45 P.M.
    B. 7:00 A.M. to 9:00 A.M.
    C. 7:00 A.M. to 1:30 P.M.
    D. The passage doesn't contain this information

81._____

82. Where were the missing magazines found?

    A. Inside the girl's backpack
    B. On the magazine stand
    C. Beneath the magazine stand
    D. They were never found

82._____

83. What did the girl do when Officer Stewart asked her about the missing magazines? She

    A. ran from the store
    B. denied stealing them
    C. confessed
    D. ran to the front counter

83._____

84. Where is the Jade Market located?

    A. On the first floor of the courthouse
    B. On the third floor of the courthouse
    C. Next to Angel High School
    D. In the plaza of Angel High School

84._____

85. When does Lola Chang work in the market?

    A. All day
    B. Afternoons
    C. Afternoons and evenings
    D. The passage doesn't contain this information

85._____

86. On what day of the week did the incident occur?

    A. Monday   B. Tuesday   C. Wednesday   D. Thursday

86._____

87. What time are students at San Gabriel High School dismissed from class? 87.___

   A. 1:30 P.M.
   B. 1:45 P.M.
   C. 2:45 P.M.
   D. The passage does not contain this information

Questions 88-89.

DIRECTIONS: Questions 88 and 89 are to be answered on the basis of the following facts.

Procedure: The Service Station at the Friendly Car Dealership has a policy which allows customers to drop off their cars the night before they are to be worked on. This allows customers the convenience of not having to take time off from work to have their cars serviced. Cars must be dropped off between 9 P.M. and 11 P.M. the night before. Keys must be labeled with the make and license plate number of the car to which they belong. They are then placed into envelopes and dropped into a locked drop box outside the service station office. Cars must be picked up by 9:00 P.M. on the day repairs are completed. If the car cannot be picked up on that day, other arrangements must be made with the service department by 3:00 P.M. of that day.

Situation: Sarah Stone drops her car off at 10:45 P.M. the night before it is to be serviced. She labels her key, places it in the envelope and leaves it in the drop box. Her car is repaired by 11:00 A.M. the next morning. Because Sarah has to catch up on a backlog of work, she is unable to pick her car up before 6:00 P.M. on the day after the repairs have been completed.

88. Based on the above procedure, which one of the following statements regarding Stone's actions is correct? 88.___
   Stone

   A. should have dropped her car off before 10:45 P.M. the night before it was to be serviced
   B. should have given her keys to someone in the service department instead of dropping them in a box
   C. should have notified the service department of her plans by 3:00 P.M. on the day the car was repaired
   D. did everything according to proper procedure

89. If Stone wishes to pick her car up at 8:00 P.M. the day the repairs are completed, which of the following things must she do? 89.___
   She

   A. must make special arrangements with the service department
   B. must wait until the following morning to pick up her car
   C. must make a special appointment to pick up her car after hours
   D. does not need to do anything

Questions 90-91.

DIRECTIONS: Questions 90 and 91 are to be answered on the basis of the following facts.

Procedure: Notification of absence due to illness must be made between 9:00 A.M. and 10:00 A.M. on the first day of illness. Illness which results in more than four days of consecutive absence must be confirmed by a doctor's note stating the nature of the illness and the approximate date of return to work.

Situation: Officer Janus Lee becomes sick on the night of June 25 while at home. At 10:15 on the morning of June 26, Lee notifies his office that he will not be in. On July 4, Lee submits a doctor's note confirming and identifying his illness and stating that Lee will return to work on July 5.

90. Based on the above procedure, which one of the following statements regarding Lee's actions is correct?
Officer Lee

   A. should have notified his office of his absence by 10:00 A.M. on the morning of June 26
   B. should have notified his office of his absence by 10:00 A.M. on the morning of June 25
   C. should have submitted the doctor's note on June 26
   D. followed the procedure correctly

91. Officer Lee's note from the doctor states that he will be absent from the office from June 26 through July 4. Which of the following notification procedures should he follow on those days?

   A. Officer Lee must notify his office of his absence on each morning between June 26 and July 4 by 10:00 A.M.
   B. Officer Lee's doctor must notify his office of Officer Lee's absence on each morning between June 26 and July 4 by 10:00 A.M.
   C. Officer Lee must contact his office periodically between June 26 and July 4 to notify them of his progress.
   D. Once he has submitted his doctor's note, Officer Lee does not need to notify his office any further so long as he returns to work on July 5.

Questions 92-93.

DIRECTIONS: Questions 92 and 93 are to be answered on the basis of the following facts.

Procedure: Court officers in Montgomery County who work overtime are awarded compensation time instead of overtime pay. Each hour of over-time is equal to one hour of compensation time. In order to use compensation time, court officers must submit a written vacation request two weeks in advance of the desired time off. The request must contain the beginning and ending dates of the requested vacation. It must be signed by the officer's supervisor before the officer may utilize the compensation time.

Situation: Officer Sabrina Hellman wishes to use compensation time for a vacation beginning October 1 and ending October 10. The vacation will require 7 days of compensation time. Officer Hellman submits her vacation request on September 24. The request contains the beginning and ending dates of her desired vacation.

18 (#1)

92. Based on the above procedure, which of the following statements regarding Officer Hellman's actions is correct?
Officer Hellman

   A. should have submitted her vacation request by September 17
   B. should have submitted her vacation request by September 1
   C. should have submitted the beginning and ending dates of her vacation
   D. followed the procedures correctly

93. How many hours of overtime must Officer Hellman have in order to accumulate 100 hours of compensation time?

   A. 50   B. 75   C. 150   D. 100

Questions 94-95.

DIRECTIONS: Questions 94 and 95 are to be answered on the basis of the following facts.

Procedure: Court officers in Salinas County who work overtime are awarded compensation time instead of overtime pay. Each hour of overtime is equal to one hour of compensation time. At the end of each calendar year, compensation time which has not been used is automatically erased unless employees submit a written request to have their compensation time rolled over to the next year. Rollover requests must be submitted no later than November 1. They must contain the employee's name, social security, and the total number of compensation hours s/he wishes to rollover.

Situation: Officer Larry Bernstein accumulated 20 hours of compensation time during calendar year 2008. In addition to that, he has 40 hours of compensation time which was rolled over from 2007. On October 30, Officer Bernstein submits a written request asking that his remaining compensation time be rolled over to calendar year 2009.

94. Based on the above procedure, which of the following statements regarding Officer Bernstein's actions is correct? Officer Bernstein

   A. should have submitted his rollover request by November 1, 2008
   B. should have submitted his vacation request by October 1, 2008
   C. should have submitted the total number of hours he wanted to be rolled over
   D. followed the procedures correctly

95. Based on the above procedure and situation, how many hours of compensation time can Officer Bernstein expect to be rolled over to calendar year 2009?

   A. 20   B. 40   C. 60   D. 80

Questions 96-97.

DIRECTIONS: Questions 96 and 97 are to be answered on the basis of the following facts.

Procedure: Court officers in Salinas County who work overtime are awarded compensation time instead of overtime pay. Each hour of overtime is equal to one hour of compensation time. If a court officer is laid off or chooses to leave his or her employment as a court officer with the county, and he or she has compensation time remaining, then he or she can choose one of two options. The first option is for the employee to use the remaining compensation time as paid vacation time. This would allow the officer to cease his or her duties early, but still be paid until the end of his or her regular employment. In order to utilize this option, employees must submit a written request 30 days before the start of the paid vacation. The second option is for the employee to remain through the end of his or her regular employment, and receive a check for any remaining compensation time. In order to utilize this option, employees must submit a written request 90 days before the scheduled departure date.

Situation: Officer Glen Regan is due to retire at the end of calendar year 2008. Through the course of his career as a court officer, Glen has accumulated 200 hours of compensation time. This equals approximately 25 standard working days.

96. If Officer Regan decides that he would like to retire early, he should submit a written request by _____ 1, 2008.

    A. December B. November C. October D. September

97. If Officer Regan decides to receive a check for his unused compensation time, he should submit a written request by _____ 1, 2008.

    A. December B. November C. October D. September

Questions 98-100.

DIRECTIONS: Questions 98 through 100 are to be answered on the basis of the following facts.

Procedure: Court officers in James County are granted 10 paid sick days each year. Sick days are to be used only in the case of unforeseen illness. Employees are also granted 5 paid personal days. Officers who work overtime are also granted compensation time instead of overtime pay. Each hour of overtime is equal to one hour of compensation time. In order to use a sick day, employees must notify a supervisor by 10:00 A.M. on the day of their absence. In order to use a personal day, employees must notify a supervisor two working days in advance. In order to use a compensation-time day, employees must notify a supervisor two weeks in advance.

Situation: Court Officer Carla Lewis has a doctor and a dentist appointment on Monday, October 5.

98. In order to use a compensation day for these appointments, by what date must Carla notify her supervisor?

    A. Friday, September 4 B. Monday, September 14
    C. 10:00 A.M. October 5 D. Thursday, September 1

99. If Officer Carla Lewis wants to use a personal day for these appointments, by what date must she notify her supervisor?

    A. Friday, September 4 B. Monday, September 14
    C. 10:00 A.M. October 5 D. Thursday, October 1

100. If Officer Carla Lewis wants to use a sick day for these appointments, by what date must she notify her supervisor?

   A. 10:00 A.M. on October 5
   B. Monday, September 14
   C. She cannot use a sick day for these appointments
   D. She does not have to notify her supervisor until after she returns to work

---

KEY (CORRECT ANSWERS)

1. B	21. A	41. D	61. B	81. D
2. D	22. C	42. B	62. D	82. C
3. C	23. B	43. A	63. D	83. B
4. A	24. D	44. D	64. A	84. A
5. D	25. A	45. C	65. B	85. C
6. B	26. C	46. B	66. D	86. D
7. A	27. D	47. A	67. C	87. A
8. D	28. A	48. D	68. A	88. C
9. C	29. C	49. B	69. B	89. D
10. A	30. A	50. C	70. D	90. A
11. D	31. D	51. B	71. C	91. D
12. B	32. C	52. D	72. A	92. A
13. C	33. B	53. C	73. B	93. D
14. C	34. D	54. A	74. D	94. D
15. B	35. A	55. B	75. B	95. C
16. A	36. C	56. D	76. C	96. B
17. D	37. B	57. A	77. B	97. C
18. A	38. A	58. A	78. A	98. B
19. B	39. D	59. C	79. A	99. D
20. C	40. C	60. C	80. B	100. C

EXAMINATION SECTION

TEST 1

DIRECTIONS: Each question or incomplete statement is followed by several suggested answers or completions. Select the one that BEST answers the question or completes the statement. *PRINT THE LETTER OF THE CORRECT ANSWER IN THE SPACE AT THE RIGHT.*

1. Forcible touching is classified as a
   A. Class A Misdemeanor
   B. Class B Misdemeanor
   C. Class C Misdemeanor
   D. Felony

   1.____

2. Inciting to riot is classified as a
   A. Class B Misdemeanor
   B. Grand Felony
   C. Class A Misdemeanor
   D. Felony

   2.____

3. A misdemeanor is defined as an offense, other than a traffic infraction, for which a sentence to a term of imprisonment in excess of _____ day(s) may be imposed, but for which a sentence to a term of imprisonment in excess of _____ year(s) cannot be imposed.
   A. six; one   B. five; one   C. fifteen; two   D. fifteen; one

   3.____

4. Fortune telling, falser personation and creating a hazard are all classified as
   A. felonies
   B. misdemeanors
   C. violations
   d. minor infractions

   4.____

5. A motorist, Jan, ran a traffic light at the intersection of Buffalo Avenue and Rochester Way. Jan is afraid that she has committed a misdemeanor because she was applying lipstick as she was driving and nearly hit a fire hydrant after she realized she blew the light.
   What is Jan guilty of committing?
   A. A traffic infraction, which is not a misdemeanor
   B. A traffic infraction, also known as a misdemeanor
   C. A Class A Misdemeanor
   D. A Class B Misdemeanor

   5.____

6. If James is sentenced to a period of probation, which of the following is MOST likely to accompany the sentence?
   A. The conditions of the sentence, including not leaving the state or abstaining from alcohol
   B. The address of James's probation officer and how to get there from James's home address
   C. The address of the judge presiding over James's probation hearing
   D. The jury instructions which were given to the jury in James's trial

   6.____

7. For a Class A Misdemeanor, other than sexual assault, what is the MAXIMUM period of probation?
   A. Two years   B. Three years   C. Four years   D. Five years

8. For a Class A Misdemeanor sexual assault, the period of probation is _____ years.
   A. four   B. five   C. six   D. seven

9. The conditions of probation or conditional discharge shall be determined by the
   A. jury
   B. parole officer
   C. court
   D. prosecuting attorney

10. When imposing a sentence of probation or conditional discharge, the court may consider restitution and require which of the following?
    A. The defendant avoid injurious habits
    B. Work in a respectable retail environment
    C. Study to become a nurse or other healthcare professional
    D. Participate in an alcohol or substance abuse program of the defendant's family's choosing

11. If Bill has been convicted of a traffic violation which caused the serious physical injury or death of another person, which of the following may the court require as a condition of probation?
    A. Anger management course
    B. Motor vehicle accident prevention course
    C. Defense driving course
    D. Motor skills and research methodology course

12. Unconditional discharge may be imposed for a felony as long as the court sets forth the
    A. actions the defendant has taken not to repeat his or her illicit behavior
    B. reasons for its actions
    C. skills or other licenses of the defendant
    D. other crimes the defendant is alleged to have committed

13. Pursuant to Article 65 of the New York Penal Law, as a condition of probation for sex offenders, the court may impose which of the following additional conditions?
    Reasonable limitation on
    A. food obtained from local grocery stores
    B. his or her use of the internet
    C. the amount of money expended on gaming devices
    D. extracurricular activities

14. Pursuant to Article 70 of the New York Penal Law, the court must inquire that parents of a minor committed to the Department of Corrections grant the minor the capacity to consent to
    A. routine dental treatment
    B. mental health treatment, but only if needed
    C. routine medical treatment, but only if required
    D. routine medical, dental, and mental health services and treatment

15. If a defendant is given a sentence of life imprisonment without parole, where will the defendant be committed?
    A. Custody of the City Department of Corrections
    B. Custody of the State Department of Corrections
    C. Custody of the State Department of Corrections and community supervisions for the remainder of the life of the defendant
    D. Rikers Island

16. A court sentence may run
    A. concurrently or consecutively
    B. concurrently or contemporaneously
    C. consecutively or respectively
    D. concurrently or coincidentally

17. Rich has been convicted of a felony murder of his cousin, Eric. While released on $5,000,000 bail, he is alleged to have murdered a shopkeeper in Albany. Rich is convicted of 25 years for the murder of Eric and 30 years for the murder of the shopkeeper. The sentences will run _____ for a total of _____ years incarceration.
    A. consecutively; 30
    B. consecutively; 55
    C. concurrently; 55
    D. contemporaneously; 30

Questions 18-19.

DIRECTIONS: Questions 18 and 19 are to be answered on the basis of the following information.

Paul and Amy have filed for divorce. Amy has been granted $450 per month in alimony, but Paul has not paid in over seven months. Amy has been living with her sister, Meredith, for over a year and because Paul has not paid Amy alimony, Amy has not been able to pay Meredith rent.

18. May Meredith petition the court to enforce the judgment against Paul?
    A. Yes, because Meredith is materially affected by Paul's nonpayment.
    B. Yes, because Meredith is Amy's sibling and thereby part of her nuclear family.
    C. No, because Amy has only been living with Meredith for a part of Paul's period of noncompliance with the court order.
    D. No.

19. A petition to enforce the judgment against Paul would need to be brought in which court?
    A. State of New York
    B. Supreme Court or a Court of Competent Jurisdiction
    C. Manhattan Family Court
    D. Criminal Court

20. During a support proceeding in family court, which of the following will MOST likely be accompanied to a sworn statement of net worth?
    A. Pay stubs from the year the individual earned the most, and the least, amount of money
    B. Tax return without any accompanying documentation
    C. W-2 tax and wage statements
    D. Current paycheck stub, most recently filed income tax returns, and the W-2 wage and income statements

Questions 21-22.

DIRECTIONS: Questions 21 and 22 are to be answered on the basis of the following information.

Candace filed for divorce from Jason last January. Jason and Candace have agreed to a support arrangement between themselves. Jason will pay Candace $300 per month, except during the summer months of June, July, and August, when Jason is temporarily out of work due to his occupation as a teaching paraprofessional.

21. What must Candace produce to the Court for approval?
    A. The agreement itself which must be reduced to writing
    B. Jason's bank statements, proving he can afford to pay $300 per month
    C. Jason's pay stubs, proving he is customarily out of work during the summer months
    D. The agreement is automatically approved given that the parties arranged the details themselves.

22. Who will approve the document Candace produces to the Court?
    A. The jury
    B. The attorney(s) representing Jason
    C. The court only
    D. The court or support magistrate

23. A summons was served on Jamal requiring him to appear for a family court proceeding involving his sister and father. Jamal failed to appear. The court may issue a(n) _____ directing that Jamal be arrested and brought before the court.
    A. indictment   B. subpoena   C. issue   D. warrant

24. With respect to the finding of the court and according to the New York Family Court Act, the effect of the issuance of a temporary order of protection is
    A. essentially a finding of guilt
    B. admission by the parties that the defendant will harm his or herself and others
    C. not a finding of wrongdoing
    D. a precursor to a felony conviction

25. Assume that a warrant is issued for Daniel in Richmond County. Where will Daniel be taken if he is taken into custody in Suffolk County?
    A. A family judge in Suffolk County
    B. A family judge in Richmond County
    C. A family judge in New York City
    D. The Supreme Court

KEY (CORRECT ANSWERS)

1.	A	11.	B
2.	C	12.	B
3.	D	13.	B
4.	B	14.	D
5.	A	15.	C
6.	A	16.	A
7.	B	17.	B
8.	C	18.	D
9.	C	19.	B
10.	A	20.	D

21.	A
22.	D
23.	D
24.	C
25.	A

TEST 2

DIRECTIONS: Each question or incomplete statement is followed by several suggested answers or completions. Select the one that BEST answers the question or completes the statement. *PRINT THE LETTER OF THE CORRECT ANSWER IN THE SPACE AT THE RIGHT.*

1. Which of the following is a defendant the LEAST likely to hear when being brought before the court pursuant to a warrant?
   He or she will be
   A. informed of the contents of the petition
   B. given the opportunity to present witnesses
   C. advised of their right to counsel
   D. given the option of having the public hear the case

   1._____

2. If the initial return of a summons or warrant is before a judge of the court, when support is an issue, the judge must make a(n) _____ order, either temporary or permanent with regard to support.
   A. reasonable   B. timely   C. immediate   D. seasoned

   2._____

3. Kevin has petitioned the court for temporary child support for his daughter, Maddie, from his ex-wife Katie. Katie objects to any determination of child support even though Maddie lives with Kevin full time. Katie argues that Kevin makes more money than her and there is no outstanding emergency or other issue that warrants the need for child support.
   May the court make an order for temporary child support?
   A. No, because Kevin earns more than Katie.
   B. No, because there is no impending emergency or issue warranting support.
   C. Yes, because Maddie lives with Kevin.
   D. Yes, because the court may make an order for temporary support sufficient to meet the needs of the child without a showing of immediate need.

   3._____

4. Dante is deemed an "eligible offender" because of his prior conviction of armed robbery. An eligible offender is an individual
   A. with a prior conviction
   B. with a prior conviction of a felony with a deadly weapon
   C. who has a prior conviction of an offense, but has not been convicted of more than once of a felony
   D. with at least one prior felony conviction

   4._____

5. How many votes are required from the State Board of Parole to issue a certificate of good conduct for an eligible offender?
   _____ unanimous votes
   A. Two   B. Three   C. Five   D. Four

   5._____

6. Jim is interested in obtaining a certificate of good conduct from the New York State Board of Parole after serving time for a Class C Felony.
   What is the MINIMUM amount of time that must pass before the Parole Board can grant Jim a certificate of good conduct, assuming he satisfies all other requirements of the Board?
   A. One year
   B. Eighteen months
   C. Two years
   D. Three years

7. Leandra's Law specifies that no person shall operate a motor vehicle while impaired or otherwise intoxicated with a child aged _____ years or less as a passenger.
   A. twelve
   B. thirteen
   C. fifteen
   D. eighteen

8. Liam was convicted of driving under the influence of alcohol when he was nineteen in California, his home state. In an attempt to escape his license suspension of one year, he moved to New York to live with his aunt.
   Is Liam's license still suspended?
   A. Yes, his license is suspended in California only
   B. Yes, his license is suspended in New York and California
   C. Yes, his license is suspended in all states
   D. No

9. An adult driving under the combination of drugs and alcohol for the first time will MOST likely be convicted of a
   A. traffic infraction
   B. sanction offense
   C. misdemeanor
   D. felony

10. James has been hired as a marketing assistant for a local pharmaceutical company. After he received his offer letter from the Human Resources Department with his starting salary and start date, he received a call from Sylvia, the HR Coordinator. She informed James that a mistake had been made and the company did not realize James had a criminal record. She rescinded the employment offer and apologized to James for the inconvenience.
    Did the company violate any law?
    A. No, the company is permitted to rescind the offer since James is a felon
    B. No, the company informed James of the situation before he started his employment
    C. Yes, the company should have completed his background search prior to sending his offer of employment
    D. Yes

11. Before Daniel started law school, he became a licensed HVAC technician working for his father's air conditioning repair business. After law school, he became a licensed attorney. Daniel also owns a handgun for which he has a permit. Which of the following are considered "licenses" under the New York Corrections Law Article 23-a?
    A. HVAC license only
    B. HVAC and Bar licenses only
    C. HVAC and Firearm licenses only
    D. HVAC, Bar and Firearm licenses

12. When Marissa was 19, she began working for a local accountant, Bill. After one year as an intern, she began to steal cash and other gifts Bill received from his clients. Bill reported her to authorities and she was convicted of larceny. Seven years later, Marissa is denied employment as an accountant with a local CPA firm.
Why is this permitted under the New York Corrections Law?
    A. There is a direct relationship between the offense she committed and the employment she is seeking.
    B. Denial of employment is only permitted after ten years has passed since the conviction, not seven years.
    C. Marissa was not a minor when she committed the crime.
    D. The CPA firm is not permitted to deny Marissa employment in this situation.

12.____

13. Once a child custody determination has been decided, it is conclusive unless and until the
    A. parents move out of state
    B. child moves out of state with one of the parents
    C. order is modified or changed
    D. judge nullifies the order due to noncompliance

13.____

14. When Bob and Sharon were dating, they lived in Connecticut and moved to Westchester County after they got married. They had their son, Jayden, soon after and when Jayden turned six years old, Bob and Sharon divorced. Bob moved back to Connecticut and has petitioned the court for full legal and physical custody of Jayden. The child custody determination hearings have started in New York and Bob would like his sister, Michelle, to testify on his behalf at the hearing. Michelle lives in Connecticut.
May Bob's sister testify?
    A. No
    B. No, because she lives in Connecticut
    C. Yes, even though she lives in Connecticut
    D. Yes, because she is a material witness to Bob and Sharon's marriage

14.____

15. A private placement adoption is MOST accurately defined as any adoption
    A. of a minor other than that placed by an authorized agency
    B. organized by three or more parties
    C. of a minor organized directly by the parties of the adoptee child
    D. of a minor other than that placed by a government agency

15.____

16. James wants to adopt his stepdaughter, Stephanie, so that he can include her in his will. James is still married to Stephanie's mother, Diane.
May James adopt Stephanie?
    A. It cannot be determined because it is not known if Stephanie is a minor.
    B. Yes, because James has a legitimate reason for adopting Stephanie.
    C. No, because James requires Diane's signature or consent to adopt Stephanie.
    D. No, because James cannot adopt Stephanie for the purpose of inheritance or support rights.

16.____

17. Which of the following individuals will be entitled to notice of adoption pursuant to the New York Domestic Relations Law?
    A. A person determined by a court to be the father of the child
    B. The great-aunt of the child
    C. The doctor, midwife, or other person who delivered the child
    D. The maternal grandfather of the child

18. Grounds for divorce in New York include all of the following EXCEPT
    A. Cruel and inhuman treatment of the plaintiff by the defendant
    B. Abandonment of the plaintiff for a period of one or more years
    C. Confinement of the defendant in prison for a period of three or more consecutive years after the marriage of the plaintiff and defendant
    D. The dissolution of the common law marriage between the plaintiff and defendant

Questions 19-20.

DIRECTIONS: Questions 19 and 20 are to be answered on the basis of the following information.

Amanda wants to file for divorce from Todd on the grounds of adultery. Todd carried on an affair with Amanda's co-worker, Rebecca, nearly six years ago. When Amanda discovered the affair six years ago, she immediately moved out.

19. Will Amanda's petition for divorce be granted?
    A. Yes, because adultery is a ground for divorce in the State of New York.
    B. No, because the affair was forgiven.
    C. No, because Amanda allowed Todd to have an affair and implicitly forgave him by living with him at the time the affair began.
    D. No, because Amanda's petition for divorce was not commenced within five years after the discovery of the affair.

20. Does Amanda have the right to a trial by jury on the issues concerning the grounds for granting her divorce from Todd?
    A. No, because the adulterous affair is settled as fact
    B. No, because the affair is presumed to have ended and/or become immaterial once the divorce petition is filed
    C. No, because there is no right to a trial by jury for divorce cases
    D. Yes, because there is a right to trial by jury of the issues of the grounds for divorce.

21. According to the New York Criminal Procedure Law, the prosecution of a petty offense must be commenced within _____ year(s).
    A. one   B. two   C. three   D. four

22. According to the New York Criminal Procedure Law, the prosecution for a misdemeanor must be commenced within _____ year(s).
    A. one   B. two   C. three   D. four

23. Joel, the treasurer for ABC Limited, Inc., has been stealing from the company for approximately three years. The CEO of ABC Limited, Billy, discovered the larceny nearly two years ago. Billy fired Joel but never brought charges for the theft.
   Will Billy be able to prosecute Joel for larceny?
   A. Yes, because prosecution for larceny committed by a person in violation of a fiduciary duty may be commenced within three years
   B. Yes, because prosecution for larceny committed by a person in violation of a fiduciary duty may be commenced within two years
   C. No, because prosecution for larceny committed by a person in violation of a fiduciary duty must commence within one year
   D. No.

24. After a criminal action is commenced, the defendant is entitled to a _____ trial.
   A. deliberate   B. quick   C. thorough   D. speedy

25. Must the court furnish a defendant with a copy of the felony complaint during arraignment?
   A. No, because a court may furnish this information but is not required to
   B. No, because a court must furnish the complaint before trial but not at arraignment
   C. No, because the court must determine whether the defendant is to be held for grand jury
   E. Yes

KEY (CORRECT ANSWERS)

1. D
2. C
3. D
4. C
5. B

6. D
7. C
8. A
9. C
10. D

11. B
12. A
13. C
14. C
15. A

16. D
17. A
18. D
19. D
20. D

21. A
22. B
23. D
24. D
25. D

TEST 3

DIRECTIONS: Each question or incomplete statement is followed by several suggested answers or completions. Select the one that BEST answers the question or completes the statement. *PRINT THE LETTER OF THE CORRECT ANSWER IN THE SPACE AT THE RIGHT.*

1. Aggravated criminal contempt, aggravated family offense, and absconding from a community treatment facility are classified as   1.____
   A. E Felonies
   B. Violent Felonies
   C. Misdemeanors
   D. Felonies

2. Aggravated harassment in the second degree and arson in the fifth degree are examples of   2.____
   A. Felonies
   B. Misdemeanors
   C. A Misdemeanors
   D. Violent Felonies

3. Murder in the first degree will always be classified as a(n)   3.____
   A. Misdemeanor
   B. E Felony
   C. Felony
   D. Minor Felony

4. A "child born out of wedlock" is   4.____
   A. any child of marriage unless dissolved
   B. any children born after the parents are married
   C. a child born after the marriage license is obtained, but before the parents are legally married
   D. any children born between two consenting adults

5. The social welfare law maintains that in the case of neglect or inability of the parents to provide for the support and education of the child, the child is supported by the   5.____
   A. next closest kin to the mother
   B. next closest kin to the father
   C. child welfare agency of the state
   D. county, city, or town chargeable under the provision of the social welfare law

6. The district attorney who conducts a hearing upon a felony complaint represents, or hears, the case on behalf of the   6.____
   A. county   B. city   C. people   D. government

7. If after a hearing on a felony complaint there is a reasonable cause to believe that a defendant committed an offense that was not a felony, the court may   7.____
   A. reduce the charge but keep the felony charge on record
   B. keep the felony charge on record until the defendant is proven innocent of the lesser crime
   C. reduce the charge to one for such non-felony offense
   D. release the defendant on his or her own recognizance

8. May a court order the removal of an action that begins in criminal court to family court?
   A. Yes, but only if the court states on record the factors upon which the determination is based
   B. Yes, but only if there are two related parties at issue
   C. Yes, but only if the complaining party consents to such a removal
   D. Yes, but only justice is better served if the case were removed to family court

9. Proceedings to establish paternity may be originated in which court? The court in the
   A. county where the mother or child resides or in the county where the putative father resides or is found
   B. city where the birth father lives
   C. county where the mother lives
   D. county where the mother birthed the child

10. If a juvenile offender defendant waives a hearing upon a felony complaint, the court must order that the defendant be held for
    A. the action of the grand jury
    B. capacity hearings
    C. guardianship determination
    D. the results of paternity

11. Bail is defined as
    A. cash or deposit
    B. deposit or bail
    C. cash or bail
    D. bail or cash

12. For the purposes recognizance, bail and commitment, an "obliger" is MOST appropriately defined as the
    A. defendant
    B. person who executes the bail bond on behalf of the defendant, assuming the undertaking
    C. co-defendant
    D. person who signs a contract indicating that they intend to post bail bond in the future

13. An appearance bond is a bail bond in which the only obligor is the
    A. defendant or principal
    B. property secured therewith
    C. defendant's co-conspirators, if any
    D. contract of appearance of the defendant

Questions 14-15.

DIRECTIONS: Questions 14 and 15 are to be answered on the basis of the following information.

Ed's mother has posted bail in the amount of $250,000 for Ed's release after he was charged with aggravated assault. The court imposed the condition that Ed appear for subsequent hearings related to the charges. Ed failed to appear for the second hearing before Judge O'Connor, who then issued a warrant for his arrest. Ed claimed his mother became gravely ill which is why he did not appear for his hearing.

14. What is the effect of Ed's failure to appear on the bail previously posted? The bail is
    A. unequivocally forfeited.
    B. generally forfeited, unless the court finds Ed had sufficient excuse for missing his appearance.
    C. reduced given the nature of Ed's mother's health condition.
    D. forfeited unless Ed's mother can produce a doctor's note.

14._____

15. Assume that the bail has been forfeited. The local criminal must pay the forfeited bail to the
    A. local village justice
    B. treasurer or other financial officer if it is a city court or the state comptroller if it is a town or village court
    C. chief justice directly
    D. treasurer of the junior congressional member of the State of New York

15._____

16. What does Leandra's Law prohibit?
    A. Driving while intoxicated with a person less than 15 years of age as a passenger in the vehicle
    B. Driving while under the influence of alcohol with other passengers in the vehicle
    C. Driving while under the influence of drugs or alcohol with a passenger less than 12 years of age in the vehicle
    D. Driving while intoxicated

16._____

17. An elderly gentleman, Dave, was assaulted at his 70th birthday celebration by another elderly man, Frank, who is ten years younger than Dave. Dave suffered various minor injuries.
    What is the MOST appropriate charge against Frank?
    A. Assault 3   B. Assault 2
    C. Harassment   D. Violent misdemeanor

17._____

18. According to the New York Civil Practice Law and Rules, when a defendant has failed to appear, plead, or proceed to trial of an action, what is the MOST appropriate remedy for a plaintiff?
    A. Resume judgment   B. Dismissal action
    C. Default judgment   D. Increase in charge

18._____

4 (#3)

19. The party responsible for adopting rules of the courts including the preparation and publication of court calendars of the unified court system is the
    A. chief justice of the Civil Courts
    B. chief administrator of the courts
    C. comptroller of the currency
    D. bailiff of the unified court system

    19.____

20. Katie sues Terry for breach of contract after Terry failed to appear for Katie's baby shower and deliver food as the contracted caterer. Terry filed a cross-claim against Samuel, whom she hired to drive her to the venue of Katie's shower. Terry alleges that because Samuel never picked her up as agreed upon, she failed to perform the catering contract for Katie.
    The action to join the claims is also known as
    A. correction of claims
    B. severance of claims
    C. joinder of claims
    D. class action

    20.____

21. Generally, when actions involving a common question of law or fact are pending before the court, the court may order the actions be _____ to avoid unnecessary costs or delay.
    A. combined
    B. categorized
    C. classified
    D. consolidated

    21.____

22. Justice O'Connor has ordered that certain claims in an action before the court be heard separately, or severed, from one another.
    Who is now responsible for determining the order of when each of the newly severed claims are heard?
    A. The chief justice, if not Justice O'Connor
    B. The constable
    C. The court
    D. The attorneys of record

    22.____

23. Which of the following is a prerequisite to the filing of a class action?
    A. The class is so numerous that joinder of all members is impracticable.
    B. The attorneys for each class member approves the joinder of the class.
    C. Less than 500 persons embody the entire class.
    D. The class acts as a whole and accept the settlement paid as a lump sum.

    23.____

24. The order permitting a class action shall do which of the following?
    A. Describe the class
    B. Set out the demand for the class
    C. Name the attorneys of record
    D. Detail the action generally

    24.____

25. A class action cannot be dismissed, discontinued, or compromised without the
    A. consent of the attorneys of record
    B. approval of the court
    C. approval of the class
    D. approval of the court after a full hearing on the merits of the defense

    25.____

KEY (CORRECT ANSWERS)

1. D
2. B
3. C
4. B
5. D

6. C
7. C
8. A
9. A
10. A

11. C
12. B
13. A
14. B
15. B

16. A
17. B
18. C
19. B
20. C

21. D
22. C
23. A
24. A
25. B

TEST 4

DIRECTIONS: Each question or incomplete statement is followed by several suggested answers or completions. Select the one that BEST answers the question or completes the statement. *PRINT THE LETTER OF THE CORRECT ANSWER IN THE SPACE AT THE RIGHT.*

1. During a criminal trial, where an error or other legal defect in the proceedings occurs that prejudices the defendant, the court must declare a _____ upon motion of the defendant.
   A. hung jury
   B. recantation
   C. mistrial
   D. error of motion

   1._____

2. Which party can file a motion for mistrial if it is physically impossible to proceed with the trial in conformity with the law?
   A. Defendant
   B. Plaintiff
   C. The court
   D. All of the above

   2._____

3. After issuing a trial order of dismissal which has the effect of dismissing the entire indictment, the court does which of the following immediately?
   A. Discharge the defendant from custody or exonerate the bail.
   B. Notify the defendant's next of kin
   C. Notify the complaining witness and/or victim of the dismissal
   D. Arrange for a possible appeal from the plaintiff and/or the people

   3._____

4. Generally, when the court has imposed a sentence of imprisonment, when is the last time the sentence can be changed, suspended, or interrupted?
   A. Before the sentence has commenced
   B. After the sentence has been served
   C. After the arraignment, but before the conclusion of the trial
   D. After the instructions on the charge(s) are read to the jury

   4._____

5. Judge Smith rendered a verdict in a criminal case in Essex County. However, the court did not have jurisdiction over the case. The PROPER remedy is
   A. dismissal
   B. hung jury
   C. mistrial
   D. vacate judgment

   5._____

6. The court may vacate a judgment, upon motion of the defendant, for which of the following grounds?
   A. The judgment was procured by duress.
   B. The material evidence at trial was true, but presented in a way that painted the defendant in a negative light.
   C. Material evidence was obtained for trial via search warrant or other lawful device.
   D. All of the above

   6._____

7. Rachel, a licensed eighth grade teacher, was recently convicted of felony larceny. Who must be notified of Rachel's felony conviction?
   A. Rachel's next of kin
   B. The New York Comptroller, who must garnish Rachel's pay
   C. The Department of Education
   D. The Parole Board of New York

7._____

8. Jamal knowingly filed a false financing statement for his contractor business, indicating that he owes more money than he actually does to his bank lender. Jamal was convicted of intentionally filing a false financing statement under the Uniform Commercial Code (UCC).
   Who must be notified of Jamal's conviction?
   A. The Office of the UCC
   B. The New York Secretary of State
   C. The Chief Justice
   D. The Parole Board of New York

8._____

9. During jury selection, Dawn's lawyer did not object to any potential jurors. Once the trial began, Dawn's attorney raised the objection that juror number 3, Richard, may be biased against Dawn.
   What is the MOST appropriate response to Dawn's attorney's objection?
   A. A challenge to the jury panel must be made before the selection of the jury commences, therefore overruled
   B. A challenge to the jury panel must be made before the selection of the jury ends, therefore overruled
   C. A challenge to the jury panel must be made before the selection of the jury commences, therefore accepted
   D. Sustained

9._____

10. A criminal trial jury consists of not less than _____ members.
    A. fourteen   B. nine   C. six   D. twelve

10._____

11. Pursuant to Article 270 of the New York Criminal Procedure Law, either party may examine prospective jurors regarding their qualifications to serve as jurors. However, the court cannot allow the questioning to
    A. become repetitious, irrelevant, or involve questioning of a juror's knowledge of the rules of law
    B. reduce to questioning of the individual's family history or other background
    C. involve asking the prospective juror about his prior service on a jury
    D. contain questions that are relevant to the case, but asked in a rude or belittling manner

11._____

12. How many peremptory challenges may either side exercise during jury selection?
    A. One   B. Two
    C. Three   D. Dependent on the type of case

12._____

13. A challenge for cause of a prospective juror which is not made before he is sworn as a trial juror shall be deemed to be
    A. accepted   B. rebuked   C. waived   D. refuted

14. According to Section 270.16 of the New York Criminal Procedure Law, the examination of prospective jurors by either party is permitted to take place outside the presence of other prospective jurors for which type of case?
    A. Matrimonial cases, involving the adoption of a stepchild or adopted child
    B. Surrogates cases, involving complicated estates
    C. Capital cases, in which the crime charged may be punishable by death
    D. All such cases as long as the defense moves first

15. A peremptory challenge is defined as a(n)
    A. objection to a prospective juror for which no reason need be assigned
    B. objection to a prospective juror for which there must be a reason assigned
    C. objection to a prospective juror for justified cause
    D. trial objection

16. At what point in a trial is the jury provided with general instructions concerning its basic functions, duties, and conduct?
    After the jury has been sworn _____ opening address.
    A. but before the people's
    B. and after the people's
    C. but before the defense's
    D. and after the defense's

17. Pursuant to Section 270.45 of the New York Criminal Procedure Law, the court may in its discretion either permit a jury to _____ during recesses and/or adjournments or direct that they be continuously kept together during such periods under the supervision of an appropriate public servant.
    A. not communicate with one another
    B. not make eye contact with one another
    C. refrain from using their mobile phones
    D. separate

18. If a defendant pleads not responsible by reason of mental disease or defect, the court will ask him or her which of the following?
    A. About the offense or offenses charged in the indictment
    B. Family background
    C. Feelings or mental state at the time of the hearing
    D. Additional information not previously asked by counsel

19. Assuming the same facts as Question 18, by answering the questions posed by the court, the defendant has effectively
    A. lost his right to appeal by waiver
    B. waived his or her right to not be compelled to incriminate him or herself
    C. harmed him or herself
    D. waived his or her rights under the Second Amendment

20. Before accepting a plea of not responsible by reason of mental disease or defect, the court must find and state which of the following on record in detail?
    A. That the affirmative defense of lack of criminal responsibility by reason of mental disease or defect would be proven by the defendant at trial by a preponderance of the evidence
    B. That the defendant entered the plea under duress
    C. That the court is satisfied the defendant has been diagnosed with a generally accepted mental disease
    D. That the defendant can speak for himself

20.____

21. Intermittent imprisonment is defined as
    A. revocable sentence of imprisonment to be served on days or during certain periods of days, or both, specified by the court
    B. irrevocable sentence of imprisonment to be served part time
    C. revocable sentence of imprisonment to be served on weekends only
    D. another form of irrevocable release based on one's own recognizance

21.____

22. If John is currently serving an intermittent sentence of imprisonment and is then sentenced to a definite sentence of three years, when will he begin his definite sentence?
    A. After the conclusion of his intermittent sentence
    B. After a hearing of the court to determine which sentence takes priority
    C. After thirty days
    D. Immediately

22.____

23. Burglary in the first, second, and third degree is classified as a
    A. misdemeanor   B. minor infraction
    C. felony   D. subordinate crime

23.____

24. The crime of conspiracy is
    A. always classified as a felony
    B. always classified as a misdemeanor
    C. sometimes classified as a felony, but in other instances classified as a misdemeanor
    D. not a crime

24.____

25. The criminal sale of a firearm is
    A. always classified as a felony
    B. always classified as a violent felony
    C. sometimes classified as a felony, but in other instances classified as a misdemeanor
    D. not a crime if there is no buyer

25.____

KEY (CORRECT ANSWERS)

1.	C		11.	A
2.	D		12.	D
3.	A		13.	C
4.	A		14.	C
5.	D		15.	A
6.	A		16.	A
7.	C		17.	D
8.	B		18.	A
9.	A		19.	B
10.	D		20.	A

21. A
22. D
23. C
24. C
25. D

EXAMINATION SECTION
TEST 1

DIRECTIONS: Each question or incomplete statement is followed by several suggested answers or completions. Select the one that BEST answers the question or completes the statement. *PRINT THE LETTER OF THE CORRECT ANSWER IN THE SPACE AT THE RIGHT.*

1. Peter Poe has been arrested on a charge of petit larceny. A search of police files indicates prior convictions for possessing a dangerous weapon and for illegally using the same. According to Criminal Procedure Law, it would be correct to state, with respect to the release of Poe on bail when arraigned in the court indicated, that he

    A. can be released on bail by a judge of the district court because such judges can admit to bail perpetrators of any crime
    B. can be released on bail by a judge of the criminal court of the City of New York because petit larceny is a misdemeanor
    C. cannot be released on bail by a judge of the criminal court of the City of New York because Poe has had two prior convictions
    D. cannot be released on bail by a judge of the district court because such judges can only admit to bail defendants charged with an offense

1.____

2. John Doe has been arrested in New York County charged therein with murder, first degree. According to Criminal Procedure Law, it would be correct to state, with respect to the release of Doe on bail, that he

    A. can be released on bail by a justice of the Supreme Court of New York State
    B. can be released on bail by a justice of the Court of Special Sessions of the City of New York
    C. cannot be released on bail by anyone if he had ever before attempted to commit a felony
    D. cannot be released on bail under any circumstances, except by a judge of the district court

2.____

3. John Doe has been arrested by an officer on patrol at night and brought to the station house for booking on a charge of disorderly conduct under Section 722 of the Penal Law. According to Criminal Procedure Law, the desk officer must release Doe on bail for appearance before a magistrate the next morning if Doe was charged with

    A. interfering with a person by placing his hand near such person's pocketbook or pocket
    B. soliciting men for lewd purposes in a public place
    C. engaging in an illegal occupation
    D. causing a disturbance in a bus or acting in a manner disturbing or offensive to others

3.____

4. John Doe has been arrested on a charge of disorderly conduct under Section 722 of the Penal Law. The one of the following offenses covered by this section for which Criminal Procedure Law requires the court's approval prior to admitting him to bail is

    A. jostling against or unnecessarily crowding a person in a public place
    B. acting in such a manner as to interfere with others

4.____

C. congregating on a public street and refusing to move on when ordered by the police
D. shouting outside a building at night to the annoyance of a considerable number of persons

5. The hours during which a police officer of superior rank must take bail for a misdemeanor are limited by Criminal Procedure Law to the hours between

   A. 11 A.M. and 8 A.M. the next morning
   B. 2 P.M. and 8 A.M. the next morning
   C. 11 A.M. and 2 P.M. the same day
   D. 2 P.M. and 11 A.M. the next morning

6. Billy Doe, a 13-year-old boy, is the only witness to a crime committed by his 22-year-old uncle with whom he has been staying while on a visit to New York City. According to Criminal Procedure Law, with respect to the production of the child in court, it would be correct to state that a

   A. personal recognizance in writing shall be accepted from Billy's parent or guardian only
   B. separate personal recognizance must be taken by the court for each production of the child pending the final termination of the proceedings
   C. personal recognizance shall not be accepted in this case from any person
   D. personal recognizance shall be vacated on failure to produce Billy in court as ordered and Billy himself taken into custody thereafter

7. The one of the following prerequisites for a permit to possess or dispose of firearms anywhere in this state, according to Penal Law is that the applicant must

   A. file a separate new application for each weapon if he wishes at any time to amend his license to include one or more weapons, if he is licensed either to possess weapons as an individual or as a dealer
   B. be a resident of the county in which the weapon is to be used, if he is applying for a license to possess and carry a weapon as a merchant or employee of a financial institution
   C. not have been convicted of either a misdemeanor or a felony, if he is applying for a permit to possess and carry concealable firearms
   D. be a citizen of the United States and over 21 years of age, if he wishes to be either a gunsmith or a dealer in firearms

8. John Doe, a barber, who has been posing as a surgeon specializing in abortions, is on trial. He is charged with having performed an illegal abortion which resulted in the death of Jane X. Before she died, Jane X made a dying declaration naming Doe as the person who had performed the illegal operation. According to Criminal Procedure Law, it would be correct to state that in this prosecution of Doe for abortion Jane X's dying declaration shall

   A. be admitted in evidence without any restrictions
   B. be admitted in evidence subject to the same restrictions as in cases of homicide
   C. not be admitted in evidence
   D. not be admitted in evidence if Jane X voluntarily submitted to the operation fully aware of its possible consequences

9. John Doe, the defendant on a robbery charge, has been released on bail in Manhattan. He goes to the farm home of his parents in Ulster County and fails to appear in court as ordered. As a result, his bail is forfeited and a bench warrant is issued in New York County for his arrest. Criminal Procedure Law provides, with respect to the service of such a bench warrant, that it may

   A. not be served outside New York County, the county of issue
   B. be served in Ulster County, but only after being endorsed by a magistrate of that county
   C. be served in Ulster County without being endorsed by a magistrate of that county
   D. be served in any county, in the same manner as a warrant of arrest, without any exceptions

10. John Smith, an accountant for the Alden Corporation, is dismissed after 20 years with the organization. Angry and disgruntled with the treatment accorded to him by the company, Smith tells Bill Jones, a neighbor, about all he had done to build up the company. He tells Jones how *cheap* the company is and how easy it would be to rob it on any pay day because of the lack of protective devices. He says he hopes someone will do it some day, and goes into great detail about how it could be done successfully. About six months later, without any knowledge on Smith's part, Jones and his brothers, Jim and Bob, successfully rob the Alden Corporation treasurer as he is about to pay off the staff. The holdup nets $40,000.
    Four years later, Bob Jones is apprehended. He involves his brothers. Bill Jones, on questioning, describes how Smith had given him the idea for the crime.
    According to the Penal Law, it would be most correct to state that Smith

    A. cannot be charged with having any connection with the crime because it took place entirely without his knowledge
    B. can no longer be arrested or charged with any crime because the statute of limitations for robbery is four years
    C. can be arrested and charged only with being an accessory because he took no part in the actual commission of the crime
    D. can be arrested and charged with being a principal to the robbery

11. Charging his pretty wife with infidelity, Joe Doakes has slashed at her face with a razor, causing severe mutilation around her eyes, mouth, and cheeks. This action results in permanent ugly scars. He is taken into custody and held for trial on a charge of maiming. In order to sustain this charge, it is necessary that intent be shown. According to the Penal Law, in connection with intent, with respect to this crime, it is most correct to state that the

    A. disfigurement need not even have been inflicted with felonious intent
    B. injury must seriously diminish the victim's physical vigor
    C. disfigurement must be incapable of being repaired by plastic surgery
    D. mere infliction of the injury is presumptive evidence of the intent

12. Arthur Mason has been released on $50,000 bail as the alleged armed-robber of a supermarket. He fails to appear in court as ordered. According to the Penal Law, it would be most correct for the police to charge Mason, in addition to the original charge, with a

    A. felony for jumping bail, if he fails to surrender himself within 30 days
    B. misdemeanor for jumping bail, if he fails to surrender himself within 30 days

C. felony for jumping bail, if he fails to surrender himself within 15 days
D. misdemeanor for jumping bail, plus the loss of the $50,000 if he fails to surrender himself within 15 days

13. Bill Walters, who has been subpoenaed as a witness to a holdup murder, is approached by two men, who offer him $10,000 to testify falsely as to what he had seen. When he refuses, they threaten his life. He then agrees, but notifies the police as soon as the two men leave.
According to the Penal Law, the two men can be charged with

A. subornation of perjury
B. perjury
C. suppressing evidence
D. dissuading witness from testifying

14. According to the Penal Law with regard to the use of force or fear in the crime of robbery, it would be most correct to state that, to constitute robbery,

A. force may have been used to obtain possession of the property, but, if this did not occur, force must have been used to escape
B. the mere snatching of the property from the hand of the victim without his resistance and without force or violence by the offender is sufficient
C. fear is a necessary ingredient regardless of the value of the property taken
D. when there is nothing to inspire fear, superior force must have been used, and the property relinquished upon a struggle and upon compulsion

15. The State Legislature amended the section of the Penal Law dealing with the making of malicious telephone calls. The amendment added a provision which made it a misdemeanor for a person to maliciously use the telephone

A. to threaten to commit a crime against the person called
B. to threaten to commit a crime against the teenage daughter of the person called
C. for the purpose of using obscene language to any person of the female sex
D. for the purpose of using obscene language to a male child under the age of 16 years

16. Jane Doe, a model, posed in the nude for several lewd photographs. Joe Hoe did the actual photographing and developed 100 prints of each pose. John Coe, the distributor, was apprehended with all the prints in his possession except for the 10 copies of one pose which he had just sold to Peter Poe. Poe was apprehended at the same time with the purchased pictures in his hand. Under Section 1141 of the Penal Law (obscene prints and articles), it would be most proper to charge a violation thereof to

A. J. Doe and J. Hoe only
B. J. Coe and P. Poe only
C. all four persons
D. J. Doe, J. Hoe, and J. Coe only

17. According to the Penal Law, the one of the following who could be charged with the misdemeanor of violating the provisions governing immoral shows and exhibitions is

    A. an actor participating in the performance
    B. the manager of the theater or place who permits the immoral show though without knowledge of the type of performance involved
    C. the advertising manager of the show
    D. the owner of the premises who rented the theater to the producers of the show though without any knowledge of the type of performance involved

18. Two officers on radio motor patrol notice four men acting suspiciously in a parked automobile near a large jewelry store. Upon questioning, the officers learn that the car and its driver had been hired for the night by the other three men. Dissatisfied with the evasiveness of the three men with respect to their answers to some of the questions, the officers frisk all four. An unlicensed .45 automatic is found on one of the passengers who states it does not belong to him. The other passengers know nothing of the presence of the gun. According to the Penal Law, the presence of the gun is presumptive evidence of its possession by

    A. all the occupants of the automobile
    B. the individual possessing it only
    C. all the occupants except the driver
    D. the individual possessing it and also the real owner

19. John Doe, who has just been convicted of a felony, is being transferred from the city prison to the state prison at Dannemora. While he is waiting under guard at Grand Central Station, his brothers, James and William, try to overpower the guards in order to help John escape. They succeed but all three are apprehended in the western part of the state two weeks later. According to the Penal Law, James and William

    A. can be charged with a misdemeanor, which is next lesser in degree than the felony for which John was convicted
    B. can be charged with a felony because John was convicted of a felony
    C. cannot be charged with a felony, because no weapons were used and the guards were not injured
    D. can be charged with either a misdemeanor or a felony, depending on who originated the conspiracy

20. Roy Brown enters a drugstore and forces the proprietor into the back room at knife point. He takes all the money he finds in the cash register and in the pharmacist's pocket. He ties the pharmacist's hands behind his back with adhesive tape and puts tape across his mouth. He sees the pharmacist's 15-year-old daughter in the back room, tapes her hands and mouth, and carnally abuses the girl with the intention of eventually raping her. Before he can rape her, he is surprised by an officer who comes into the store to check whether anyone had come in for treatment of a stab wound. The would-be rapist is apprehended while in the act of carnally abusing the girl.
    According to the Penal Law, Brown, if convicted,

    A. cannot be considered within the province of the law dealing with sexual abuse unless he administered or forced the girl to take a poison or narcotic intended to weaken her resistance
    B. may be sentenced for each crime separately, but the sentences must run consecutively

C. must be given a definite sentence for armed robbery and also an indeterminate sentence for the sex offense
D. may, in place of the penalty for armed robbery, receive an indefinite sentence of one day to life for the sexual abuse

---

KEY (CORRECT ANSWERS)

1.	B	11.	D
2.	A	12.	A
3.	D	13.	C
4.	A	14.	D
5.	B	15.	D
6.	C	16.	C
7.	D	17.	C
8.	B	18.	B
9.	C	19.	B
10.	A	20.	D

EXAMINATION SECTION
TEST 1

DIRECTIONS: Each question or incomplete statement is followed by several suggested answers or completions. Select the one that BEST answers the question or completes the statement. *PRINT THE LETTER OF THE CORRECT ANSWER IN THE SPACE AT THE RIGHT.*

1. What is the typical time between an arrest and arraignment? 1.____
   A. 90 days B. 30 days C. 24 hours D. 6 days

2. A court order issued for a defendant's arrest if he or she fails to appear for a court proceeding other than an arraignment is also known as a 2.____
   A. subpoena B. indictment
   C. deposition D. bench warrant

3. A _____ fee is imposed upon conviction of a felony, miscemeanor, or violation. 3.____
   A. criminal assistance B. criminal action
   C. crime victim assistance D. crime novice

4. Barr is caught drinking in public and issued a DAT by the arresting officer. A DAT is an acronym for which notice that will require Barry to appear in court at a later date for arraignment? 4.____
   A. Desk Appearance Ticket B. Desk Arraignment Ticket
   C. Direct Appearance Toll D. Desk Appearance Toll

5. Maria is a journalist conducting research on a current case that is taking place at the New York City Criminal Court. Maria needs to obtain an official court document that indicates the current status of a case or its final disposition. 5.____
   Which of the following documents would be the MOST helpful in Maria's research?
   A. Certificate of Disposition B. Docket number
   C. Index number D. Trial exhibits

Questions 6-7.

DIRECTIONS: In answering Questions 6 and 7, use the following list.

The order of a jury trial, in general, is as follows:
  I. The jury must be selected and sworn
  II. The people must deliver an opening address to the jury
  III. The court must deliver preliminary instructions to the jury
  IV. The defendant may deliver an opening address to the jury

6. Which of the following is the CORRECT order of events in a jury trial? 6.____
   A. I, II, III, IV   B. IV, II, III, I   C. I, III, II, IV   D. I, III, IV, II

7. Which of the following is the next step in the jury trial? 7.____
   A. The defendant may offer evidence in his defense.
   B. The people may offer evidence in rebuttal of the defendant's evidence.
   C. The people must offer evidence in support of the indictment.
   D. The trial concludes.

8. A trial jury consists of _____ jurors, but _____ jurors may be selected and sworn pursuant to Section 270.30 of the New York Criminal Procedure Law. 8.____
   A. six; alternative
   B. six; alternate
   C. twelve; rendering
   D. twelve; alternate

9. Which of the following is a challenge for cause to a prospective juror? 9.____
   A. He or she does not have the qualifications required by the judiciary law
   B. He or she was a witness at the preliminary examination
   C. He or she served on the grand jury which found the indictment in issue
   D. All of the above

10. A(n) _____ is a written accusation by a grand jury, filed with a superior court, charging a person, or two or more persons jointly, with the commission of a crime, or with the commission of two or more offenses at least one of which is a crime. 10.____
    A. subpoena   B. indictment   C. return   D. information

11. A court sentence may run 11.____
    A. directly or indirectly
    B. contemporaneously or simultaneously
    C. concurrently or consecutively
    D. consecutively or respectively

12. Upon the taking of fingerprints of an arrested person or defendant, the appropriate police officer or agency must, without unnecessary delay, forward two copies of such fingerprints to the 12.____
    A. Child Welfare Services
    B. Division of Social Services Law
    C. Criminal Justice Services
    D. Criminal Welfare and Domestic Services

13. Rebecca alleges that she is the victim of a sexual assault which occurred on her walk back to her apartment two nights ago. After taking Rebecca's statement, the arresting officer requests that Rebecca submit to a polygraph test regarding the incident. Is Rebecca's polygraph examination admissible at trial? 13.____
    A. Yes, but only if Rebecca submits to the test
    B. Yes, but only if Rebecca consents to the test's admission into evidence
    C. Unequivocally yes
    D. No

14. Jason is convicted of possession of a controlled substance, completed his sentence, and now would like his record sealed. Which of the following is MOST likely required to be fulfilled before the court, in its discretion, can seal Jason's record?
    A. Completion of a judicial diversion program
    B. Secure permanent employment within close proximity to Jason's primary residence
    C. Demonstrate through financial or other banking statements that Jason has successfully paid probation fees and related expenses
    D. The court's determination is solely one of discretion

15. When a court orders sealing, all official records and papers relating to the arrests, _____, including all duplicates and copies thereof, on file with the division of criminal justice services or any court shall be sealed and not made available to any person or public or private agency.
    A. prosecutions, and convictions
    B. dockets, and interrogatories
    C. allegations, and convictions
    D. forgeries, and docket entries

16. Can a criminal record be sealed while the charged offense is still pending?
    A. Yes, if the outcome is favorable to the defendant
    B. Yes, if the alleged victim withdraws his or her complaint
    C. Yes, if the alleged victim consents to the sealing of the record
    D. No

17. During jury deliberations, who is permitted to communicate with the jurors?
    A. Only their immediate family to the extent that can prove they are related by blood
    B. No one may communicate with the jurors
    C. The court officer may communicate with them as long as it is related to the case
    D. The judge's clerk may communicate with the jurors as long as it is related to the case

18. The verdict must be rendered and announced by the _____ of the jury in the courtroom in the presence of the court, a prosecutor, the defendant's counsel, and the defendant.
    A. primary person
    B. indicative person
    C. designated member
    D. foreperson

19. If the court accepts a verdict which is defective or incomplete by reason of the jury's failure to render a verdict upon every count upon which it was instructed to do so, such verdict is deemed to constitute a(n) _____ upon every such count improperly ignored in the verdict.
    A. finding of guilt   B. acquittal   C. mistrial   D. hung jury

20. Under what circumstances will a jury be discharged without having rendered a verdict?
    A. The jury has deliberated for an extensive period of time without agreeing on a verdict and the court is satisfied that any agreement is unlikely within a reasonable amount of time
    B. The court, the defendant, and the people all consent to such discharge
    C. A mistrial is declared
    D. All of the above

21. After a jury trial where the jury found Mr. Smith guilty of the crime charged, the defendant's counsel requests to poll the jury. During a polling of the jury, juror #4 indicates that he voted "not guilty".
    What is the MOST appropriate response of the court after this revelation?
    A. Sentence the defendant as the guilty verdict was already read in open court
    B. Declare a mistrial given that one of the jurors' votes was improperly counted
    C. Ask that juror #4 elaborate on his vote to ensure that he or she is not confused by the question
    D. Refuse to accept the verdict and direct the jury to resume its deliberations

22. Must a motion to set aside a verdict based upon the ground that one of the jurors is actually related to the defendant be in writing?
    A. No, as long as the people are given reasonable notice and an opportunity to appear in opposition
    B. Yes, all requests made to the court must be in writing
    C. Yes, all requests in the form of motions must be in writing
    D. Yes, all requests to set aside a verdict must be in writing

23. If a defendant is ordered to pay a fine, which of the following payment methods may the court require of the defendant?
    A. Pay the entire amount at the time the sentence is pronounced
    B. Pay the entire amount at some later date
    C. Pay a specified portion at designated periodic intervals
    D. Any of the above

24. Brian is ordered to pay restitution to the victim of his crime, Sarah. Sarah dies before the full payment of restitution is made. Must Brian continue to pay restitution?
    A. No, because Sarah died
    B. Yes, because Sarah died the restitution is doubled
    C. Yes, the remaining payments are made to Sarah's estate
    D. Yes, unless Sarah relieved Brian of further payments in her will

25. The prosecution for a felony must be commenced within ____ years after the commission of the crime itself.
    A. two   B. three   C. four   D. five

KEY (CORRECT ANSWERS)

1.	C	11.	C
2.	D	12.	C
3.	C	13.	D
4.	A	14.	A
5.	A	15.	A
6.	C	16.	D
7.	C	17.	B
8.	D	18.	D
9.	D	19.	B
10.	B	20.	D

21.	D
22.	A
23.	D
24.	C
25.	D

TEST 2

DIRECTIONS: Each question or incomplete statement is followed by several suggested answers or completions. Select the one that BEST answers the question or completes the statement. *PRINT THE LETTER OF THE CORRECT ANSWER IN THE SPACE AT THE RIGHT.*

1. Which of the following must be specified in the sentence of probation? 1.____
    A. The conditions to be complied with
    B. The age of the offender at the time of the commission of the crime
    C. The gender of the alleged victim of the underlying crime
    D. The statute which the probationary sentence derives from

2. The court may modify or enlarge the conditions of a sentence of probation or of conditional discharge at any time prior to the expiration of termination of the period of the sentence, but only if the defendant 2.____
    A. consents
    B. is personally present
    C. submits to drug testing
    D. submits to polygraph testing

3. If at any time during the period of a sentence of probation or of conditional discharge the court has reasonable cause to believe that the defendant has violated a condition of the sentence, it may file a written 3.____
    A. declaration of incumbency
    B. warrant for arrest
    C. modification of order for cause
    D. declaration of delinquency

4. Bryan was sentenced to a period five years' probation, during which time he is prohibited from leaving the State of New York. During a bachelor party, and unbeknownst to him, his brother-in-law drives Bryan and three of his closest friends to a nightclub in Connecticut. Bryan was unaware he was not in New York. On the way back from the nightclub, Bryan's brother-in-law was pulled over for speeding and Bryan was arrested. 4.____
    May the court order Bryan to appear before it in connection with his arrest?
    A. No, because Bryan was unaware he was in Connecticut
    B. No, because Bryan did not consent to violating his probation
    C. No, because Bryan was not the driver of the vehicle when it was stopped
    D. Yes

5. Where the probation officer has requested that a probation warrant be issued, the court shall within _____ hours of its receipt of the request, issue or deny the warrant or take any other lawful action. 5.____
    A. 24   B. 35   C. 48   D. 72

6. The duty of supervision of the defendant after the imposition of a sentence of probation belongs to the 6.____
    A. probation department serving the court that imposed the sentence
    B. defendant's legal counsel
    C. judge's office including the legal staff, just as the clerk and associate clerk
    D. judge

7. Can supervision of a defendant be transferred if the defendant moves to another state?
   A. No, the sentence of probation is automatically dismissed if he or she moves
   B. No, the sentence of probation is stayed until the individual moves or returns back to New York
   C. No, unless the defendant consents in writing to the continued supervision in order to complete the sentence of probation expediently
   D. Yes

8. John has been on probation for the last eight years, with two more years left of his 10-year sentence. John has requested that the court terminate the remainder of his probation sentence.
   Can the court, in its discretion, grant a request for termination of a sentence of probation?
   A. No
   B. No, unless John's probation officer consents in writing
   C. Yes, if John posts bail in the amount of $50,000 which will be returned to him at the end of the final two years
   D. Yes, if the court determines John no longer needs such supervision, diligently complied with the conditions of the problems and the termination is not adverse to the protection of the public

Questions 9-10.

DIRECTIONS: Questions 9 and 10 are to be answered on the basis of the following fact pattern.

Angelo, 15, and his brother Dave, 18, decide to rob a convenience store. When Angelo and Dave entered the convenience store, the store owner shot and killed Dave before the plot unraveled. The store owner called the police after Angelo fled the scene. When Angelo was apprehended by the police, he had a gun in his pants.

9. Assume a criminal case has been brought against Angelo for robbery. However, the criminal court directs that the action be moved to the family court for adjudication because the store owner was Angelo's uncle.
   Which document is issued to move the case from criminal court to the family court?
   A. Order of removal
   B. Order of detention
   C. Order of discharge
   D. Order of retention

10. When an action is moved to the family court, what is the effect of the action in the original court?
    A. The action in the original court continues.
    B. The store owner can elect to continue the case in criminal court if he so chooses.
    C. The store owner can choose which court to continue the case in.
    D. The action in the criminal court ceases.

11. An "incapacitated person" is defined as a(n)
    A. individual in prison or otherwise under the custody of the bureau of prisons
    B. incarcerated person, interchangeably defined as incapacitated
    C. defendant who as a result of mental disease lacks capacity to understand against him
    D. defendant who has surrendered his or her rights to handle their legal matters

12. A warrant of arrest must be subscribed by the
    A. issuing court
    B. arresting officer
    C. issuing judge
    D. court clerk

13. Which of the following is NOT required to be included in a warrant of arrest?
    A. The date of issuance of the warrant
    B. The name or title of an offense charged in the underlying accusatory instrument
    C. The age of the defendant
    D. The police officer to whom the warrant is addressed

14. A non-jury trial of an indictment must be conducted by
    A. a panel of judges
    B. one judge
    C. assistant district attorneys
    D. a panel of court clerks

15. In any case in which the defendant's appearance is required by a summons or an appearance ticket, the court in its discretion may, for good cause shown, permit the defendant to appear by _____ instead of in person.
    A. telephone
    B. facsimile
    C. teleconference
    D. counsel

16. May a prosecutor's information or misdemeanor complaint be removed from one local criminal court to another?
    A. No
    B. Not unless the judge becomes ill
    C. Yes, under certain circumstances
    D. Yes, but only if the original court is closed

17. A(n) _____, which replaces a misdemeanor complaint, need not charge the same offense or offenses, but at least one count thereof must charge the commission by the defendant of an offense based upon conduct which was the subject of the misdemeanor complaint.
    A. subpoena
    B. warrant
    C. information
    D. order

18. Celeste was sentenced to 60 months' imprisonment. After she begins her sentence, she petitions the court to pause her sentence so that she can take care of her terminally ill mother. May Celeste's sentence be interrupted?
    A. No, because she has commenced the sentence
    B. No, because her mother has not passed away

C. No, because Celeste has not appealed the sentence and asked for a pause, or interruption
D. Yes

19. A "resentence" is MOST closely defined as a(n)
    A. replacement sentence
    B. intermittent sentence
    C. sentence that must be served within 60 days of final judgment
    D. sentence of imprisonment of less than one year

20. In counties within New York City, what party is responsible for the detention of defendants in criminal actions?
    A. Justice of the peace   B. Commissioner of correction
    C. Sheriff   D. Park ranger

21. The court may not revoke a sentence of probation or a sentence of conditional discharge, or extend a period of probation, unless (a) the court has _____ and (b) the defendant has had an opportunity to be heard.
    A. found that the defendant has violated a condition of the sentence
    B. found that the defendant has moved out of the area
    C. found that the defendant has requested a different probation officer
    D. lost or otherwise forfeited original jurisdiction

22. In general, the court may hear all legally relevant facts except those that are
    A. damaging to the defendant's reputation in the business community
    B. revealing of the defendant's age or occupation
    C. privileged
    D. facts that are material to the case, but may need an expert to explain in greater detail

23. At what point in a criminal proceeding is a defendant entitled to counsel?
    A. After arraignment   B. At the trial
    C. Before jury selection   D. At all stages

24. The court may terminate a period of probation for a person who is subject to _____ probation and who has been on unrevoked probation for at least five consecutive years.
    A. unspecified   B. lifetime   C. uninterrupted   D. suspended

25. A defendant may waive indictment and consent to be prosecuted by superior court information when a local criminal court has held the defendant for the action of a grand jury, the defendant is not charged with a Class A felony, and the
    A. district attorney consents to the waiver
    B. defendant consents in writing to the waiver
    C. district attorney submits an order in support of the waiver
    D. commissioner submits an order in support of the waiver

KEY (CORRECT ANSWERS)

1.	A	11.	C
2.	B	12.	C
3.	D	13.	C
4.	D	14.	B
5.	D	15.	D
6.	A	16.	C
7.	D	17.	C
8.	D	18.	A
9.	A	19.	A
10.	D	20.	B

21. A
22. C
23. D
24. B
25. A

EXAMINATION SECTION

TEST 1

DIRECTIONS: Each question or incomplete statement is followed by several suggested answers or completions. Select the one that BEST answers the question or completes the statement. *PRINT THE LETTER OF THE CORRECT ANSWER IN THE SPACE AT THE RIGHT.*

1. Which method below can be used to require a defendant's appearance in local criminal court for arraignment?
    A. Issuance of a warrant of arrest
    B. Issuance of a summons
    C. An accusatory instrument
    D. All of the above

2. May an arrest be made without a warrant?
    A. No, in all circumstances a person can only be arrested with a warrant
    B. No, unless the person consents to the arrest
    C. No, unless there is a warrant or otherwise a desk appearance ticket
    D. Yes

3. Which of the following individuals is MOST likely to be fingerprinted?
    A. Bill, who is arrested for felony sexual assault
    B. Sarah, who is given a desk appearance ticket for drinking in public
    C. Amy, who has been pulled over for running a red light
    D. Tom, who has a suspended license for unpaid parking tickets

4. Must a defendant appear personally for an arraignment?
    A. Yes, in all circumstances
    B. Yes, but in limited circumstances counsel may appear on the defendant's behalf
    C. Yes, unless the court consents to their lack of appearance
    D. No

5. At any time before entry of a plea of guilty to or commencement of a trial of a local criminal court accusatory instrument containing a charge of misdemeanor, a superior court having jurisdiction to prosecute such misdemeanor charge by indictment may order that such charge be prosecuted by _____ and that the district attorney present it to the grand jury for such purpose.
    A. indictment   B. information   C. affidavit   D. warrant

6. A(n) _____ ticket is a written notice issued and subscribed by a police officer directing a designated person to appear in a designated local criminal court at a designated future time in connection with his alleged commission of a designated offense.
    A. appearance   B. information   C. warrant   D. summons

7. Which of the following is MOST likely to occur at an arraignment? The court will
   A. inform the defendant of the charges against him
   B. begin the voir dire process for trial
   C. set a trial date
   D. direct the clerk to take testimony from the complaining victim

8. What is the MAXIMUM number of jurors that can empanel a grand jury?
   A. 8   B. 16   C. 23   D. 32

9. Proceedings of a grand jury are not valid unless at least _____ of its members are present.
   A. twelve   B. fourteen   C. sixteen   D. twenty

10. A written accusation by a grand jury, filed with a superior court, charging a person, or two or more persons jointly, with the commission of a crime, or with the commission of two or more offenses at least one of which is a crime is called a(n)
    A. information   B. charge   C. indictment   D. arraignment

11. Which of the following must be included in an indictment?
    A. Name of the superior court in which it is filed
    B. Title of the action
    C. A list of counts addressing each charged offense
    D. All of the above

12. A defendant may waive an indictment and choose to be prosecuted by superior court information in which circumstance?
    A. The district attorney consents to a waiver.
    B. The defendant is charged with a Class A felony.
    C. The defendant is over the age of 35.
    D. The defendant is not a resident of New York City.

13. Can an indictment be amended?
    A. No
    B. Not unless the defendant consents
    C. Not unless the court of the clerk consents
    D. Yes, in limited circumstances

14. When can an indictment be amended?
    A. An indictment cannot be amended
    B. At any time before or during trial
    C. At any time before arraignment
    D. At any time in the voir dire process

15. Generally, every trial of an indictment must be a _____ trial.
    A. jury   B. bench   C. waivable   D. expedited

16. What takes place immediately after a jury is selected and sworn?   16.____
    A. The people deliver an opening address to the jury.
    B. The court delivers preliminary instructions to the jury.
    C. Then defendant may deliver an opening address to the jury.
    D. Then people offer evidence in support of the indictment.

17. Under what circumstances may a motion for mistrial be made during the   17.____
    trial by the defendant?
    A. When an error in the proceedings occurs which is prejudicial to the
       defendant
    B. When a legal defect in the proceedings occurs which is prejudicial to the
       defendant
    C. Conduct inside or outside the courtroom occurs which is prejudicial to the
       defendant
    D. All of the above

18. At the conclusion of the summations, the court must deliver a _____ to the jury.   18.____
    A. charge   B. summons   C. information   D. deposition

19. Two counts that are inconsistent when guilt of the offense charged in one   19.____
    necessarily negates guilt of the offense charged in the other are deemed
    inconsistent
    A. offenses   B. counts   C. allegations   D. consequences

20. In a trial where both parties deliver an opening address, which party goes   20.____
    first?
    A. The people
    B. The defendant
    C. The order is decided by the court
    D. The order is decided in a preliminary conference prior to the trial

21. If both parties deliver summations, otherwise known as closing arguments,   21.____
    which party goes first?
    A. The order is decided by the court
    B. The defendant
    C. The people
    D. The order is decided in a preliminary conference prior to the trial

22. When cases where a trial is assigned to a judicial hearing officer, what   22.____
    must a judicial officer decide?
    A. Determine all questions of law
    B. Act as the exclusive trier of all issues of fact
    C. Render a verdict
    D. All of the above

23. If at any time during the period of a sentence of probation or of conditional discharge the court has reasonable cause to believe that the defendant has violated a condition of the sentence, it may declare the defendant delinquent and file a written
    A. declaration of delinquency
    B. affidavit of suspension
    C. declaration of insufficiency
    D. affidavit of insufficiency

23.____

24. Where a violation of probation petition and report has been filed and the person has not been taken into custody nor has a warrant been issued, an initial court appearance shall occur within _____ days.
    A. five business
    B. five calendar
    C. ten business
    D. ten calendar

24.____

25. How many jurors can be appointed as alternates?
    A. Up to two
    B. Up to three
    C. Up to four
    D. Up to five

25.____

KEY (CORRECT ANSWERS)

1.	D		11.	D
2.	D		12.	A
3.	A		13.	D
4.	B		14.	B
5.	A		15.	A
6.	A		16.	B
7.	A		17.	D
8.	C		18.	A
9.	C		19.	B
10.	C		20.	A

21.	B
22.	D
23.	A
24.	C
25.	A

TEST 2

DIRECTIONS: Each question or incomplete statement is followed by several suggested answers or completions. Select the one that BEST answers the question or completes the statement. *PRINT THE LETTER OF THE CORRECT ANSWER IN THE SPACE AT THE RIGHT.*

1. Which of the following statements is CORRECT regarding alternate jurors? 1.____
   A. They are chosen prior to the selection of the regular jury.
   B. They are chosen in the same manner as the regular jury.
   C. They are not subject to preemptory challenge.
   D. They must be over the age of 55 or otherwise retired.

2. Before a sentence can be pronounced, for certain offenses, a fingerprint report of the defendant must be presented to ascertain which of the following? Defendant's 2.____
   A. genetic disposition   B. prior arrest record
   C. DNA sampling   D. family history

3. For which of the following offenses is a pre-sentence report required? 3.____
   A. Felonies   B. Violations
   C. Traffic infractions   D. Misdemeanors

4. A pre-sentence investigation and report will contain which of the following information? 4.____
   A. Defendant's employment history
   B. Defendant's social history
   C. Circumstances attending the commission of the crime
   D. All of the above

5. What information is generally included in a victim impact statement? 5.____
   A. Victim's version of the offense
   B. Extent of the victim's injury\
   C. Amount of restitution or reparation sought by the victim
   D. All of the above

6. Which part prepares a pre-sentence memorandum? 6.____
   A. Defendant only   B. Prosecutor only
   C. Judge   D. Defendant and/or prosecutor

7. What is the purpose of a pre-sentence memorandum? 7.____
   A. Offer information the court may deem relevant in sentencing
   B. To offer a prolonged probationary period for the defendant
   C. To offer the court additional evidence and testimony not presented at trial
   D. To offer the court depositions that were conducted prior to trial

8. When the court pronounces a sentence of probation or of conditional discharge, it must specify which of the following?
   A. The conditions to be complied with
   B. The offense that is relevant to the sentence
   C. The age of the defendant
   D. The propensity of the defendant to commit similar crimes

9. A "youthful offender" is between the ages of _____ when the crime was committed.
   A. 15 and 17   B. 16 and 19   C. 16 and 20   D. 15 and 21

10. If a youthful offender has committed a second offense, can he or she still be classified as a youthful offender?
    A. No, they must be classified as an adult if they committed a second offense
    B. No, unless he or she is under the age of 21
    C. No, unless the court grants him continued youthful offender status
    D. Yes, as it does not matter if he or she commits a second offense

11. Which of the following individuals is deemed a "principal" in the matter New York v. Smith, an action involving the murder of a shopkeeper allegedly by Jones Smith?
    A. Jones Smith, the defendant in the action
    B. Barry Alexander, a material witness to the crime
    C. Mary Martin, Jones' live-in girlfriend and character witness in the case
    D. All of the above

12. A court will release a defendant, James, on his own recognizance if James
    A. will appear whenever his attendance is required and will make himself amenable to the court's orders
    B. has posted bail within 48 hours
    C. has been granted unsupervised probation, thereby proving the lesser nature of the crime committed
    D. has secured a favorable pre-sentence report

13. Bail can be either
    A. mortgage or cash bail
    B. promissory note or bail bond
    C. cash bail or bail bond
    D. debenture or mortgage note

14. Which of the following is MOST likely to be security in a "secured bail bond" for $50,000?
    A. A watch
    B. A mortgaged property
    C. A handbag
    D. A leased car

15. An affirmative action taken or directed by an appellate court upon reversing or modifying a judgement, sentence, or order of another court is known as a(n)
    A. administrative judgment
    B. corrective action
    C. rehabilitative means
    D. surety bond

16. In an appeal, a reversal or a modification of judgment, sentence or order must be based upon which determination?
    A. The law
    B. The facts
    C. A matter of discretion in the interest of justice
    D. Any or all of the above

17. What is the effect of a mistrial on the indictment in the second trial? The indictment is deemed
    A. null and void
    B. fact
    C. to contain the same number of counts as in the first trial
    D. affirmative evidence of guilt

18. In the lower courts, defendant Michael James is found guilty of assault in the second degree. New evidence of Mr. James' involvement in the commission of the crime was discovered after the trial and on appeal the appellate court declared Mr. James not guilty. In this instance, the appellate court found that the new evidence would prove Mr. James was incapable is deemed to have _____ the lower court's judgment.
    A. remanded   B. reversed   C. appended   D. reconstituted

19. Potential testimony is information or factual knowledge of a person who
    A. is definitely available as a witness
    B. is a material witness
    C. may be available as a witness
    D. is a witness for the prosecution only

20. In what court must a non-jury trial of an indictment be conducted?
    A. The superior court in which the indictment is pending
    B. The district court in which the indictment is pending
    C. The appellate court in which the indictment is pending
    D. The federal court in which the indictment is pending

21. How many judges preside in a non-jury trial of an indictment?
    A. Three   B. Five   C. One   D. Two

22. Must a motion to set aside a verdict due to the improper conduct by a juror be in writing?
    A. Yes, and reasonable notice must be given to the people
    B. No, as long as reasonable notice is given to the people
    C. No, if the court allows verbal motions
    D. No, if the court allows electronic filing of motions

23. The act of surrendering an alleged criminal by one state or other authority to another authority having jurisdiction to try the charge is called
    A. interrogation   B. interstate movement
    C. extradition   D. recompense

24. A written notice issued by a police officer instructing an individual to appear in a designated local criminal court at a future time in connection with the commission of a designated offense is a(n)
    A. summons
    B. subpoena
    C. appearance ticket
    D. deposition

25. A partially secured bail bond is secured only by a deposit of a sum of money not exceeding _____ percent of the total amount of the undertaking.
    A. five
    B. ten
    C. twenty
    D. forty

KEY (CORRECT ANSWERS)

1.	B	11.	D
2.	B	12.	A
3.	A	13.	C
4.	D	14.	B
5.	D	15.	B
6.	D	16.	D
7.	A	17.	C
8.	A	18.	B
9.	B	19.	C
10.	D	20.	A

21. C
22. A
23. C
24. C
25. B

EXAMINATION SECTION

TEST 1

DIRECTIONS: Each question or incomplete statement is followed by several suggested answers or completions. Select the one that BEST answers the question or completes the statement. *PRINT THE LETTER OF THE CORRECT ANSWER IN THE SPACE AT THE RIGHT.*

1. Which class of felonies are divided into subclasses?
    A. Class A   B. Class B   C. Class C   D. Class D   1.____

2. Can a traffic infraction be classified as a misdemeanor? 2.____
    A. Yes, if the punishment is less than one year of imprisonment
    B. Yes, if the punishment is less than fifteen months of imprisonment
    C. No, unless specified in the judgment
    D. No

3. Bryan smuggles cocaine out of Mexico in his infant daughter's diaper. He and his daughter are caught de-boarding from a plane at John F. Kennedy Airport. 3.____
    At arraignment, Bryan will MOST likely be charged with a
    A. misdemeanor   B. traffic infraction
    C. traffic violation   D. drug trafficking felony

4. A "juvenile offender" is defined as a person _____ years old who is criminally responsible for an act constituting murder in the second degree or such conduct as a sexually motivated felony. 4.____
    A. twelve   B. thirteen   C. fourteen   D. fifteen

5. The New York Penal Law defines "child day care provider" by the definition used in what other law? 5.____
    A. Child Welfare Act   B. Social Services Law
    C. Family Court Act   D. Surrogates Court Clerk Law

6. Pursuant to the New York Penal Law, a felony without specification of the classification is deemed a Class _____ felony. 6.____
    A. A   B. B   C. D   D. E

7. The MAXIMUM penalty for a Class B felony is _____ thousand dollars. 7.____
    A. ten   B. twenty   C. thirty   D. fifty

8. Tony was convicted of stealing a car, which carries a felony designation. Tony maintains that he simply wanted to go for a joyride, but the victim alleges that $4,000 was in the car when it was stolen. The car was eventually returned to the victim; however, the cash was never recovered. 8.____
    Can the court legally demand that Tony replay the cash that was never recovered?

A. Yes, because that is the amount gained from the commission of the crime
B. No, because one cannot prove he stole the cash
C. No, because Tony simply wanted a joyride
D. No, because the cash was not insured by the vehicle's owner

9. A sentence to pay a fine for a Class A misdemeanor shall not exceed _____ dollars or an amount equivalent to double the value of the property unlawfully disposed of in the commission of the crime.
   A. five hundred
   B. eight hundred
   C. one thousand
   D. two thousand

10. Marcel posted an advertisement on social media selling a new guitar. A buyer forwarded Marcel $500 and Marcel never delivered the product as he never had a guitar to sell. Marcel was later convicted of the misdemeanor of false advertising. The court imposes an alternative sentence for the crime.
    What is the MOST likely fine Marcel will need to pay?
    A. $250, half the amount he received from the crime
    B. $750, a 50% increase in the amount of money he received from the crime
    C. $1,000, double the amount of money he received from the crime
    D. Marcel will not have to pay any money as he was convicted of a misdemeanor

11. Which of the following are classified as Class A misdemeanors?
    A. Escape in the third degree
    B. Perjury in the third degree
    C. Identify theft in the third degree
    D. All of the above

12. Which of the following is a Class B misdemeanor?
    A. Reckless endangerment of property
    B. Coercion in the second degree
    C. Making graffiti
    D. Arson in the fifth degree

13. Tim is convicted of two misdemeanors, one which is classified as Class A and the other is classified as Class B. For the Class A misdemeanor, the court imposes a term of eight months imprisonment.
    Can the court impose a fine of $500 for the Class B misdemeanor?
    A. Yes, the court can impose a fine in addition to the term of imprisonment
    B. No, the court cannot impose a fine in excess of $250 as this is deemed excessive punishment and not available for appeal
    C. No, the court cannot impose a fine in excess of $400 as this is deemed excessive punishment and not available for appeal
    D. No, the court cannot impose a fine in addition to the term of imprisonment if the offenses were committed through a single act and one offense is a material element of the other

14. If ABC Corporation is convicted of a felony, what is the maximum amount the company will have to pay? 14.____
    A. Five thousand dollars
    B. Ten thousand dollars
    C. Fifteen thousand dollars
    D. An amount not to exceed double the amount of shareholders the company has on record as of the date of the commission of the crime

15. Soliciting or providing support for an act of terrorism in the second degree is classified as a 15.____
    A. misdemeanor
    B. violation
    C. Class D felony
    D. felony of an unspecified degree

16. Richie is convicted of making a terrorist threat. What is this offense classified as? 16.____
    A. Class D felony
    B. Unclassified felony
    C. Unclassified misdemeanor
    D. Civil offense

17. A firearm that is actually shared, made available, sold, exchanged, given or disposed of among or between two or more persons, at least one of whom is not authorized pursuant to law possess such firearm is defined as a 17.____
    A. roundabout gun
    B. community gun
    C. shared gunner
    D. civil weapon

18. Judge O'Neill is currently presiding over a murder trial, where the defendant ran over a young child with his car. The defense alleges the crime was an accident and that the defendant should be found guilty, if at all, of a lesser offense. The prosecution argues that the defendant intended to kill the victim. In chambers, Judge O'Neill explains to his law clerk that in order to find the defendant guilty of the more serious crime charged, he must have the culpable mental state during the commission of the crime. 18.____
    A culpable mental state means
    A. intentionally, knowingly or recklessly or with criminal negligence
    B. knowingly but not intentionally
    C. negligent intent but not knowingly or recklessly
    D. none of the above

19. Derek wants to kill Al who works at the local gym. Al's twin brother exits the gym at 11:45 P.M. and Derek shoots him. Derek alleges that because he meant to kill Al and not Al's twin brother, he should not be found guilty of murder. 19.____
    What is the likely verdict?
    A. Not guilty, because of a mistake of fact
    B. Not guilty, because Derek has confessed to his crimes
    C. Guilty, because of a mistake of fact
    D. Guilty, because the crime of murder still occurred

20. Any article or thing which a person confined in a detention facility is prohibited from obtaining or possessing by statute, rule, regulation or order is known as
   A. illicit materials
   B. contraband
   C. magazines
   D. weaponry

21. Which of the following offenses relating to custody is classified as a misdemeanor?
   A. Escape in the third degree
   B. Absconding from temporary release in the second degree
   C. Resisting arrest
   D. All of the above

Questions 22-25.

DIRECTIONS: Questions 22 through 25 are to be answered on the basis of the following fact pattern.

Ralph was kidnapped at gunpoint outside of Syracuse. He was taken to an abandoned warehouse by his captors and kept for nearly three days without food or water. Ralph never saw the gun or any other weapons while he was in captivity, but was told he would be killed if he did not go to the bank and empty his bank accounts. After his captors dropped him off at a local bank, Ralph went inside and closed all of his accounts and left the cash outside of the bank in an envelope and ran. Later, Ralph was able to identify all of his captors and at trial alleged that he emptied his bank accounts in duress.

22. Under these circumstances, can Ralph allege that he was under duress?
   A. Yes, he can assert duress as an affirmative defense
   B. No, because Ralph never saw a weapon after the initial kidnapping
   C. No, because Ralph emptied his account on his own free will
   D. No, because Ralph does not know for sure if the captors ever received the cash

23. When is duress NOT available as a defense?
   A. When a person intentionally or recklessly places himself in a situation in which it is probable that he will be subjected to duress
   B. Duress is always available as a defense
   C. Duress is a rarely used defense and is not available for adults who are capable of acting of their own free will
   D. Duress is not available as a defense if the defense of intentional negligence is also used

24. If Ralph's captors are convicted of a Class B violent felony, what is the MOST likely outcome of the sentencing in terms of imprisonment?
   A. 1-3 years   B. 5-10 years   C. 5-25 years   D. 25 years to life

25. Which of the following is MOST likely to be considered in the sentencing of Ralph's captors?
    A. Familial relationship to Ralph, if any
    B. The location Ralph was abducted and how far that location is from Ralph's primary residence or domiciliary
    C. Prior criminal history of each offender
    D. Ralph's age

25.____

KEY (CORRECT ANSWERS)

1.	A	11.	D
2.	D	12.	A
3.	D	13.	D
4.	B	14.	B
5.	B	15.	C
6.	D	16.	A
7.	C	17.	B
8.	A	18.	A
9.	C	19.	D
10.	C	20.	B

21.	D
22.	A
23.	A
24.	C
25.	C

TEST 2

DIRECTIONS: Each question or incomplete statement is followed by several suggested answers or completions. Select the one that BEST answers the question or completes the statement. *PRINT THE LETTER OF THE CORRECT ANSWER IN THE SPACE AT THE RIGHT.*

1. Prosecutors must prove that Abe and Luke's conspiracy derived from an intentional scheme to defraud investors.
 Which of the following is the MOST appropriate definition of scheme?
 A. A plan between two people to do an agreed upon activity
 B. Any plan, pattern device, contrivance, or course of action intended to deceive others
 C. A plan between three or more people to do something one of them is intent on finishing
 D. A topic of conversation shared between two or more people

 1.____

2. Corrupting the government in the fourth degree is classified as a Class ____ felony and requires that the individual committing the crime either be, or act in concert with a ____.
 A. E; public servant
 B. D; person of interest
 C. E; person of interest
 D. D; public servant

 2.____

3. A person commits the crime of ____ when being a public servant he or she commits a specified offense through the use of his or her public office.
 A. private coercion
 B. public corruption
 C. sentencing
 D. acting in dangerous concert

 3.____

4. Arson in the first degree and aggravated enterprise corruption are examples of
 A. A-1 felonies
 B. Class C felonies
 C. misdemeanors
 D. traffic violations

 4.____

5. If a felon sentence does not carry a term of imprisonment, which of the following will MOST likely be required of the defendant in lieu of jail?
 A. Parole
 B. Probation
 C. Active custody
 D. Recognizance

 5.____

6. Which of the following is a violation?
 A. Loitering
 B. Criminal solicitation in the second degree
 C. Welfare fraud in the third degree
 D. Bribing a labor official

 6.____

7. Maurice is found guilty of intentionally, and for no legitimate purpose, engaging in a course of conduct directed at his former co-worker, Michelle, that he knows is likely to cause reasonable fear of material harm. Maurice is convicted of which crime?
 A. Battery   B. Negligence   C. Stalking   D. Trespass

 7.____

8. Which of the following carries the LOWEST sanction and is not defined as a crime?
   A. Felony
   B. Misdemeanor
   C. Class A felony
   D. Violation

9. Which felony class is the MOST serious?
   A. Class B
   B. Class A
   C. Class E
   D. Class D

10. An "act" is considered the opposite of a(n) _____. As an example, during an interrogation into the disappearance of Andrew's cousin, Andrew fails to mention that he was the last person to see his cousin alive.
    A. response
    B. omission
    C. redaction
    D. impactful

11. A person acts _____ when his conscious objective is to cause such result or to engage in such conduct, whereas a person acts _____ when he is aware that his conduct is of such nature or that such circumstance exists.
    A. knowingly; recklessly
    B. knowingly; negligently
    C. knowingly; criminally
    D. intentionally; knowingly

12. Kristin was driving under the influence of alcohol when she crashed her brand new car into the front yard of Joe's house, killing his outdoor cat and knocking over his mailbox. Kristin argues that she is not liable for her actions because she was intoxicated at the time of the accident. Joe argues that Kristin intentionally crashed into his house.
    What is the effect of intoxication or liability?
    Evidence of intoxication
    A. may be offered whenever it is relevant to negate an element of the crime charged
    B. is always relevant in disputes involving a vehicle
    C. is only relevant if raised in the initial complaint or otherwise raised prior to opening arguments at trial
    D. never has any material effect on the defendant's liability

13. Any contest, game, gaming scheme or gaming device in which the outcome depends in a material degree upon an element of change is known as
    A. gambling
    B. illicit arson
    C. restriction to chance
    D. contest of chance

14. If the court imposes a fine for a felony, the court must also make a finding as to the _____ the crime.
    A. amount of the defendant's gain from
    B. defendant's age at the time of
    C. defendant's height at the time of
    D. financial liabilities of the defendant at the time of

15. Jeremy is convicted of a felony and required to pay $15,000 in fines, or double the amount of money he gained in the commission of his crime. The state comptroller is responsible for collecting moneys in excess of _____ received or collected in payment of a fine and depositing the same into the rehabilitative alcohol and substance treatment fund established by the state finance law.
    In other words, the total sum of _____ will be deposited into the treatment fund.
    A. $5,000; $10,000
    B. $2,000; $13,000
    C. $14,000; $1,000
    D. $1,000; $14,000

16. Which of the following is MOST likely a condition of probation?
    A. Answer all reasonable inquiries by the probation officer
    B. Notify the probation officer prior to any change in address
    C. Notify the probation officer prior to any change in employment
    D. All of the above

17. When can a sentence requiring the defendant to submit to the use of an electronic monitoring device be imposed?
    A. Only where the court determines that such condition will advance public safety, probationer control or probationer surveillance
    B. Whenever the court pleases and for every type of offense involving a minor
    C. Electronic monitoring devices were deemed unlawful in the State of New York in 2005
    D. Only where the court determines that the defendant's family or alleged victim is in imminent danger

18. A condition of probation for a convicted sex offender, when the victim of the crime was under the age of eighteen, will always include a prohibition against which of the following?
    Knowingly entering into
    A. or upon school grounds
    B. a movie theater
    C. or upon a library
    D. or upon a grocery store or other marketplace

19. Amara's trial begins on April 1, 2017 and lasts for three months. Amara is found guilty of the crime charged on June 1, 2017 but is not sentenced until September 15th. Amara is sentenced to probation on September 15, 2017 for a period of twelve months.
    When does Amara's probation end?
    A. April 1, 2018
    B. June 1, 2018
    C. September 15, 2018
    D. August 1, 2018

20. A revocable sentence of imprisonment to be served on days or during certain periods of days, or both, specified by the court as part of the sentence is deemed a(n)
    A. conditional release
    B. unconditional sentence
    C. intermittent imprisonment
    D. restless release

21. A conviction of a violation shall be punishable by a fine not to exceed 21._____
   A. $250   B. $500   C. $1,000   D. $5,000

Questions 22-25.

DIRECTIONS: Questions 22 through 25 are to be answered on the basis of the following fact pattern.

Tom and Hank are hanging out after school when Tom dares Hank to steal graffiti on the side of an apartment building. Tom and Hank are both eighteen and graduating from high school in the spring. Tom and Hank are both apprehended during the commission of the crime.

22. A person is guilty of _____ when, with intent that another person engage in conduct constituting a crime, he solicits, requests, commands, importunes, or otherwise attempts to cause such other person to engage in such conduct. 22._____
    This crime is a violation of
    A. criminal solicitation in the fifth degree
    B. criminal trespass
    C. criminal restitution in the first degree
    D. burglary with an accessory

23. Hank alleges that he did not know that making graffiti is a crime, because he sees graffiti in New York City all the time. 23._____
    Has Hank proffered an affirmative defense to the crime of making graffiti?
    A. Yes, he can commit a crime if he did not know what he was doing was criminal
    B. Yes, because he offered his defense prior to the start of the trial and in all honesty
    C. No, because he was caught in the commission of the crime with another person
    D. No, because now knowing he was committing a crime does not absolve him of liability

24. Tom insists that he also did know that making graffiti is a crime. Tom is also being charged with possession of graffiti instruments. Making graffiti is a Class _____ misdemeanor whereas possession of graffiti instruments is a Class _____ misdemeanor. 24._____
    A. B; C   B. C; D   C. A; B   D. E; D

25. Given that the crimes Tom is being charged with are misdemeanors, what is the MAXIMUM term of imprisonment Tom is facing (in months)? 25._____
    A. Six   B. Twelve   C. Eighteen   D. Twenty-four

KEY (CORRECT ANSWERS)

1.	B	11.	D
2.	A	12.	A
3.	B	13.	D
4.	A	14.	A
5.	B	15.	A
6.	A	16.	D
7.	C	17.	A
8.	D	18.	A
9.	B	19.	D
10.	B	20.	C

21.	C
22.	A
23.	D
24.	C
25.	B

EXAMINATION SECTION
TEST 1

DIRECTIONS: Each question or incomplete statement is followed by several suggested answers or completions. Select the one that BEST answers the question or completes the statement. *PRINT THE LETTER OF THE CORRECT ANSWER IN THE SPACE AT THE RIGHT.*

Questions 1-3.

DIRECTIONS: Questions 1 through 3 are to be answered on the basis of the following fact pattern.

Dave asks his son, Junior, to drop off a package to their neighbor. Dave knows there are drugs in the package. Dave's neighbor, Tom, is expecting the package. However, Junior is intercepted by a police officer who happened to be driving by at the time of the delivery.

1. When charged, what will Dave MOST likely be accused of committing? 1.____
   A. Drug trafficking violation   B. Drug offense
   C. Drug trafficking felony   D. Misdemeanor

2. Which of the following scenarios also falls under the same category as described above? 2.____
   A. Criminal sale of a controlled substance in or near schools
   B. Sexual assault of a minor
   C. Burglary of a senior citizen or assisted living facility
   D. Burglary of a school

3. At trial, Dave argues that he did not possess any drugs at the time of his arrest. Which of the following is the BEST argument that Dave was in possession of the drugs? 3.____
   A. Possession requires only physical custody.
   B. Possession can be physical custody, dominion or control which he had until the time of delivery
   C. Possession is not necessary to charge Dave with a crime.
   D. Possession is a requirement to prove all crimes.

4. If John is sentenced to a term of imprisonment of more than six months, he has been convicted of a 4.____
   A. misdemeanor   B. violation
   C. serious offense   D. felony

Questions 5-7.

DIRECTIONS: Questions 5 through 7 are to be answered on the basis of the following fact pattern.

Amy ran a stop sign in her suburban neighborhood as she was driving to visit her boyfriend in Manhattan. While driving in Manhattan, Amy also runs a red light. In running the red light, she hit a bicyclist. The bicyclist did not want to file a report, although he suffered minor injuries. Amy drove away and a week later received a ticket in the mail for running the red light.

5. Amy's running of a red light is a
   A. violation
   B. traffic infraction
   C. misdemeanor
   D. not a crime

6. What is the BEST argument that Amy's collision with the bicyclist is a crime?
   A. No crime was committed because the accident was not fatal.
   B. No crime was committed because the bicyclist was uninsured.
   C. A crime is a misdemeanor or a felony; Amy may have committed a misdemeanor.
   D. A crime is a misdemeanor or a felony; Amy most likely committed a felony.

7. Amy's running of the stop sign in her own neighborhood is
   A. not a crime because she was in her own neighborhood
   B. not a crime because no one reported her and she did not report herself
   C. a traffic infraction
   D. a more serious violation, which is punishable by a term of imprisonment

8. Which of the following is classified as a "deadly weapon"?
   A. Metal knuckles
   B. Switchblade knife
   C. Plastic knuckles
   D. All of the above

9. Physical force which, under the circumstances in which it is used, is readily capable of causing death or other serious physical injury is deemed
   A. deadly physical force
   B. force that is sustainable
   C. serious force
   D. tangle force

10. Anthony, Carl, and Dave are called for jury duty at the federal courthouse. Anthony is impaneled to serve on a grand jury. Carl and Dave are still waiting to be called. Who is considered a juror?
    A. Anthony, Carl, and Dave
    B. Anthony only
    C. Carl and Dave only
    D. None of them are jurors

11. If Jackie is charged as a juvenile offender, what is the MAXIMUM age Jackie can be?
    A. Fifteen   B. Fourteen   C. Thirteen   D. Twelve

12. Which designation includes a "Class D" category? 12.____
    A. Felony
    B. Misdemeanor
    C. Violation
    D. Offense

13. Forcible touching is classified as a 13.____
    A. misdemeanor
    B. Class A felony
    B. Class B felony
    D. Class C felony

Questions 14-17.

DIRECTIONS: Questions 1 through 17 are to be answered on the basis of the following fact pattern.

Bill, nineteen, is on trial for conspiracy to commit murder. During Bill's trial, his best friend Alex testifies for the defense. Under oath, Alex states that Bill was with him the night of the murder and the two of them never left Alex's house. In fact, Alex and Bill had not seen one another for months before the murder. After the trial ended, but before deliberations concluded, Alex garnered the name of the jury foreperson and attempted to pay him in exchange for swinging the jury in Bill's favor.

14. Bill is being charged with a 14.____
    A. felony, because the intent was to commit a felonious crime
    B. felony, because all conspiracy charges are felonies
    C. misdemeanor, because all conspiracy charges are misdemeanors
    D. misdemeanor, because the murder did not take place

15. Where can Bill be tried for conspiracy? 15.____
    A. The county where the conspiracy was entered into
    B. The county where an overt act in furtherance of the conspiracy was committed

16. At the conclusion of the trial, Alex will be charged with _____, which in the first degree is a _____. 16.____
    A. perjury; Class D felony
    B. perjury; Class A felony
    C. negligence; Class C felony
    D. tortious act; Class C felony

17. Alex's attempted involvement with a juror is deemed 17.____
    A. tampering with a juror
    B. influencing a juror
    C. improper juror gifting
    D. forcible tampering

18. May a fine be imposed as a sentence for a felony conviction? 18.____
    A. No, only imprisonment can be a sentence for a felony
    B. No, unless the convicted felon consents to the alternate sentence
    C. Yes, and it may not exceed $50,000
    D. Yes

19. Suppose Damien is convicted of armed robbery and assault, stemming from a single act, both of which are felonies. After conviction, assume the judge imposes a sentence of $5,000 for the armed robbery conviction. What will be the sentence for the assault?
    A. An additional fine
    B. There will be no sentence for the assault conviction
    C. There will be a reduced sentence for the assault conviction
    D. A fine cannot be imposed for the assault conviction

20. If a person has gained money or property through the commission of any misdemeanor or violation, the court may sentence the defendant to pay an amount not exceeding _____ the amount of the defendant's gain from the commission of the offense.
    A. double   B. triple   C. half   D. four times

21. Assume the same facts as Question 20. The imposition of this sentence, as opposed to the sentence prescribed by the penal code is known as a(n)
    A. sustainable charge
    B. alternate sentence
    C. alternative imposition
    D. resistant change

22. Fines for corporations will generally not exceed _____ for a misdemeanor.
    A. $100,000   B. $50,000   C. $5,000   D. $1,000

23. The fine for a Class B misdemeanor shall not exceed
    A. $1,000   B. $750   C. $500   D. $250

24. Menacing in the second degree and hazing in the first degree are both considered
    A. serious violations
    B. misdemeanors
    C. felonies
    D. minor violations

25. Promoting a suicide attempt and stalking in the first degree are both considered
    A. minor violations
    B. minor felonies
    C. major felonies
    D. felonies

KEY (CORRECT ANSWERS)

1. C
2. A
3. B
4. D
5. B

6. C
7. C
8. D
9. A
10. A

11. C
12. A
13. A
14. A
15. A

16. A
17. A
18. D
19. D
20. A

21. B
22. C
23. C
24. B
25. D

TEST 2

DIRECTIONS: Each question or incomplete statement is followed by several suggested answers or completions. Select the one that BEST answers the question or completes the statement. *PRINT THE LETTER OF THE CORRECT ANSWER IN THE SPACE AT THE RIGHT.*

Questions 1-3.

DIRECTIONS: Questions 1 through 3 are to be answered on the basis of the following fact pattern.

Olivia and Amy, both nineteen, have conspired to assault one of their classmates. They enlist the help of Amy's sister, Jane, to help them carry out the assault. Amy does not tell Jane what her and Olivia are attempting to do, but instead instructs Jane to pretend that she is lost and lure the classmate to the parking lot where Olivia and Amy will be waiting.

1. The scenario described involves the implication of which two crimes? 1.____
   A. Solicitation and conspiracy
   B. Perjury and conspiracy
   C. Negligence and conspiracy
   D. Conspiracy only

2. Assuming that assault is a felony, which is Amy MOST likely to be guilty of? 2.____
   A. A misdemeanor
   B. A serious violation
   C. A felony
   D. An infraction

3. At trial, Amy and Olivia claim that they are not guilty of any crime because they did not know conspiracy was a crime. Is this a defense? 3.____
   A. No
   B. Not unless they can prove they did not know the law
   C. Yes, ignorance is always a defense
   D. Yes

4. Matt stole a garden gnome, worth $700, from his stepdad's neighbor's lawn. He is charged with a misdemeanor. The court can charge Matt with which of the following? 4.____
   A. $5,500
   B. $1,000
   C. $1,400, equal to double the amount of the stolen good
   D. Any of the above

5. The MAXIMUM fine for a Class B misdemeanor is 5.____
   A. $100   B. $150   C. $200   D. $500

6. Criminally negligent homicide is classified as a 6.____
   A. Class E felony
   B. Class B felony
   C. Class A felony
   D. misdemeanor

7. A person is guilty of issuing abortion articles when he manufactures, sells, or delivers any instrument, article, medicine, drug or substance with intent that the same be used in unlawfully procuring the miscarriage of a female, which is a
   A. Class A misdemeanor
   B. Class B misdemeanor
   C. Class A felony
   D. Class B felony

7.____

8. Issuing a bad check and false personation are both deemed Class _____ misdemeanors.
   A. A
   B. B
   C. C
   D. D

8.____

9. James writes a check for $75 at the grocery store, knowing that he does not have the funds in his account to cover the check. He realizes he has his credit card in his wallet and decides, instead, to pay with his credit card. What crime has James committed?
   A. Issuing a bad check
   B. Conspiracy to defraud
   C. Attempting to issue a bad check
   D. No crime was committed

9.____

10. Criminal sale of a police uniform is
    A. not a crime
    B. a minor violation
    C. a felony in New York City only
    D. a misdemeanor

10.____

11. Susan and James's father suddenly passed away. As Susan was cleaning out their father's home, she discovered his last will which left all of his possessions to James only. Susan does not tell anyone that she discovered her father's will and takes it home with an intent to destroy it. What crime is Susan guilty of?
    A. Unlawfully concealing a will
    B. Tampering with evidence
    C. Conspiracy to impersonate
    D. Fraud

11.____

12. Assume the same facts as in Question 11. Susan's crime is deemed a
    A. Class A misdemeanor
    B. Class C misdemeanor
    C. Class E felony
    D. Unclassified misdemeanor

12.____

13. Which one of the following individuals qualifies as a corporate official for the purposes of the crime of misconduct by a corporate official?
    A. Director of a stock corporation
    B. Receptionist of a stock corporation
    C. Consultant at a private company
    D. Part-time employee of a bank

13.____

14. A person is guilty of _____ when, not being authorized or permitted by law to do so, he knowingly charges, takes, or receives any money or other property as interest on the loan or forbearance of any money or other property, at a rate exceeding twenty-five per centum per annum or the equivalent rate for a longer or shorter period.
    A. Criminal trespass
    B. Criminal usury in the second degree
    C. Criminal negligence
    D. Civil tort

14.____

15. Unlawful collection practices are always classified as
    A. violations
    B. infractions
    C. misdemeanors
    D. felonies

    15.____

16. Making a false statement of credit terms violates which law?
    A. Truth in Lending Act
    B. Dodd Frank
    C. Bank Secrecy Act
    D. Humanitarian Relief Act

    16.____

17. Identity theft can be charged as a misdemeanor or a felony. A person who obtains goods, money, property, or services or uses credit in the name of such other person in an aggregate amount that exceeds five hundred dollars has committed a
    A. petty misdemeanor
    B. misdemeanor
    C. minor felony
    D. felony

    17.____

18. A person is guilty of _____ when he or she knowingly and with intent to defraud assumes the identity of another person by presenting himself as that other person, or by acting as that other person or by using personal identifying information of that other person, and knows that such person is a member of the armed forces.
    A. Armed theft
    B. Minor identify theft
    C. Aggravated identity theft
    D. Unlawful impersonation

    18.____

19. Dave, seventeen, used a stolen drivers license to buy alcohol. The store owner called the police, suspecting that Dave was underage, and Dave was charged with identity theft. What is Dave's BEST defense?
    A. Dave was under 21 and only used the ID to purchase alcohol
    B. Dave found the ID on the ground and thought it was abandoned
    C. Dave was under 18 at the time of the offense
    D. There is no affirmative defense for the alleged crime

    19.____

20. Daniel has filed for bankruptcy. After the commencement of the bankruptcy petitions, Daniel is prohibited from moving or concealing any assets that may be available to his creditors. Daniel decides to withdraw $5,000 out of his checking account and hide the money in his home so that creditors cannot get to it. What crime has Daniel committed?
    A. Banking fraud
    B. Truth in Lending violation
    C. Fraud in Insolvency
    D. Negligent fraud

    20.____

21. Assume the same facts as in Question 20. What is the category of crime Daniel has committed?
    A. Class A felony
    B. Class B felony
    C. Class A misdemeanor
    D. Violation

    21.____

22. A person is guilty of _____ when he renders criminal assistance to a person who has committed a Class B or Class C felony.
    A. hindering prosecution in the second degree
    B. tampering with evidence
    C. harboring a fugitive
    D. criminal solicitation

23. A person is guilty of _____ when he intentionally prevents or attempts to prevent a police office or peace officer from effecting an authorized arrest of himself or another person.
    A. fraud
    B. negligence
    C. resisting arrest
    D. trespass

24. After Dalia is arrested, she escapes from the cop car. She is guilty of _____, which is a _____.
    A. escape; misdemeanor
    B. escape; violation
    C. escape; infraction
    D. absconding; misdemeanor

25. Marlene performs a marriage ceremony for Bob and Danielle. Marlene charges a fee of $125 for the ceremony and performs the ceremony in front of the courthouse. Marlene is not authorized by the state to perform marriage ceremonies. Marlene has committed what crime?
    A. Unlawfully solemnizing a marriage
    B. Fraud of a civil union
    C. Identity theft
    D. Unlawful impersonation

KEY (CORRECT ANSWERS)

1. A
2. C
3. A
4. D
5. D

6. A
7. B
8. B
9. D
10. D

11. A
12. C
13. A
14. B
15. C

16. A
17. D
18. C
19. A
20. C

21. C
22. A
23. C
24. A
25. A

EXAMINATION SECTION
TEST 1

DIRECTIONS: Each question or incomplete statement is followed by several suggested answers or completions. Select the one that BEST answers the question or completes the statement. *PRINT THE LETTER OF THE CORRECT ANSWER IN THE SPACE AT THE RIGHT.*

1. As a superior officer, you have the responsibility of deciding whether some of your duties should be delegated to subordinate officers.
   The delegation of certain duties to subordinates is GENERALLY considered

    A. *inadvisable;* subordinates should not share your responsibilities
    B. *advisable;* this will help to prevent you from getting bogged down with minor details and problems
    C. *inadvisable;* you can probably do all parts of your job better than anyone else can
    D. *advisable;* more time can therefore be devoted to day-to-day operations and less to long-range planning

    1._____

2. Assume that you are a superior officer and that one of your subordinates is careless in the performance of his job.
   Of the following, it would be MOST important for you, when helping this employee, to realize that

    A. punitive methods produce better long-term results than non-punitive methods
    B. most problem officers require strict supervision rather than counseling and training
    C. the superior can often play a large part in changing employee patterns of work
    D. if orders are given in detail, carelessness will be eliminated

    2._____

3. One of the key qualities of a good superior officer is his ability to balance his work load against the time available to him to complete the job.
   Of the following, the BEST procedure for a superior to follow in establishing his work priorities is to

    A. organize tasks according to urgency without regard to importance
    B. undertake all important, difficult tasks in any order and delegate the routine work to subordinates
    C. assign all work to various subordinates and guide their handling of the problems
    D. delegate those problems that can be solved by others and personally handle the difficult, most pressing issues first

    3._____

4. It is generally CORRECT to state that the planning process within an organization

    A. is a management responsibility and should not involve the participation of operating personnel
    B. should include long-range programs and goals, and should not include activities which can be carried out within a few weeks or months
    C. is to be used in order to develop and improve practices and procedures but is not to be used in applying these procedures in actual operations
    D. should be used at all supervisory levels since each superior officer must determine how to accomplish tasks and what resources are needed

    4._____

5. Assume you are a superior officer and one of your subordinates, who has a low performance rating, has made a good suggestion that will make his job easier.
The BEST course of action for you to take in this situation is to

   A. disregard his suggestion, since he is only trying to do as little work as possible
   B. use his suggestion, since it is a positive suggestion and could motivate him to do better work
   C. use his suggestion, but transfer him to a position where he will not benefit from it
   D. disregard his suggestion, and have a talk with him about his poor performance

6. The use of different criteria to rate employees in different jobs is GENERALLY considered

   A. *desirable,* chiefly because people should be treated as individuals with varying strengths and weaknesses
   B. *undesirable,* chiefly because the use of different criteria results in unfair evaluations
   C. *desirable,* chiefly because people in different jobs cannot always be rated on the basis of the same criteria
   D. *undesirable,* chiefly because ratings that are standardized cannot be compared

7. In preparing an annual division budget for equipment and supplies, the one of the following methods that is MOST appropriate to use is to

   A. combine the previous year's division budget with the estimate of any additional or reduced needs for the coming year
   B. determine what amount the department will approve and use that figure
   C. overestimate division needs by 10% because the department will automatically reduce the figure that is first submitted
   D. underestimate division needs because a reduction in the budget indicates increased efficiency

8. All of the following are objectives of in-service training EXCEPT

   A. discovering and developing skills
   B. providing better service to the public
   C. raising the status of the service
   D. eliminating the need for performance evaluations

9. From a management point of view, the one of the following that is the MOST important advantage of regular personnel performance appraisals is that they

   A. help an officer to prepare for promotion examinations
   B. pinpoint an officer's personality weaknesses
   C. provide an opportunity for regular discussions, including counseling, between an officer and his superior
   D. provide the setting to explain the reasons for disciplinary actions which an officer might not understand

10. Assume that an officer arrests a man for assaulting a woman in the building he is guarding. Later, while the suspect is being searched, the officer finds a switchblade knife, four bags of heroin, and three hypodermic syringes in his clothing.
    In these circumstances, the possession of which of the following items might indicate a violation of some law?

    A. Only the heroin
    B. The heroin, the hypodermic syringes, but not the switchblade knife
    C. The switchblade knife, the heroin, but not the hypocermic syringes
    D. The switchblade knife, the heroin, and the hypodermic syringes

11. Upon arriving at the scene of a serious crime, a superior officer SHOULD instruct his subordinates to

    A. protect the crime scene
    B. collect, mark, and evaluate evidence
    C. brief the news media on the status of the crime
    D. prevent medical personnel from entering the crime scene

12. In standard police terminology, the term *fugitive warrant* refers to

    A. any type of warrant that is not a local warrant
    B. a written request for the detention of a suspect
    C. a warrant for a person who leaves his local jurisdiction and commits an offense in another jurisdiction
    D. a type of booking made when a person wanted by an out-of-state jurisdiction is arrested by local officers

13. The one of the following actions with respect to an offender that an officer should NOT take when an infraction has been committed is to

    A. inform the offender of his rights
    B. punish the offender
    C. warn the offender of possible consequences
    D. apprehend the offender using appropriate force

14. Perimeter barriers, intrusion devices, protective lighting, and a personnel identification system are used for good physical security of a building.
    An objective of personnel identification and control is to

    A. exempt authorized personnel from compliance with annoying entry and departure procedures
    B. detect unauthorized persons who attempt to gain entry
    C. eliminate the need for expensive perimeter barriers and intrusion alarms
    D. allow an increased number of gates and perimeter entrances to be operated at the same time during peak activity hours

15. A true copy of the testimony taken in a criminal action is known as a(n)

    A. verdict   B. transcript
    C. judgment   D. indictment

16. The process of gathering information during an investigation usually involves interviewing or interrogating witnesses.
Interviews or interrogations are *primarily* used for all of the following purposes EXCEPT to

   A. establish the facts of a possible crime to provide the investigator with leads
   B. verify information already known to the police
   C. secure evidence that may establish the guilt or complicity of a suspect
   D. prevent the person questioned from giving an account of the incident under investigation to newspapers

17. Of the following, the BEST reason to apprehend a narcotics violator out of view of the public is to

   A. prevent the drug user from becoming violent
   B. allow the suspect to *save face* with his friends
   C. prevent the knowledge of his apprehension from reaching any collaborators
   D. keep the suspect from disposing of evidence

18. Assume that you, a superior officer, are planning the physical security operation at a facility. One of the problems you are faced with is that of casual thievery by staff.
Of the following, the BEST means of discouraging such thievery is by establishing

   A. an aggressive security education program
   B. adequate inventory control measures
   C. spot search procedures
   D. an effective key control system

19. Under an officer's scope of authority, all of the following actions would be proper EXCEPT

   A. apprehending persons attempting to gain unauthorized access to any work location
   B. enforcing the traffic control rules applicable to the work location
   C. removing persons suspected of theft with a warning to them not to return
   D. responding to protective alarm signals and other warning devices

20. One of the ways of deploying an officer force at the scene of a demonstration is called *strength in reserve*. This procedure involves having only a few officers police the demonstration while most are being held in reserve. Which one of the following is a DISADVANTAGE of this type of deployment?
It

   A. permits the demonstrators to estimate the number of officers available
   B. might result in a delay between a violent outbreak and the arrival of enough officers to handle the situation
   C. prevents the superior officer from deploying his forces
   D. does not permit rotation of the officers confronting the demonstrators

21. Of the following, the MOST important principle to keep in mind when making arrests is that

    A. the absence of force will discourage resistance on the part of the offender
    B. the arresting officer should assume, for his own safety, that the person to be arrested is dangerous
    C. once the offender is arrested he should be kept at the scene of the arrest and questioned
    D. in order to prevent violence, it is better to have too few officers making arrests than too many

22. Of the following steps, the one that an officer should take FIRST upon discovering a broken electrical power line while on duty is to

    A. notify his supervisor
    B. notify the electrical company
    C. determine whether it is a live wire
    D. take measures to protect and barricade the area

23. Assume you are a superior officer interrogating a suspect. The FIRST question you ask him should usually pertain to

    A. his name and address
    B. a package which he may be carrying
    C. where he has been
    D. where he is going

24. Which one of the following statements concerning the interrogation of a juvenile is INCORRECT?

    A. The juvenile should be advised of his rights.
    B. The juvenile should be told as little as possible about the case.
    C. A bond of mutual interest should be established with the juvenile.
    D. The juvenile should be encouraged to ask the interrogator questions.

25. Assume that an intoxicated man has wandered into a center and is begging for money and harassing clients. Of the following, the MOST effective action to take in this situation would be to

    A. call immediately for police assistance
    B. take the man aside quietly and try to persuade him to move along
    C. ask two or three male clients to help you take the man outside
    D. arrest the man at once so that drunks will know they should stay away

KEY (CORRECT ANSWERS)

1.	B		11.	A
2.	C		12.	D
3.	D		13.	B
4.	D		14.	B
5.	B		15.	B
6.	C		16.	D
7.	A		17.	C
8.	D		18.	C
9.	C		19.	C
10.	D		20.	B

21. B
22. D
23. A
24. D
25. B

———

TEST 2

DIRECTIONS: Each question or incomplete statement is followed by several suggested answers or completions. Select the one that BEST answers the question or completes the statement. *PRINT THE LETTER OF THE CORRECT ANSWER IN THE SPACE AT THE RIGHT.*

1. Assume that you, a superior officer, have received a communication from one of your subordinates that his center has just received a *ticking* package.
   Of the following steps, the one that he should take FIRST is to

   A. notify the Police Department
   B. remove the package and soak it in water
   C. check the contents of the package
   D. evacuate the area

2. Assume that an individual suspected of drug abuse is apprehended. The suspect produces a prescription which he claims is for the drug found on his person.
   Which of the following actions should be taken NEXT?

   A. The prescription should be disregarded and the suspect should be arrested.
   B. Release the individual, but confiscate the drug in order to have a laboratory check its composition.
   C. The opinion of a medical doctor should be obtained.
   D. The suspect should be released since he has a prescription.

3. A mob has been defined as a group of individuals who commit lawless acts under the stimulus of intense excitement or agitation.
   All of the following are generally considered characteristics of a mob EXCEPT

   A. some degree of organization
   B. one or more leaders
   C. a common motive for action
   D. unemotional behavior

4. Which of the following would be IMPROPER for an officer to do while apprehending a suspect?

   A. Maintain a quiet voice and manner
   B. Remove the person from the scene as soon as possible in order to avoid conflict with the suspect and bystanders
   C. Allow the suspect to realize that the officer does not like persons who commit crimes
   D. Direct and accompany the person to an appropriate location

5. Which of the following is MOST appropriate for an officer to do while testifying as a witness in court?

   A. State the facts only of your own knowledge
   B. Argue with the defense attorney in order to show that your actions were proper
   C. Deny that you have discussed the case outside of court even if you have done so only with close friends
   D. Use as much technical language as possible in order to impress the jury with your knowledge

6. It is sometimes inadvisable to arrest the leaders of an unlawful demonstration immediately.
   Of the following, the BEST reason to delay arresting the leaders of a demonstration is to

   A. permit them to restrain their followers who might threaten violence
   B. avoid unfavorable coverage by the press
   C. determine whether there is more than one charge involved
   D. let them get deeper in trouble so they will receive longer sentences when convicted

7. The one of the following approaches which would BEST foster good human relations when dealing with the public is for an officer to

   A. act very self-assured, thus gaining respect
   B. learn how to appeal to the biases and prejudices of others
   C. treat everyone in exactly the same way since everyone has the same needs
   D. appeal to the positive interests of others

8. The causes of many job complaints come not just from wages and working conditions but also from contacts with people on and off the job and from the officer's background and outlook on life.
   Because of this, the BEST of the following ways for a superior officer to handle a complaint from a subordinate is generally to

   A. talk to the officer for the purpose of getting him to withdraw his complaint
   B. get as much information as possible to try to determine the real causes of the complaint
   C. postpone action on the complaint since conditions change so rapidly that it is useless to try to act quickly on a complaint
   D. handle each complaint as quickly as possible without looking into the motives for the complaint

9. In every unit certain officers are more cooperative than others.
   The one of the following that is MOST likely to occur with regard to supervising such cooperative officers is that they

   A. are more easily intimidated
   B. are often assigned to difficult jobs
   C. are unfriendly to the general public
   D. assume a supervisor's position in dealing with others

10. Assume that you are a superior officer and that one of your subordinate officers comes to you with a complaint about an officer under his command. After listening to a few of the details, you suspect that his complaint is not justified.
    Considering this, you should do all of the following during this initial conversation EXCEPT

    A. listen with interest until the subordinate officer finishes making his complaint
    B. tell the subordinate officer that you will investigate the matter further
    C. inform the subordinate that his complaint is invalid
    D. ask the subordinate officer further questions about his complaint

11. As a superior officer, you may receive complaints about the department or individual officers from the public.
    Of the following, the PROPER attitude to take with regard to such complaints is that they

    A. are often helpful in determining how to give the public better service
    B. cause poor morale in the service and should not be revealed to subordinates
    C. are useful as a basis for disciplining officers who have been troublesome in the past
    D. take up too much of an officer's time and should not be accepted

11._____

12. One of the people present at a local parent-teacher organization meeting complained about the time it took for him to be taken care of at an agency office. A superior officer, present at the meeting, stood up and explained to the person and the group that there was no personal discrimination involved because the normal procedures took a while and that everyone spent about the same amount of time in the office.
    In this situation, the action of the superior officer was

    A. *proper,* mainly because it will show the group how much he knows about agency operations
    B. *improper,* mainly because he should tell the man who complained to check first with the agency before complaining
    C. *proper,* mainly because he helped to clear up a misunderstanding
    D. *improper,* mainly because the officer should not discuss his agency in public

12._____

13. Assume that you are a superior officer and that you have begun a campaign to encourage your subordinates to be prompt in reporting for work. One of your subordinates requests that he be allowed to arrive a half hour late in the morning while his wife is in the hospital as a maternity patient.
    Of the following actions, it would be BEST in this situation for you to

    A. *refuse* the request, claiming it would be unfair to others to make an exception
    B. *grant* the request, telling your other subordinates the reason for this exception
    C. *refuse* the request, blaming the central office for having inflexible rules
    D. *grant* the request, making it clear to all that this will be the last exception

13._____

14. Authorities agree that keeping rumors to a minimum is one of the goals of communication.
    Which of the following is NOT consistent with this goal?

    A. Distribute information that will tend to make rumors unnecessary
    B. Reduce the social distance between top management and the lower supervisors
    C. Stress the development of downward rather than upward channels of communication
    D. Understand the emotional elements that cause stress

14._____

15. Of the following, the MOST important factor in determining the success or failure of communication between officers and the public is the

    A. attitude of the public toward the officers prior to and during the communication
    B. use of proper channels of communication within the organization
    C. use of the mass media to change the public's attitude from negative to positive
    D. increase in opportunities for personal contact between the officers and the public

15._____

16. Assume that you are a superior officer concerned with the effective use of praise and criticism to motivate your subordinates.
Of the following statements, the one that is EQUALLY TRUE of praise and criticism is that both should generally be

    A. directed mainly toward the act instead of the person
    B. given often and with no restrictions
    C. given in public for the greatest effect
    D. directed toward group efforts rather than individual efforts

17. Which of the following actions on the part of a superior officer is MOST likely to improve upward communication between his subordinates and himself?

    A. Delay acting on undesirable working conditions until complaints from subordinates have reached top management
    B. Make the time to listen to subordinates' ideas
    C. Resist becoming involved with the personal problems of subordinates
    D. Discourage communications that indicate which policies may have resulted in poor performance

18. Assume that you are a recently appointed superior officer and are told that one of your subordinates is a chronic complainer.
In this situation, which of the following steps should you take FIRST?

    A. Report your subordinate to higher authority
    B. Discipline your subordinate for his poor performance
    C. Change your subordinate's tour of duty
    D. Ask your subordinate for a list of his complaints

19. In addition to formal supervision, every group of officers soon develops informal leaders who influence the other members of the group.
Of the following statements about informal leaders, the one that is GENERALLY correct is that they

    A. provide supervision when the regular supervisor is absent
    B. are entitled to special benefits for their services
    C. can be used to help settle disputes between employees
    D. prevent the rapid transmission of orders

20. The grapevine is a frequently used means of informal communication in any work location.
The one of the following statements that BEST describes the attitude a superior officer should take in relation to the grapevine is that it is

    A. unreliable and should not be trusted
    B. useful and should be recognized
    C. valuable and should be the chief method of transmitting orders
    D. insignificant and should be ignored

21. As a supervising officer, it may be useful for you to conduct periodic interviews with each of your subordinates to discuss his job performance in broad perspective.
All of the following are ground rules to follow during such an interview EXCEPT

    A. showing him how he compares in work performance with other supervisors in your district
    B. giving him a chance to talk
    C. focusing on what can be learned from any mistakes discussed rather than on the mistakes themselves
    D. avoiding a discussion of personalities

22. When you, as a superior officer, are correcting the errors of a supervisor in your district, which of the following is NOT a good point to keep in mind?

    A. Find something on which to compliment the supervisor before you correct him
    B. Watch yourself carefully to avoid the mistake of overcorrecting
    C. Correct the supervisor at the same time as you correct other supervisors who make similar mistakes
    D. Induce the supervisor to correct himself if possible

23. Following are four steps to be used when instructing a subordinate in the performance of his job:
    I. Observe the subordinate doing the job
    II. Compare his performance to established standards
    III. Explain the purpose of the job to the subordinate
    IV. Demonstrate each step of the job

    Which of the following choices lists the CORRECT order in which the above steps should be taken?

    A. III, IV, I, II B. IV, III, I, II
    C. III, IV, II, I D. IV, III, II, I

24. Of the following leadership characteristics, the one that is generally considered PRIMARY for a supervisor is the ability to

    A. achieve good working relations with fellow supervisors
    B. get subordinates to air their personal problems
    C. take action to get the job done
    D. plan his work efficiently

25. A recently appointed supervising officer is placed in charge of a district which includes several senior employees. He finds that while these subordinates are able to learn new tasks and methods, some of them tend to take longer to learn procedural changes than newer, younger workers.
Of the following, the MAIN reason for this is that senior workers

    A. are embarrassed by younger workers' intelligence
    B. have to *unlearn* what was taught them in the past
    C. form learning blocks when they are supervised by a younger person
    D. are more interested in doing the work than in academic discussion

KEY (CORRECT ANSWERS)

1.	D	11.	A
2.	C	12.	C
3.	D	13.	B
4.	C	14.	C
5.	A	15.	A
6.	A	16.	A
7.	D	17.	B
8.	B	18.	D
9.	B	19.	C
10.	C	20.	B

21. A
22. C
23. A
24. C
25. B

EXAMINATION SECTION
TEST 1

DIRECTIONS: Each question or incomplete statement is followed by several suggested answers or completions. Select the one that BEST answers the question or completes the statement. *PRINT THE LETTER OF THE CORRECT ANSWER IN THE SPACE AT THE RIGHT.*

1. When training your subordinates in a new method of crowd control, which one of the following techniques SHOULD be used? 1.____

   A. Teach them the whole job at one time, whether it contains a great many steps or only a few
   B. Issue orders without giving reasons because this will result in more questions and delays
   C. Explain and demonstrate, one step at a time
   D. Use technical language in order to make instructions precise

2. It is sometimes necessary to provide additional training for staff members who are poor in their performance of specific tasks. 2.____
   Of the following, the MOST effective way of improving staff performance is to

   A. use visual aids along with reading material to train staff on the general subject involved
   B. train subordinates to perform only those tasks which they normally perform
   C. plan and carry out programs to meet the subordinates' real work needs
   D. provide training only for staff members performing critical tasks

3. Assume that as a superior officer you confront one of your subordinate officers with the fact that he is not performing his job effectively. The officer tries to avoid the blame and shifts the criticism to other officers including yourself. 3.____
   Which one of the following is NOT a good way of handling this situation?

   A. Speaking and acting in an impartial and fair-minded manner
   B. Trying to determine why the officer finds it difficult to accept justifiable criticism
   C. Calling in the other officers whom this subordinate has criticized and having them discuss the matter with him
   D. Listening to the officer, at least at the outset, rather than interrupting his statement

4. For a superior officer to discuss a subordinate's performance evaluation with him is GENERALLY 4.____

   A. *inadvisable;* such a discussion will discourage a good worker
   B. *advisable;* the subordinate must know about the quality of his performance for improvement to occur
   C. *inadvisable;* a good performance evaluation will result in the subordinate's asking for more responsibility
   D. *advisable;* such discussions generally lead to a change in the subordinate's evaluation

5. The one of the following which is the MAJOR cause of employee lateness is

   A. low morale
   B. excessive fatigue
   C. accidents
   D. sickness

6. For officers to work together smoothly, teamwork is necessary.
   Which one of the following statements BEST describes the relationship between leadership and teamwork?

   A. Leadership cannot exist without teamwork.
   B. Teamwork cannot exist without leadership.
   C. Leadership and teamwork are one and the same.
   D. There is no relationship between leadership and teamwork.

7. For superiors who wish to achieve proper discipline among subordinates, it is generally MOST difficult to

   A. obtain rapid compliance with orders and directives
   B. prevent subordinates from questioning orders that are issued to them
   C. achieve compliance with orders while encouraging individual initiative
   D. use punishment to prevent infractions of the rules

8. Of the following, it is MOST likely that laxity in administering discipline will result in

   A. a loss of respect for their superior on the part of subordinates
   B. the satisfactory completion of the organization's job
   C. an increase in the number of disturbances at centers
   D. the establishment of proper conditions for successful administration

9. In dealing with a subordinate who shows a lack of interest in performing his duties, a superior officer should GENERALLY

   A. assign to him all the difficult work
   B. give him more responsibility
   C. inspect his performance more often than usual
   D. give him direct, detailed orders

10. A superior officer who has a highly motivated group of officers under his command GENERALLY

    A. shows an interest in how they are doing and is willing to back them up
    B. spends most of his time in closely supervising his subordinates
    C. supervises mainly through one of his subordinate officers
    D. is management-oriented rather than subordinate-oriented

11. As a superior, you might have to supervise subordinate officers who are very enthusiastic and ambitious.
    Which one of the following is the BEST reason for carefully watching the work of such officers?
    They

    A. may produce so much work that other officers resent them
    B. may appear to be overly concerned about being promoted
    C. might make decisions before obtaining the necessary information
    D. may be seeking the superior's job

12. In dealing with the public, officers should behave with courtesy.
    Which one of the following practices would be LEAST effective in promoting courtesy?

    A. Giving advice on subjects about which you are not well informed
    B. Learning to take constructive criticism intelligently
    C. Avoiding discussions of a personal nature
    D. Treating members of the public as you would like to be treated

13. When directing the officers under your command, which one of the following is generally the MOST effective method of supervision?

    A. Provide your directions through written orders to prevent misunderstanding
    B. Supervise every detail of the work closely so that it is carried out exactly as you want it
    C. Limit your concern to getting the job done and not to the people doing the work
    D. Set up general standards and goals so that officers have leeway as to how to achieve them

14. Leadership is particularly important in the security field.
    Of the following, people GENERALLY expect their leader to

    A. state, *Do as I say, not as I do*
    B. refuse to allow changes in orders
    C. get many of his ideas from his subordinates
    D. take his feelings out on those who make mistakes

15. The MOST important single factor in the selection of a person for assignment to a position of greater responsibility should be his

    A. demonstrated ability to do the job
    B. schooling, both civilian and military
    C. training and experience on the job
    D. length of service

16. Security training received by security officers and noted in their personnel charts or records should NOT be used as a basis for

    A. indicating individual degrees of skill
    B. assigning officers to particular shifts
    C. establishing priorities of instruction
    D. presenting a consolidated picture of the training status

17. As a superior officer, you note that one of your subordinates has not been performing his job properly. You discover that the cause of this problem seems to be that he drinks excessively when off duty.
    Of the following, the BEST way to handle this situation is to

    A. discipline the officer to the fullest extent possible
    B. discuss the problem and possible solutions with the officer's fellow workers
    C. wait until the officer has straightened himself out and then counsel him
    D. have a blunt and firm talk with the officer and direct him to seek treatment

18. Officers who are overly sensitive to criticism are one of the problems that superiors must deal with.
Of the following, which is the BEST way to handle such officers?
They should

    A. not be talked to differently from other officers
    B. be criticized only on serious mistakes
    C. not be criticized at all
    D. be reassured of their worth to their unit

19. A superior officer who suspects an employee of petty office theft calls the employee to his office and questions him directly.
In this situation, the superior's action is

    A. *desirable,* primarily because the subordinate should be allowed to answer these accusations privately
    B. *desirable,* primarily because confrontation will persuade the employee to tell the truth
    C. *undesirable,* primarily because line department personnel should handle such matters
    D. *undesirable,* primarily because direct confrontation might unnecessarily embarrass the employee

20. Assume that a certain superior officer assigns a task, without explanation, to a new subordinate who is not yet accepted by the work group.
Of the following, the MOST likely result of this action would be to

    A. encourage the subordinate to perform at his best
    B. make the subordinate feel insecure about proving himself
    C. stimulate other officers to do their best to impress the new staff member
    D. cause the experienced officers to feel inferior

21. A newly appointed superior officer often faces the problem of supervising officers who were formerly close personal friends of his.
In this situation, the one of the following which is the BEST approach to take toward these officers is to

    A. break all ties with former friends
    B. stay personally close with friends as this is always an advantage on the job
    C. maintain a relationship of easy, occasional familiarity
    D. become businesslike on the job but remain close socially

22. Assume that you, as a superior officer, are talking over a proposed change in procedure with your subordinates which would require their full cooperation.
Which one of the following actions would be MOST appropriate for you to take if your subordinates suggest modifications in the procedure?

    A. Prepare arguments against your subordinates' suggestions while you are listening to them
    B. Refuse to accept suggestions for changes since procedures can't be modified
    C. Listen carefully since your subordinates' suggestions may have merit
    D. Accept the recommendations of your more experienced subordinates

23. The successful supervisor should be aware that two of his most important assets are patience and understanding.
Of the following actions by a supervisor, the one that is LEAST likely to demonstrate these qualities would be to

    A. make deadlines realistic and reachable
    B. reprimand an employee the minute he makes a mistake
    C. assist employees in work-related problems
    D. discuss changes in procedures with subordinates

23.____

24. One of a supervisor's goals should be to create and maintain a force of loyal subordinates with high morale. This objective is likely to be achieved by all of the following EXCEPT

    A. making subordinate officers feel that their job is an important one
    B. encouraging supervisors to be concerned with the individual needs of subordinates
    C. giving subordinate officers an opportunity to express their thoughts, likes, and interests to their supervisors
    D. having supervisors rely only on the advice of trusted employees when resolving disputes between subordinates

24.____

25. One of a supervisor's major responsibilities is to evaluate the performance of his subordinates.
Which one of the following practices would be LEAST productive in developing meaningful evaluations from performance interviews?

    A. Make positive statements only
    B. Outline the points to discuss
    C. Adjust to the individual and situation
    D. Allow the employee to participate

25.____

KEY (CORRECT ANSWERS)

1. C
2. C
3. C
4. B
5. A

6. B
7. C
8. A
9. B
10. A

11. C
12. A
13. D
14. C
15. A

16. B
17. D
18. D
19. A
20. B

21. C
22. C
23. B
24. D
25. A

TEST 2

DIRECTIONS: Each question or incomplete statement is followed by several suggested answers or completions. Select the one that BEST answers the question or completes the statement. *PRINT THE LETTER OF THE COREECT ANSWER IN THE SPACE AT THE RIGHT.*

1. Assume that you are a superior officer concerned with improving the attitude of your subordinates toward their work.
   Of the following, the action that is MOST likely to improve this attitude would be for you to

   A. allow your subordinates to take extra time off
   B. interpret rules and regulations leniently
   C. request a merit increase in salary for your subordinates
   D. train your subordinates to perform at the highest possible level

   1._____

2. Assume that two of the officers under your command are hotly disputing the accuracy of a log book entry. One of the officers asks for your opinion.
   Which of the following would be LEAST advisable for you to do in this situation?

   A. Ask the officers to present their views calmly
   B. Keep your temper and remain impartial
   C. Stop the argument and then give your decision
   D. Judge the argument in proportion to its importance

   2._____

3. A superior officer notices that one of his subordinates is not doing his job.
   In this situation, it would be MOST appropriate for the superior officer to

   A. caution the subordinate officer promptly
   B. ignore the incident this time
   C. check on the subordinate officer's behavior in an hour
   D. warn the subordinate officer at the end of his work day that a report may be filed

   3._____

4. A recently appointed superior officer finds it difficult to make the decisions required in his new position.
   Which one of the following suggestions would be MOST helpful to him in overcoming this problem?

   A. Don't be concerned because everyone makes mistakes, and any mistake caused by your decisions will be ignored.
   B. Remember that you will be judged by the long-range soundness of all of your decisions.
   C. Since you are now in charge of a number of officers, let them bear the decision-making responsibility.
   D. Remember that you have a superior and that he can make the decision for you.

   4._____

5. Of the following, the BEST reason for a superior officer to make inspections and rounds is to

   A. observe the physical appearance of personnel
   B. determine whether communication equipment is working properly

   5._____

C. decide whether adequate records are being kept
D. see that the performance of subordinates conforms with departmental standards

6. Assume that you, as a superior officer, have made an inspection and have submitted recommendations for improvements.
Which one of the following actions should be taken to assure that the desired results are obtained from the inspection?
You should

   A. distribute copies of the recommendations to all members of the force
   B. follow-up to determine whether the recommended improvements have been made
   C. give credit to other officers when it is due in order to help increase morale
   D. set up a schedule so that you inspect once a week

7. Assume that you have noticed that one of your subordinates has been quiet and rather depressed for two to three days with no change in his usual satisfactory job performance.
Of the following, the BEST action for you to take in this situation is to

   A. ask him to describe his feelings in detail
   B. act as if you noticed no change in the subordinate's behavior
   C. tell him to forget what's bothering him
   D. recommend that he seek professional guidance

8. Assume that you wish to introduce a change in your subordinates' work procedures in order to improve their performance.
Of the following, the BEST way to gain acceptance of this change is for you to

   A. stress its positive aspects
   B. downgrade past practices
   C. delay discussing it for a while
   D. order your subordinates to follow the new procedure at once

9. Suppose you come across two of your subordinate officers having an argument about the boundaries of their patrol posts.
Which of the following is the LEAST advisable course of action for you to take after stopping the argument?

   A. Tell the officers to speak with you individually
   B. Have the officers submit their views in writing for you to evaluate properly when you have time
   C. Meet with both officers in your office after they finish their tours
   D. Tell the officers to consult you on such matters in the future

10. Assume that a superior officer is explaining a new rule to his men at roll call. One officer states that he does not like the rule. The superior tells the officer that he agrees with him, but that the rule must be followed anyway. In this situation, the superior officer's statement was

    A. *proper*, chiefly because the men should know where superiors stand on rules and regulations
    B. *improper*, chiefly because superiors should not indicate disagreement with a change in rules since they must enforce them

C. *proper,* chiefly because efficiency improves when supervisors and subordinates agree on new rules
D. *improper,* chiefly because questions regarding rule changes should be answered at staff meetings rather than at roll call

11. Assume that you find that several of your subordinate officers have not performed satisfactorily during the last few emergency situations at your work location. The one of the following actions which is LEAST likely to improve their performance is for you to

    A. keep the subordinates informed about how they performed after each emergency
    B. stay alert for officers who are having difficulty with their work
    C. circulate among the officers at emergencies
    D. avoid the use of criticism

11.____

12. Of the following qualifications for an officer, the one that is MOST important is the ability to

    A. understand and get along with people
    B. write a good report
    C. overcome resistance to arrest
    D. solve crimes

12.____

13. Assume that you have noticed that one of your subordinate officers makes errors when questioning clients. You discuss with him the proper method to use when questioning clients.
Of the following, your NEXT step should be to

    A. ask another officer to check on your subordinate's procedure when questioning clients
    B. tell the officer to discuss with others how they question clients
    C. have the officer report regularly to you about the clients he questions
    D. watch the officer to see how he questions clients

13.____

14. One of the MOST important rules to follow when communicating with your superior is:

    A. Report everything that happens at your work location to him
    B. Pass on to him rumors and gossip heard within your center
    C. Let him hear from you first about any unusual success, problem or error
    D. Assign to one of your subordinates the responsibility of communicating with your supervisor

14.____

15. A superior officer may be required to instruct subordinates in the performance of their tasks.
Which of the following would NOT be proper when instructing a small group of employees?

    A. Use simple language
    B. Explain the procedure and the reason for the procedure
    C. Demonstrate one step at a time
    D. Use the lecture method instead of the discussion method whenever possible

15.____

16. Assume that a new officer has joined your unit. Which of the following approaches should you, as his superior officer, use in introducing him to the job?

    A. Put him right to work; he will learn best through his mistakes
    B. Act sternly, thereby gaining his respect and indicating the proper supervisor-subordinate relationship
    C. Give him the overall picture of the department and unit he is in
    D. Praise him, even when he makes errors, in order to gain his confidence

17. When a new officer begins work, he will often perform tasks ineffectively, thus requiring corrective action by his supervisor.
    In this situation, which one of the following represents the MOST desirable course of action for the supervisor?

    A. Point out specific errors in performance and how to correct them
    B. Tell the new officer that he is not doing the job properly and assign him to a new task
    C. Avoid criticism in the beginning since it may result in bitterness
    D. Do not criticize because criticism is not currently considered an acceptable tool of management

18. Of the following types of work, the one that is MOST likely to lead to dissatisfaction is work that is

    A. difficult to perform
    B. tiring to complete
    C. uncomplicated
    D. unimportant

19. When instructing subordinates to perform new tasks, the one of the following that is LEAST important in helping then to learn is to

    A. explain the procedure to them in a step-by-step manner
    B. show them what they must do
    C. let them do the task under guidance
    D. have them perform the task without supervision so they may learn from their mistakes

20. Which one of the following is the MOST important single thing to bear in mind about giving orders?

    A. An order should be given to a capable employee, not an uncooperative one.
    B. If an order is given correctly, you will not have to check the work.
    C. An order should be given in as forceful a manner as possible to assure that it is understood.
    D. An order is given because it is necessary to bring about certain results.

21. Suppose that a subordinate asks you about a rumor he has heard. The rumor deals with a subject which your superiors consider *confidential.*
    Which of the following BEST describes how you should answer the officer?
    Tell

    A. the officer that you don't make the rules and that he should speak to higher ranking officers
    B. the officer that you will ask your superior for information

C. him only that you cannot comment on the matter
D. him the rumor is not true

22. Superior officers often find it difficult to *get their message across* when instructing newly appointed officers in their various duties.
The MAIN reason for this is generally that the

   A. duties of the officers have increased
   B. superior officer is often so expert in his area that he fails to see it from the learner's point of view
   C. superior officer adapts his instruction to the slowest learner in the group
   D. new officers are younger, less concerned with job security, and more interested in fringe benefits

23. Assume that you are discussing a security problem with an officer under your command. During the discussion, you see that the officer's eyes are turning away from you and that he is not paying attention.
In order to get the officer's attention, you should FIRST

   A. ask him to look you in the eye
   B. talk to him about sports
   C. tell him he is being very rude
   D. change your tone of voice

24. As a superior officer, you may find it necessary to conduct meetings with your subordinates.
Of the following, which would be MOST helpful in assuring that a meeting accomplishes the purpose for which it was called?

   A. Give notice of the conclusions you would like to reach at the start of the meeting
   B. Delay the start of the meeting until everyone is present
   C. Write down points to be discussed in proper sequence
   D. Make sure everyone is clear on whatever conclusions have been reached and on what must be done after the meeting

25. Every superior officer will occasionally be called upon to deliver a reprimand to a subordinate. If done properly, this can greatly help an officer improve his performance.
Which one of the following is NOT a good practice to follow when giving a reprimand?

   A. Maintain your composure and temper
   B. Reprimand a subordinate in the presence of other officers so they can learn the same lesson
   C. Try to understand why the officer was not able to perform satisfactorily
   D. Let your knowledge of the officer involved determine the exact nature of the reprimand

KEY (CORRECT ANSWERS)

1.	D	11.	D
2.	C	12.	A
3.	A	13.	D
4.	B	14.	C
5.	D	15.	D
6.	B	16.	C
7.	B	17.	A
8.	A	18.	D
9.	B	19.	D
10.	B	20.	D

21. B
22. B
23. D
24. D
25. B

TEST 3

DIRECTIONS: Each question or incomplete statement is followed by several suggested answers or completions. Select the one that BEST answers the question or completes the statement. *PRINT THE LETTER OF THE CORRECT ANSWER IN THE SPACE AT THE RIGHT.*

1. Of the following, the PRIMARY purpose of communications between subordinates and superiors is to

    A. develop language skills
    B. enable subordinates to air their grievances
    C. help establish friendly ties
    D. solve job problems

2. Of the following, the MOST necessary elements of good communication are

    A. openness and form
    B. details and subjectivity
    C. speed and dependability
    D. length and appearance

3. Of the following, the MOST important role of a supervisor is that of

    A. being able to understand how his men feel about their assignments
    B. establishing good contacts with the administration
    C. fulfilling his responsibility to the assigned position
    D. presenting a good public image on the behalf of his organization

4. Of the following, the LEAST desirable behavior of a senior officer would be for him to

    A. attempt to gain the respect of superiors
    B. attempt to find causes of high employee turnover
    C. ignore infrequent latenesses
    D. ignore suggestions which may prove unworthy

5. A senior officer who consults with his subordinates about operational planning is GENERALLY

    A. attempting to prove his supervisory ability
    B. developing their job participation and cooperation
    C. passing down his responsibilities to others
    D. searching for an employee with supervisory ability

6. If a senior officer conducted supervision and inspection programs in order to become aware of his men's conduct, he would GENERALLY be considered to be

    A. excessively strict and authoritarian
    B. looking for potential troublemakers
    C. overconscientious in his work
    D. performing a vital duty

7. Of the following, the BEST reason for a supervisor's evaluation of his own on-the-job performance is to enable him to

    A. find the best methods of supervising his men and in getting the job done
    B. give the impression that he is sincere in trying to become a better supervisor

C. make a favorable impression on his superiors
D. make his work seem more important than it actually is

8. Assume that you are a senior officer making a performance evaluation of an officer. The reason for NOT drawing conclusions too quickly is CHIEFLY that

    A. without due consideration of all the facts, you are likely to evaluate the officer on biased personal judgment
    B. evaluation reports take a great deal of time and thought
    C. senior officers must consult with superiors before drawing conclusions about a subordinate's performance
    D. the officer might try to disprove any wrong information which you may have obtained about him

9. A senior officer notices two officers, known to be good workers, playing practical jokes and pranks on the other employees.
In this case, disciplinary action is

    A. *desirable,* chiefly because horseplay on the job is not, strictly speaking, against the rules
    B. *undesirable,* chiefly because good workers tend to correct their own improper actions
    C. *desirable,* chiefly because horseplay could provoke other employees and that would disrupt normal work routine
    D. *undesirable,* chiefly because a supervisor should not get involved with employees' affairs

10. Resistance to or resentment of training is likely to be an attitude shown by many officers. Therefore, it is important for a senior officer to understand the causes of his men's attitudes and learn how to deal with them. Of the following, which is the BEST method of lessening an officer's resentment of training?

    A. Give the officers extra time off for taking part in the training program
    B. Openly criticize the officer who often makes mistakes during training
    C. Recommend promotions for those who complete the training program quickest
    D. Explain that the purpose of the training is to help them perform their jobs more efficiently

11. A senior officer required all officers under his supervision to submit a weekly report based on information from their daily log (memo) entries. The senior officer did not examine these reports, but he did file them as proof that the officers were not *sleeping* on the job.
In general, this practice of the senior officer is considered

    A. *correct,* chiefly because the senior officer has little need of the reports since he is usually on the scene to observe the performance of his men
    B. *incorrect,* chiefly because, if the senior officer asked for reports, he should read or use the information they contain
    C. *correct,* chiefly because any information an officer had could only be based on daily occurrences
    D. *incorrect,* chiefly because the senior officer is placing too much emphasis on accuracy of paper work

12. Selecting an employee to be trained for performing the supervisor's duties is generally considered

    A. *desirable*, chiefly because it allows the supervisor to avoid many of his duties
    B. *undesirable*, chiefly because it creates the impression that the supervisor is showing favoritism
    C. *desirable*, chiefly because supervisory coverage is assured in the absence of the supervisor
    D. *undesirable*, chiefly because the trainee will cause the supervisor to worry about possible competition and thus neglect the performance of his duties

13. When discussing lateness with an employee, a supervisor should take the employee to an area where the problem can be discussed privately
    Generally, this practice is considered

    A. *desirable*, chiefly because it gives the employee an opportunity to converse with the supervisor in a very casual way
    B. *desirable*, chiefly because it keeps the problem from being discussed in front of an audience
    C. *undesirable*, chiefly because isolating an employee from his co-workers causes the *rumor-mongers* to spread false gossip about the matter
    D. *undesirable*, chiefly because trivial matters can be mentioned in the open without any repercussions

14. When an officer shows a pattern of abuse in his use of sick leave, a senior officer should

    A. ask the officer for medical proof of all future illnesses
    B. discourage other officers from abusing sick leave by giving the offending officer a public warning
    C. interview the officer and inquire about the reasons for his behavior
    D. acknowledge the officer's right to sick leave as set forth in departmental rules and regulations

15. Of the following, the MAJOR reason why grapevines generally develop in an agency is that

    A. employees have too much idle time
    B. employees want to socialize and gossip with other employees while working
    C. superior officers avoid reporting bad news downward from management to subordinates
    D. there is a communication gap between management and employees

16. If a newly-assigned senior officer is doubtful about the exact details of the assignment he is about to give to an officer, he should GENERALLY

    A. ask to speak to the officer in private and give him another assignment
    B. delay giving the assignment until he clears up his own doubt
    C. attempt to explain to the officer what he knows about the assignment in the best possible way
    D. put the assignment in writing

17. Of the following situations, which one would justify a supervisor's giving direct orders to another supervisor's subordinate?

    A. A supervisor away from his normal assignment observes a serious disturbance and gives orders to the officers in that area.
    B. A supervisor foresees a problem that will arise the next day in another district and immediately proceeds to inform the other supervisor's officers of the action they should take.
    C. A supervisor tells an officer under another supervisor to perform a duty a week from today because he feels it is an urgent matter.
    D. None of the above situations would justify direct supervision by any senior officer.

18. In the planning process, which of the following is NOT a recommended practice in preparing your final plan of action?

    A. Obtain all important available facts related to the problem
    B. Clarify the problem before any plan is created
    C. Make the plan easy to understand so that it can be carried out efficiently
    D. Never make assumptions or forecasts about what could occur

19. Of the following, the BEST way for a senior officer to get his subordinates to carry out his orders is to

    A. explain whenever possible why the orders are being given
    B. let subordinates know in advance the penalties for disobeying his orders
    C. describe the steps that must be followed in performing each order
    D. issue all orders in the form of direct and positive commands

20. It is MOST correct to state that race prejudice is to the GREATEST extent

    A. an inborn human characteristic
    B. the result of training and group association
    C. the product of ghetto areas
    D. a condition limited to adults only

21. *Scapegoating* is a form of prejudice which results MAINLY from

    A. degrading minority groups in an effort to secure status for one's own group
    B. shifting the blame for social inadequacies and ills from oneself to others
    C. thinking of people not as individual persons but rather placing them in carelessly formed, all-embracing classifications
    D. maintaining the existing order to prevent other groups from rising in social and economic status

22. The MOST important step in democratic supervision is

    A. allowing the employee a chance to apologize whenever he makes an error
    B. keeping tight control over employees
    C. making the employee realize that he needs your approval in order to keep his position
    D. showing an interest in the welfare of the employee

23. Evaluating a subordinate's likes and dislikes concerning his work is GENERALLY considered to be　　23.____

    A. valuable in assigning work details to the subordinate
    B. necessary only when the subordinate complains of dissatisfaction with his daily duties
    C. unnecessary and a waste of time
    D. useful only in establishing a good relationship with the subordinate

24. Employee motivation is very critical in keeping up the morale of employees.　　24.____
    Of the following, which is generally the BEST method of supervision which both motivates and maintains high morale?

    A. Aid employees in finding satisfaction in their assignments even if it requires extra time and responsibility
    B. Allow employees to work with a free hand and without daily interruptions
    C. Don't get involved or become concerned with interests or problems of employees outside the job
    D. Prove your friendship to a select number of employees so that the remainder of the staff will feel you are a *good guy* to work for

25. When attempting to motivate an experienced individual, it is BEST for a senior officer to appeal to the person's　　25.____

    A. emotions   B. positive interests
    C. negative feelings   D. inhibitions

KEY (CORRECT ANSWERS)

1.	D	11.	B
2.	C	12.	C
3.	C	13.	B
4.	D	14.	C
5.	B	15.	D
6.	D	16.	B
7.	A	17.	A
8.	A	18.	D
9.	C	19.	A
10.	D	20.	B

21. B
22. D
23. A
24. A
25. B

170

PREPARING WRITTEN MATERIALS
EXAMINATION SECTION
TEST 1

DIRECTIONS: Each question consists of a sentence which may be classified appropriately under one of the following four categories:
- A. Incorrect because of faulty grammar or sentence structure.
- B. Incorrect because of faulty punctuation.
- C. Incorrect because of faulty spelling or capitalization.
- D. Correct

Examine each sentence carefully. Then, in the space at the right, print the capital letter preceding the option which is the BEST of the four suggested above. All incorrect sentences contain only one type of error. Consider a sentence correct if it contains none of the types of errors mentioned, although there may be other correct ways of expressing the same thought.

1. The fire apparently started in the storeroom, which is usually locked. 1.____
2. On approaching the victim two bruises were noticed by this officer. 2.____
3. The officer, who was there examined the report with great care. 3.____
4. Each employee in the office had a separate desk. 4.____
5. The suggested procedure is similar to the one now in use. 5.____
6. No one was more pleased with the new procedure than the chauffeur. 6.____
7. He tried to pursuade her to change the procedure. 7.____
8. The total of the expenses charged to petty cash were high. 8.____
9. An understanding between him and I was finally reached. 9.____
10. It was at the supervisor's request that the clerk agreed to postpone his vacation. 10.____
11. We do not believe that it is necessary for both he and the clerk to attend the conference. 11.____
12. All employees, who display perseverance, will be given adequate recognition. 12.____
13. He regrets that some of us employees are dissatisfied with our new assignments. 13.____

14. "Do you think that the raise was merited," asked the supervisor? 14._____

15. The new manual of procedure is a valuable supplement to our rules and regulation. 15._____

16. The typist admitted that she had attempted to pursuade the other employees to assist her in her work. 16._____

17. The supervisor asked that all amendments to the regulations be handled by you and I. 17._____

18. They told both he and I that the prisoner had escaped. 18._____

19. Any superior officer, who, disregards the just complaints of his subordinates, is remiss in the performance of his duty. 19._____

20. Only those members of the national organization who resided in the Middle west attended the conference in Chicago. 20._____

21. We told him to give the investigation assignment to whoever was available. 21._____

22. Please do not disappoint and embarass us by not appearing in court. 22._____

23. Despite the efforts of the Supervising mechanic, the elevator could not be started. 23._____

24. The U.S. Weather Bureau, weather record for the accident date was checked. 24._____

3 (#1)

KEY (CORRECT ANSWERS)

1.	D		11.	A
2.	A		12.	B
3.	B		13.	D
4.	D		14.	B
5.	D		15.	C
6.	D		16.	C
7.	C		17.	A
8.	A		18.	A
9.	A		19.	B
10.	D		20.	C

21. D
22. C
23. C
24. B

———

TEST 2

DIRECTIONS: Each question consists of a sentence. Some of the sentences contain errors in English grammar or usage, punctuation, spelling, or capitalization. A sentence does not contain an error simply because it could be written in a different manner. Choose answer:
- A. If the sentence contains an error in English grammar or usage.
- B. if the sentence contains an error in punctuation.
- C. If the sentence contains an error in spelling or capitalization
- D. If the sentence does not contain any errors.

1. The severity of the sentence prescribed by contemporary statutes—including both the former and the revised New York Penal Laws—do not depend on what crime was intended by the offender.   1._____

2. It is generally recognized that two defects in the early law of attempt played a part in the birth of burglary: (1) immunity from prosecution for conduct short of the last act before completion of the crime, and (2) the relatively minor penalty imposed for an attempt (it being a common law misdemeanor) vis-à-vis the completed offense.   2._____

3. The first sentence of the statute is applicable to employees who enter their place of employment, invited guests, and all other persons who have an express or implied license or privilege to enter the premises.   3._____

4. Contemporary criminal codes in the United States generally divide burglary into various degrees, differentiating the categories according to place, time and other attendent circumstances.   4._____

5. The assignment was completed in record time but the payroll for it has not yet been prepaid.   5._____

6. The operator, on the other hand, is willing to learn me how to use the mimeograph.   6._____

7. She is the prettiest of the three sisters.   7._____

8. She doesn't know; if the mail has arrived.   8._____

9. The doorknob of the office door is broke.   9._____

10. Although the department's supply of scratch pads and stationery have diminished considerably, the allotment for our division has not been reduced.   10._____

11. You have not told us whom you wish to designate as your secretary.   11._____

12. Upon reading the minutes of the last meeting, the new proposal was taken up for consideration.   12._____

13. Before beginning the discussion, we locked the door as a precautionary measure. 13._____

14. The supervisor remarked, "Only those clerks, who perform routine work, are permitted to take a rest period." 14._____

15. Not only will this duplicating machine make accurate copies, but it will also produce a quantity of work equal to fifteen transcribing typists. 15._____

16. "Mr. Jones," said the supervisor, "we regret our inability to grant you an extention of your leave of absence." 16._____

17. Although the employees find the work monotonous and fatigueing, they rarely complain. 17._____

18. We completed the tabulation of the receipts on time despite the fact that Miss Smith our fastest operator was absent for over a week. 18._____

19. The reaction of the employees who attended the meeting, as well as the reaction of those who did not attend, indicates clearly that the schedule is satisfactory to everyone concerned. 19._____

20. Of the two employees, the one in our office is the most efficient. 20._____

21. No one can apply or even understand, the new rules and regulations. 21._____

22. A large amount of supplies were stored in the empty office. 22._____

23. If an employee is occassionally asked to work overtime, he should do so willingly. 23._____

24. It is true that the new procedures are difficult to use but, we are certain that you will learn them quickly. 24._____

25. The office manager said that he did not know who would be given a large allotment under the new plan. 25._____

KEY (CORRECT ANSWERS)

1.	A	11.	D
2.	D	12.	A
3.	D	13.	C
4.	C	14.	B
5.	C	15.	A
6.	A	16.	C
7.	D	17.	C
8.	B	18.	B
9.	A	19.	D
10.	A	20.	A

21.	B
22.	A
23.	C
24.	B
25.	D

TEST 3

DIRECTIONS: Each of the following sentences may be classified MOST appropriately under one of the following categories:
  A. Faulty because of incorrect grammar
  B. Faulty because of incorrect punctuation
  C. Faulty because of incorrect capitalization
  D. Correct

Examine each sentence carefully. Then, in the space at the right, print the capital letter preceding the option which is the BEST of the four suggested above. All incorrect sentence contain but one type of error. Consider a sentence correct if it contains none of the types of errors mentioned, even though there may be other correct ways of expressing the same thought.

1. The desk, as well as the chairs, were moved out of the office. 1._____

2. The clerk whose production was greatest for the month won a day's vacation as first prize. 2._____

3. Upon entering the room, the employees were found hard at work at their desks. 3._____

4. John Smith our new employee always arrives at work on time. 4._____

5. Punish whoever is guilty of stealing the money. 5._____

6. Intelligent and persistent effort lead to success no matter what the job may be. 6._____

7. The secretary asked, "can you call again at three o'clock?" 7._____

8. He told us, that if the report was not accepted at the next meeting, it would have to be rewritten. 8._____

9. He would not have sent the letter if he had known that it would cause so much excitement. 9._____

10. We all looked forward to him coming to visit us. 10._____

11. If you find that you are unable to complete the assignment please notify me as soon as possible. 11._____

12. Every girl in the office went home on time but me; there was still some work for me to finish. 12._____

13. He wanted to know who the letter was addressed to, Mr. Brown or Mr. Smith. 13._____

14. "Mr. Jones, he said, please answer this letter as soon as possible." 14._____

177

15. The new clerk had an unusual accent inasmuch as he was born and educated in the south. 15.____

16. Although he is younger than her, he earns a higher salary. 16.____

17. Neither of the two administrators are going to attend the conference being held in Washington, D.C. 17.____

18. Since Miss Smith and Miss Jones have more experience than us, they have been given more responsible duties. 18.____

19. Mr. Shaw the supervisor of the stock room maintains an inventory of stationery and office supplies. 19.____

20. Inasmuch as this matter affects both you and I, we should take joint action. 20.____

21. Who do you think will be able to perform this highly technical work? 21.____

22. Of the two employees, John is considered the most competent. 22.____

23. He is not coming home on tuesday; we expect him next week. 23.____

24. Stenographers, as well as typists must be able to type rapidly and accurately. 24.____

25. Having been placed in the safe we were sure that the money would not be stolen. 25.____

KEY (CORRECT ANSWERS)

1.	A	11.	B
2.	D	12.	D
3.	A	13.	A
4.	B	14.	B
5.	D	15.	C
6.	A	16.	A
7.	C	17.	A
8.	B	18.	A
9.	D	19.	B
10.	A	20.	A

21. D
22. A
23. C
24. B
25. A

TEST 4

DIRECTIONS: Each of the following sentences consist of four sentences lettered A, B, C, and D. One of the sentences in each group contains an error in grammar or punctuation. Indicate the INCORRECT sentence in each group. *PRINT THE LETTER OF THE CORRECT ANSWER IN THE SPACE AT THE RIGHT.*

1. A. Give the message to whoever is on duty.
   B. The teacher who's pupil won first prize presented the award.
   C. Between you and me, I don't expect the program to succeed.
   D. His running to catch the bus caused the accident.

   1.____

2. A. The process, which was patented only last year is already obsolete.
   B. His interest in science (which continues to the present) led him to convert his basement into a laboratory.
   C. He described the book as "verbose, repetitious, and bombastic".
   D. Our new director will need to possess three qualities: vision, patience, and fortitude.

   2.____

3. A. The length of ladder trucks varies considerably.
   B. The probationary fireman reported to the officer to who he was assigned.
   C. The lecturer emphasized the need for we firemen to be punctual.
   D. Neither the officers nor the members of the company knew about the new procedure.

   3.____

4. A. Ham and eggs is the specialty of the house.
   B. He is one of the students who are on probation.
   C. Do you think that either one of us have a chance to be nominated for president of the class?
   D. I assume that either he was to be in charge or you were.

   4.____

5. A. Its a long road that has no turn.
   B. To run is more tiring than to walk.
   C. We have been assigned three new reports: namely, the statistical summary, the narrative summary, and the budgetary summary.
   D. Had the first payment been made in January, the second would be due in April.

   5.____

6. A. Each employer has his own responsibilities.
   B. If a person speaks correctly, they make a good impression.
   C. Every one of the operators has had her vacation.
   D. Has anybody filed his report?

   6.____

7. A. The manager, with all his salesmen, was obliged to go.
   B. Who besides them is to sign the agreement?
   C. One report without the others is incomplete.
   D. Several clerks, as well as the proprietor, was injured.

   7.____

8. A. A suspension of these activities is expected.   8._____
    B. The machine is economical because first cost and upkeep are low.
    C. A knowledge of stenography and filing are required for this position.
    D. The condition in which the goods were received shows that the packing was not done properly.

9. A. There seems to be a great many reasons for disagreement.   9._____
    B. It does not seem possible that they could have failed.
    C. Have there always been too few applicants for these positions?
    D. There is no excuse for these errors.

10. A. We shall be pleased to answer your question.   10._____
    B. Shall we plan the meeting for Saturday?
    C. I will call you promptly at seven.
    D. Can I borrow your book after you have read it?

11. A. You are as capable as I.   11._____
    B. Everyone is willing to sign but him and me.
    C. As for he and his assistant, I cannot praise them too highly.
    D. Between you and me, I think he will be dismissed.

12. A. Our competitors bid above us last week.   12._____
    B. The survey which was began last year has not yet been completed.
    C. The operators had shown that they understood their instructions.
    D. We have never ridden over worse roads.

13. A. Who did they say was responsible?   13._____
    B. Whom did you suspect?
    C. Who do you suppose it was?
    D. Whom do you mean?

14. A. Of the two propositions, this is the worse.   14._____
    B. Which report do you consider the best—the one in January or the one in July?
    C. I believe this is the most practicable of the many plans submitted.
    D. He is the youngest employee in the organization.

15. A. The firm had but three orders last week.   15._____
    B. That doesn't really seem possible.
    C. After twenty years scarcely none of the old business remains.
    D. Has he done nothing about it?

KEY (CORRECT ANSWERS)

1.	B	6.	B	11.	C
2.	A	7.	D	12.	B
3.	C	8.	C	13.	A
4.	C	9.	A	14.	B
5.	A	10.	D	15.	C

PREPARING WRITTEN MATERIALS

EXAMINATION SECTION

TEST 1

DIRECTIONS: Each question or incomplete statement is followed by several suggested answers or completions. Select the one that BEST answers the question or completes the statement. *PRINT THE LETTER OF THE CORRECT ANSWER IN THE SPACE AT THE RIGHT.*

Questions 1-25.

DIRECTIONS: Questions 1 through 25 consist of sentences which may or may not be examples of good English usage. Consider grammar, punctuation, spelling, capitalization, awkwardness, etc. Examine each sentence and then choose the correct statement about it from the four choices below it. If the English usage in the sentence given is better than it would be with any of the changes suggested in options B, C, and D, choose option A. Do not choose an option that will change the meaning of the sentence.

1. According to Judge Frank, the grocer's sons found guilty of assault and sentenced last Thursday.
    A. This is an example of acceptable writing.
    B. A comma should be placed after the word *sentenced*.
    C. The word *were* should be placed after *sons*.
    D. The apostrophe in grocer's should be placed after the *s*.

1.____

2. The department heads assistant said that the stenographers should type duplicate copies of all contracts, leases, and bills.
    A. This is an example of acceptable writing.
    B. A comma should be placed before the word "*contracts*.
    C. An apostrophe should be placed before the *s* in *heads*.
    D. Quotation marks should be placed before the *stenographers* and after *bills*.

2.____

3. The lawyers questioned the men to determine who was the true property owner?
    A. This is an example of acceptable writing.
    B. The phrase *questioned the men* should be changed to *asked the men questions*.
    C. The word *was* should be changed to *were*.
    D. The question mark should be changed to a period.

3.____

4. The terms stated in the present contract are more specific than those stated in the previous contract.   4.____
   A. This is an example of acceptable writing,
   B. The word *are* should be changed to *is*.
   C. The word *than* should be changed to *then*.
   D. The word *specific* should be changed to *specified*.

5. Of the few lawyers considered, the one who argued more skillful was chosen for the job.   5.____
   A. This is an example of acceptable writing.
   B. The word *more* should be replaced by the word *most*.
   C. The word *skillful* should be replaced by the word *skillfully*.
   D. The word *chosen* should be replaced by the word *selected*.

6. Each of the states has a court of appeals; some states have circuit courts.   6.____
   A. This is an example of acceptable writing
   B. The semi-colon should be changed to a comma.
   C. The word *has* should be changed to *have*.
   D. The word *some* should be capitalized.

7. The court trial has greatly effected the child's mental condition.   7.____
   A. This is an example of acceptable writing.
   B. The word *effected* should be changed to *affected*.
   C. The word *greatly* should be placed after *effected*.
   D. The apostrophe in *child's* should be placed after the *s*.

8. Last week, the petition signed by all the officers was sent to the Better Business Bureau.   8.____
   A. This is an example of acceptable writing.
   B. The phrase *last week* should be placed after *officers*.
   C. A comma should be placed after *petition*.
   D. The word *was* should be changed to *were*.

9. Mr. Farrell claims that he requested form A-12, and three booklets describing court procedures.   9.____
   A. This is an example of acceptable writing.
   B. The word *that* should be eliminated.
   C. A colon should be placed after *requested*.
   D. The comma after *A-12* should be eliminated.

10. We attended a staff conference on Wednesday the new safety and fire rules were discussed.   10.____
    A. This is an example of acceptable writing.
    B. The words *safety*, *fire*, and *rules* should begin with capital letters.
    C. There should be a comma after the word *Wednesday*.
    D. There should be a period after the word *Wednesday*, and the word *the* should begin with a capital letter.

11. Neither the dictionary or the telephone directory could be found in the office library.
    A. This is an example of acceptable writing.
    B. The word *or* should be changed to *nor*.
    C. The word *library* should be spelled *libery*.
    D. The word *neither* should be changed to *either*.

11._____

12. The report would have been typed correctly if the typist could read the draft.
    A. This is an example of acceptable writing.
    B. The word *would* should be removed.
    C. The word *have* should be inserted after the word *could*.
    D. The word *correctly* should be changed to *correct*.

12._____

13. The supervisor brought the reports and forms to an employees desk.
    A. This is an example of acceptable writing.
    B. The word *brought* should be changed to *took*.
    C. There should be a comma after the word *reports* and a comma after the word *forms*.
    D. The word *employees* should be spelled *employee's*.

13._____

14. It's important for all the office personnel to submit their vacation schedules on time.
    A. This is an example of acceptable writing.
    B. The word *It's* should be spelled *Its*.
    C. The word *their* should be spelled *they're*.
    D. The word *personnel* should be spelled *personal*.

14._____

15. The supervisor wants that all staff members report to the office at 9:00 A.M.
    A. This is an example of acceptable writing.
    B. The word *that* should be removed and the word *to* should be inserted after the word *members*.
    C. There should be a comma after the word *wants* and a comma after the word *office*.
    D. The word *wants* should be changed to *want* and the word *shall* should be inserted after the word *members*.

15._____

16. Every morning the clerk opens the office mail and distributes it.
    A. This is an example of acceptable writing.
    B. The word *opens* should be changed to *letters*.
    C. The word *mail* should be changed to *letters*.
    D. The word *it* should be changed to *them*.

16._____

17. The secretary typed more fast on a desktop computer than on a tablet.
    A. This is an example of acceptable writing.
    B. The words *more fast* should be changed to *faster*.
    C. There should be a comma after the words *desktop computer*.
    D. The word *than* should be changed to *then*.

17._____

18. The typist used an extention cord in order to connect her typewriter to the outlet nearest to her desks.
    A. This is an example of acceptable writing.
    B. A period should be placed after the word *cord*, and the word *in* should have a capital *I*.
    C. A comma should be placed after the word *typewriter*.
    D. The word *extention* should be spelled *extension*.

19. He would have went to the conference if he had received an invitation.
    A. This is an example of acceptable writing.
    B. The word *went* should be replaced by the word *gone*.
    C. The word *had* should be replaced by *would have*.
    D. The word *conference* should be spelled *conferance*.

20. In order to make the report neater, he spent many hours rewriting it.
    A. This is an example of acceptable writing.
    B. The word *more* should be inserted before the word *neater*.
    C. There should be a colon after the word *neater*.
    D. The word *spent* should be changed to *have spent*.

21. His supervisor told him that he should of read the memorandum more carefully.
    A. This is an example of acceptable writing.
    B. The word *memorandum* should be spelled *memorandom*.
    C. The word *of* should be replaced by the word *have*.
    D. The word *carefully* should be replaced by the word *careful*.

22. It was decided that two separate reports should be written.
    A. This is an example of acceptable writing.
    B. A comma should be inserted after the word *decided*.
    C. The word *be* should be replaced by the word *been*.
    D. A colon should be inserted after the word *that*.

23. She don't seem to understand that the work must be done as soon as possible.
    A. This is an example of acceptable writing.
    B. The word *doesn't* should replace the word *don't*.
    C. The word *why* should replace the word *that*.
    D. The word *as* before the word *soon* should be eliminated.

24. He excepted praise from his supervisor for a job well done.
    A. This is an example of acceptable writing.
    B. The word *excepted* should be spelled *accepted*.
    C. The order of the words *well done* should be changed to *done well*.
    D. There should be a comma after the word *supervisor*.

25. What appears to be intentional errors in grammar occur several times in the passage.
    A. This is an example of acceptable writing.
    B. The word *occur* should be spelled *occur*.
    C. The word *appears* should be changed to *appear*.
    D. The phrase *several times* should be changed to *from time to time*.

25.____

KEY (CORRECT ANSWERS)

1.	C		11.	B
2.	C		12.	C
3.	D		13.	D
4.	A		14.	A
5.	C		15.	B
6.	A		16.	A
7.	B		17.	B
8.	A		18.	D
9.	D		19.	B
10.	D		20.	A

21. C
22. A
23. B
24. B
25. C

TEST 2

DIRECTIONS: Each question consists of a sentence which may or may not be an example of good formal English usage. Examine each sentence, considering grammar, punctuation, spelling, capitalization, and awkwardness. Then choose the CORRECT statement about it from the four options below it. If the English usage in the sentence given is better than any of the changes suggested in options B, C, or D, pick option A. Do not pick an option that will change the meaning of the sentence. *PRINT THE LETTER OF THE CORRECT ANSWER IN THE SPACE AT THE RIGHT.*

1. I don't know who could possibly of broken it.
   A. This is an example of acceptable writing.
   B. The word *who* should be replaced by the word *whom*.
   C. The word *of* should be replaced by the word *have*.
   D. The word *broken* should be replaced by the word *broke*.

   1.____

2. Telephoning is easier than to write.
   A. This is an example of acceptable writing.
   B. The word *telephoning* should be spelled *telephoneing*.
   C. The word *than* should be replaced by the word *then*.
   D. The words *to write* should be replaced by the word *writing*.

   2.____

3. The two operators who have been assigned to these consoles are on vacation.
   A. This is an example of acceptable writing.
   B. A comma should be placed after the word *operators*.
   C. The word *who* should be replaced by the word *whom*.
   D. The word *are* should be replaced by the word *is*.

   3.____

4. You were suppose to teach me how to operate a plugboard.
   A. This is an example of acceptable writing,
   B. The word *were* should be replaced by the word *was*.
   C. The word *suppose* should be replaced by the word *supposed*.
   D. The word *teach* should be replaced by the word *team*.

   4.____

5. If you had taken my advice; you would have spoken with him.
   A. This is an example of acceptable writing.
   B. The word *advice* should be spelled *advise*.
   C. The words *had taken* should be replaced by the word *take*.
   D. The semicolon should be changed to a comma.

   5.____

6. The clerk could have completed the assignment on time if he knows where these materials were located.
   A. This is an example of acceptable writing.
   B. The word *knows* should be replaced by *had known*.
   C. The word "were" should be replaced by *had been*.
   D. The words *where these materials were located* should be replaced by *the location of these materials*.

   6.____

188

7. All employees should be given safety training. Not just those who have accidents. 7._____
   A. This is an example of acceptable writing.
   B. The period after the word *training* should be changed to a colon.
   C. The period after the word *training* should be changed to a semicolon, and the first letter of the word *Not* should be changed to a small *n*.
   D. The period after the word *training* should be changed to a comma, and the first letter of the word *Not* should be changed to a small *n*.

8. This proposal is designed to promote employee awareness of the suggestion program, to encourage employee participation in the program, and to increase the number of suggestions submitted. 8._____
   A. This is an example of acceptable writing.
   B. The word *proposal* should be spelled *proposal*.
   C. The words *to increase the number of suggestions submitted* should be changed to *an increase in the number of suggestions is expected*.
   D. The word *promote* should be changed to *enhance*, and the word *increase* should be changed to *add to*.

9. The introduction of inovative managerial techniques should be preceded by careful analysis of the specific circumstances and conditions in each department. 9._____
   A. This is an example of acceptable writing.
   B. The word *techniques* should be spelled *techneques*.
   C. The word *inovative* should be spelled *innovative*.
   D. A comma should be placed after the word *circumstances* and after the word *conditions*.

10. This occurrence indicates that such criticism embarrasses him. 10._____
    A. This is an example of acceptable writing.
    B. The word *occurrence* should be spelled *occurrence*.
    C. The word *criticism* should be spelled *creticism*.
    D. The word *embarrasses* should be spelled *embarasses*.

11. He can recommend a mechanic whose work is reliable. 11._____
    A. This is an example of acceptable writing.
    B. the word *reliable* should be spelled *relyable*.
    C. The word *whose* should be spelled *who's*.
    D. The word *mechanic* should be spelled *mecanic*.

12. She typed quickly; like someone who had not a moment to lose. 12._____
    A. This is an example of acceptable writing.
    B. The word *not* should be removed.
    C. The semicolon should be changed to a comma.
    D. The word *quickly* should be placed before instead of after the word *typed*.

13. She insisted that she had to much work to do. 13.____
    A. This is an example of acceptable writing.
    B. The word *insisted* should be spelled *insisted*.
    C. The word *to* used in front of *much* should be spelled *too*.
    D. The word *do* should be changed to *be done*.

14. The report, along with the accompanying documents, were submitted for review. 14.____
    A. This is an example of acceptable writing.
    B. The words *were submitted* should be changed to *was submitted*.
    C. The word *accompanying* should be spelled *accompaning*.
    D. The comma after the word *report* should be taken out.

15. If others must use your files, be certain that they understand how the system works, but insist that you do all the filing and refiling. 15.____
    A. This is an example of acceptable writing.
    B. There should be a period after the word *works*, and the word *but* should start a new sentence.
    C. The words *filing* and *refiling* should be spelled *fileing* and *refileing*.
    D. There should be a comma after the word *but*.

16. The appeal was not considered because of its late arrival. 16.____
    A. This is an example of acceptable writing.
    B. The word *its* should be changed to *it's*.
    C. The word *its* should be changed to *the*.
    D. The words *late arrival* should be changed to *arrival late*.

17. The letter must be read carefully to determine under which subject it should be filed. 17.____
    A. This is an example of acceptable writing.
    B. The word *under* should be changed to *at*.
    C. The word *determine* should be spelled *determin*.
    D. The word *carefully* should be spelled *carefully*.

18. He showed potential as an office manager, but he lacked skill in delegating work. 18.____
    A. This is an example of acceptable writing.
    B. The word *delegating* should be spelled *delagating*.
    C. The word *potential* should be spelled *potencial*.
    D. The words *he lacked* should be changed to *was lacking*.

19. His supervisor told him that it would be all right to receive personal mail at the office. 19.____
    A. This is an example of acceptable writing.
    B. The words *all right* should be changed to *alright*.
    C. The word *personal* should be spelled *personel*.
    D. The word *mail* should be changed to *letters*.

20. The report, along with the accompanying documents, were submitted for review.   20.____
    A. This is an example of acceptable writing.
    B. The words *were submitted* should be changed to *was submitted*.
    C. The word *accompanying* should be spelled *accompaning*.
    D. The comma after the word *report* should be taken out.

KEY (CORRECT ANSWERS)

1.	C	11.	A
2.	D	12.	C
3.	A	13.	C
4.	C	14.	B
5.	D	15.	A
6.	B	16.	A
7.	D	17.	D
8.	A	18.	A
9.	C	19.	A
10.	A	20.	B

PREPARING WRITTEN MATERIAL

PARAGRAPH REARRANGEMENT
COMMENTARY

The sentences that follow are in scrambled order. You are to rearrange them in proper order and indicate the letter choice containing the correct answer at the space at the right.

Each group of sentences in this section is actually a paragraph presented in scrambled order. Each sentence in the group has a place in that paragraph; no sentence is to be left out. You are to read each group of sentences and decide upon the best order in which to put the sentences so as to form a well-organized paragraph.

The questions in this section measure the ability to solve a problem when all the facts relevant to its solution are not given.

More specifically, certain positions of responsibility and authority require the employee to discover connection between events sometimes, apparently, unrelated. In order to do this, the employee will find it necessary to correctly infer that unspecified events have probably occurred or are likely to occur. This ability becomes especially important when action must be taken on incomplete information.

Accordingly, these questions require competitors to choose among several suggested alternatives, each of which presents a different sequential arrangement of the events. Competitors must choose the MOST logical of the suggested sequences.

In order to do so, they may be required to draw on general knowledge to infer missing concepts or events that are essential to sequencing the given events. Competitors should be careful to infer only what is essential to the sequence. The plausibility of the wrong alternatives will always require the inclusion of unlikely events or of additional chains of events which are NOT essential to sequencing the given events.

It's very important to remember that you are looking for the best of the four possible choices, and that the best choice of all may not even be one of the answers you're given to choose from.

There is no one right way to solve these problems. Many people have found it helpful to first write out the order of the sentences, as they would have arranged them, on their scrap paper before looking at the possible answers. If their optimum answer is there, this can save them some time. If it isn't, this method can still give insight into solving the problem. Others find it most helpful to just go through each of the possible choices, contrasting each as they go along. You should use whatever method feels comfortable and works for you.

While most of these types of questions are not that difficult, we've added a higher percentage of the difficult type, just to give you more practice. Usually there are only one or two questions on this section that contain such subtle distinctions that you're unable to answer confidently. And you then may find yourself stuck deciding between two possible choices, neither of which you're sure about.

EXAMINATION SECTION
TEST 1

DIRECTIONS: Each question consists of several sentences which can be arranged in a logical sequence. For each question, select the choice which places the numbered sentences in the MOST logical sequence. *PRINT THE LETTER OF THE CORRECT ANSWER IN THE SPACE AT THE RIGHT.*

1. I. A body was found in the woods.
    II. A man proclaimed innocence.
    III. The owner of a gun was located.
    IV. A gun was traced.
    V. The owner of a gun was questioned.
    The CORRECT answer is:
    A. IV, III, V, II, I   B. II, I, IV, III, V   C. I, IV, III, V, II
    D. I, III, V, II, IV   E. I, II, IV, III, V

2. I. A man is in a hunting accident.
    II. A man fell down a flight of steps.
    III. A man lost his vision in one eye.
    IV. A man broke his leg.
    V. A man had to walk with a cane.
    The CORRECT answer is:
    A. II, IV, V, I, III   B. IV, V, I, III, II   C. III, I, IV, V, II
    D. I, III, V, II, IV   E. I, III, II, IV, V

3. I. A man is offered a new job.
    II. A woman is offered a new job.
    III. A man works as a waiter.
    IV. A woman works as a waitress.
    V. A woman gives notice.
    The CORRECT answer is:
    A. IV, II, V, III, I   B. IV, II, V, I, III   C. II, IV, V, III, I
    D. III, I, IV, II, V   E. IV, III, II, V, I

4. I. A train let the station late.
    II. A man was late for work.
    III. A man lost his job.
    IV. Many people complained because the train was late.
    V. There was a traffic jam.
    The CORRECT answer is:
    A. V, II, I, IV, III   B. V, I, IV, II, III   C. V, I, II, IV, III
    D. I, V, IV, II, III   E. II, I, IV, V, III

5.
I. The burden of proof as to each issue is determined before trial and remains upon the same party throughout the trial.
II. The jury is at liberty to believe one witness' testimony as against a number of contradictory witnesses.
III. In a civil case, the party bearing the burden of proof is required to prove his contention by a fair preponderance of the evidence.
IV. However, it must be noted that a fair preponderance of evidence does not necessarily mean a greater number of witnesses.
V. The burden of proof is the burden which rests upon one of the parties to an action to persuade the trier of the facts, generally the jury, that a proposition he asserts is true.
VI. If the evidence is equally balanced, or if it leaves the jury in such doubt as to be unable to decide the controversy either way, judgment must be given against the party upon whom the burden of proof rests.
The CORRECT answer is:
A. III. II, V, IV, I, VI   B. I, II, VI, V, III, IV   C. III, IV, V, I, II, VI
D. V, I, III, VI, IV, II   E. I, V, III, VI, IV, II

6.
I. If a parent is without assets and is unemployed, he cannot be convicted of the crime of non-support of a child.
II. The term *sufficient ability* has been held to mean sufficient financial ability.
III. It does not matter if his unemployment is by choice or unavoidable circumstances.
IV. If he fails to take any steps at all, he may be liable to prosecution for endangering the welfare of a child.
V. Under the penal law, a parent is responsible for the support of his minor child only if the parent is of *sufficient ability*.
VI. An indigent parent may meet his obligation by borrowing money or by seeking aid under the provisions of the Social Welfare Law.
The CORRECT answer is:
A. VI, I, V, III, II, IV   B. I, III, V, II, IV, VI   C. V, II, I, III, VI, IV
D. I, VI, IV, V, II, III   E. II, V, I, III, VI, IV

7.
I. Consider, for example, the case of a rabble rouser who urges a group of twenty people to go out and break the windows of a nearby factory.
II. Therefore, the law fills the indicated gap with the crime of *inciting to riot*.
III. A person is considered guilty of inciting to riot when he urges ten or more persons to engage in tumultuous and violent conduct of a kind likely to create public alarm.
IV. However, if he has not obtained the cooperation of at least four people, he cannot be charged with unlawful assembly.
V. The charge of inciting to riot was added to the law to cover types of conduct which cannot be classified as either the crime of *riot* or the crime of *unlawful assembly*.
VI. If he acquires the acquiescence of at least four of them, he is guilty of unlawful assembly even if the project does not materialize.
The CORRECT answer is:
A. III, V, I, VI, IV, II   B. V, I, IV, VI, II, III   C. III, IV, I, V, II, VI
D. V, I, IV, VI, III, II   E. V, III, I, VI, IV, II

8. I. If, however, the rebuttal evidence presents an issue of credibility, it is for the jury to determine whether the presumption has, in fact, been destroyed.
    II. Once sufficient evidence to the contrary is introduced, the presumption disappears from the trial.
    III. The effect of a presumption is to place the burden upon the adversary to come forward with evidence to rebut the presumption.
    IV. When a presumption is overcome and ceases to exist in the case, the fact or facts which gave rise to the presumption still remain.
    V. Whether a presumption has been overcome is ordinarily a question for the court.
    VI. Such information may furnish a basis for a logical inference.
    The CORRECT answer is:
    A. IV, VI, II, V, I, III B. III, II, V, I, IV, VI C. V, III, VI, IV, II, I
    D. V, IV, I, II, VI, III E. II, III, V, I, IV, VI

8.____

9. I. An executive may answer a letter by writing his reply on the face of the letter itself instead of having a return letter typed.
    II. This procedure is efficient because it saves the executive's time, the typist's time, and saves office file space.
    III. Copying machines are used in small offices as well as large offices to save time and money in making brief replies to business letters.
    IV. A copy is made on a copying machine to go into the company files, while the original is mailed back to the sender.
    The CORRECT answer is:
    A. I, II, IV, III B. I, IV, II, III C. III, I, IV, II D. III, IV, II, I

9.____

10. I. Most organizations favor one of the types but always include the others to a lesser degree.
    II. However, we can detect a definite trend toward greater use of symbolic control.
    III. We suggest that our local police agencies are today primarily utilizing material control.
    IV. Control can be classified into three types: physical, material, and symbolic.
    The CORRECT answer is:
    A. IV, II, III, I B. II, I, IV, III C. III, IV, II, I D. IV, I, III, II

10.____

11. I. Project residents had first claim to this use, followed by surrounding neighborhood children.
    II. By contrast, recreation space within the project's interior was found to be used more often by both groups.
    III. Studies of the use of project grounds in many cities showed grounds left open for public use were neglected and unused, both by residents and by members of the surrounding community.
    IV. Project residents had clearly laid claim to the play spaces, setting up and enforcing unwritten rules for use.
    V. Each group, by experience, found their activities easily disrupted by other groups, and their claim to the use of space for recreation difficult to enforce.

11.____

The CORRECT answer is:
A. IV, V, I, II, III
B. V, II, IV, III, I
C. I, IV, III, II, V
D. III, V, II, IV, I

12. I. They do not consider the problems correctable within the existing subsidy formula and social policy of accepting all eligible applicants regardless of social behavior.
II. A recent survey, however, indicated that tenants believe these problems correctable by local housing authorities and management within the existing financial formula.
III. Many of the problems and complaints concerning public housing management and design have created resentment between the tenant and the landlord.
IV. This same survey indicated that administrators and managers do not agree with the tenants.
The CORRECT answer is:
A. II, I, III, IV   B. I, III, IV, II   C. III, II, IV, I   D. IV, II, I, III

13. I. In single-family residences, there is usually enough distance between tenants to prevent occupants from annoying one another.
II. For example, a certain small percentage of tenant families has one or more members addicted to alcohol.
III. While managers believe in the right of individuals to live as they choose, the manager becomes concerned when the pattern of living jeopardizes others' rights.
IV. Still others turn night into day, staging lusty entertainments which carry on into the hours when most tenants are trying to sleep.
V. In apartment buildings, however, tenants live so closely together that any misbehavior can result in unpleasant living conditions.
VI. Other families engage in violent argument.
The CORRECT answer is:
A. III, II, V, IV, VI, I
B. I, V, II, VI, IV, III
C. II, V, IV, I, III, VI
D. IV, II, V, VI, III, I

14. I. Congress made the commitment explicit in the Housing Act of 194, establishing as a national goal the realization of a *decent home and suitable environment for every American family*.
II. The result has been that the goal of decent home and suitable environment is still as far distant as ever for the disadvantaged urban family.
III. In spite of this action by Congress, federal housing programs have continued to be fragmented and grossly underfunded.
IV. The passage of the National Housing Act signaled a few federal commitment to provide housing for the nation's citizens.
The CORRECT answer is:
A. I, IV, III, II   B. IV, I, III, II   C. IV, I, II, III   D. II, IV, I, III

15. I. The greater expense does not necessarily involve *exploitation*, but it is often perceived as exploitative and unfair by those who are aware of the price differences involved, but unaware of operating costs.
   II. Ghetto residents believe they are *exploited* by local merchants, and evidence substantiates some of these beliefs.
   III. However, stores in low-income areas were more likely to be small independents, which could not achieve the economies available to supermarket chains and were, therefore, more likely to charge higher prices, and the customers were more likely to buy smaller-sized packages which are more expensive per unit of measure.
   IV. A study conducted in one city showed that distinctly higher prices were charged for goods sold in ghetto stores in other areas.

   The CORRECT answer is:
   A. IV, II, I, III B. IV, I, III, II C. II, IV, III, I D. II, III, IV, I

KEY (CORRECT ANSWERS)

1.	C	6.	C	11.	D
2.	E	7.	A	12.	C
3.	B	8.	B	13.	B
4.	B	9.	C	14.	B
5.	D	10.	D	15.	C

PREPARING WRITTEN MATERIAL

EXAMINATION SECTION

TEST 1

DIRECTIONS: The following groups of sentences need to be arranged in an order that makes sense. Select the letter preceding the sequence that represents the BEST sentence order. *PRINT THE LETTER OF THE CORRECT ANSWER IN THE SPACE AT THE RIGHT.*

1.
   I. A large Naval station on Alameda Island, near Oakland, held many warships in port, and the War Department was worried that if the bridge were to be blown up by the enemy, passage to and from the bay would be hopelessly blocked.
   II. Though many skeptics were opposed to the idea of building such an enormous bridge, the most vocal opposition came from a surprising source: the United States War Department.
   III. The War Department's concerns led to a showdown at San Francisco City Hall between Strauss and the Secretary of War, who demanded to know what would happen if a military enemy blew up the bridge.
   IV. In 1933, by submitting a construction cost estimate of $17 million, an engineer named Joseph Strauss won the contract to build the Golden Gate Bridge of San Francisco, which would then become one of the world's largest bridges.
   V. Strauss quickly ended the debate by explaining that the Golden Gate Bridge was to be a suspension bridge, whose roadway would hang in the air from cables strung between two huge towers, and would immediately sink into three hundred feet of water if it were destroyed.

   The BEST order is:
   A. II, III, I, IV, V   B. I, II, III, V, IV   C. IV, II, I, III, V   D. IV, I, III, V, II

2.
   I. Plastic surgeons have already begun to use virtual reality to map out the complex nerve and tissue structures of a particular patient's face, in order to prepare for delicate surgery.
   II. A virtual reality program responds to these movements by adjusting the images that a person sees on a screen or through goggles, thereby creating an "interactive" world in which a person can see and touch three-dimensional graphic objects.
   III. No more than a computer program that is designed to build and display graphic images, the virtual reality program takes graphic programs a step further by sensing a person's head and body movements.
   IV. The computer technology known as virtual reality, now in its very first stages of development, is already revolutionizing some aspects of contemporary life.
   V. Virtual reality computers are also being used by the space program, most recently to simulate conditions for the astronauts who were launched on a repair mission to the Hubble telescope.

The BEST order is:
A. IV, II, I, V, III B. III, I, V, II, IV C. IV, III, II, I, V D. III, I, II, IV, V

3. I. Before you plant anything, the soil in your plant bed should be carefully raked level, a small section at a time, and any clods or rocks that can't be broken up should be removed.
    II. Your plant should be placed in a hole that will position it at the same level it was at the nursery, and a small indentation should be pressed into the soil around the plant in order to hold water near its roots.
    III. Before placing the plant in the soil, lightly separate any roots that may have been matted together in the container, cutting away any thick masses that can't be separated, so that the remaining roots will be able to grow outward.
    IV. After the bed is ready, remove your plant from its container by turning it upside down and tapping or pushing on the bottom —never remove it by pulling on the plant.
    V. When you bring home a small plant in an individual container from the nursery, there are several things to remember while preparing to plant it in your own garden.
    The BEST order is:
    A. V, IV, III, II, I B. V, II, IV, III, II C. I, IV, II, III, V D. I, IV, V, II, III

4. I. The motte and its tower were usually built first, so that sentries could use it as a lookout to warn the castle workers of any danger that might approach the castle.
    II. Though the moat and palisade offered the bailey a good deal of protection, it was linked to the motte by a set of stairs that led to a retractable drawbridge at the motte's gate, to enable people to evacuate onto the motte in case of an attack.
    III. The motte of these early castles was a fortified hill, sometimes as high as one hundred feet, on which stood a palisade and tower.
    IV. The bailey was a clear, level spot below the motte, also enclosed by a palisade, which in turn was surrounded by a large trench or moat.
    V. The earliest castles built in Europe were not the magnificent stone giants that still tower over much of the European landscape, but simpler wooden constructions called motte-and-bailey castles.
    The BEST order is:
    A. V, III, I, IV, II B. V, IV, I, II, III C. I, IV, III, II, V D. I, III, II, IV, V

5. I. If an infant is left alone or abandoned for a short while, its immediate response is to cry loudly, accompanying its screams with aggressive flailing of its legs and limbs.
    II. If a child has been abandoned for a longer period of time, it becomes completely still and quiet, as if realizing that now its only chance for survival is to shut its mouth and remain motionless.
    III. Along with their intense fear of the dark, the crying behavior of human infants offers insights into how prehistoric newborn children might have evolved instincts that would prevent them from becoming victims of predators.

IV. This behavior often surprises people who enter a hospital's maternity ward for the first time and encounter total silence from a roomful of infants.
V. This violent screaming response is quite different from an infant's cries of discomfort or hunger, and seems to serve as either the child's first line of defense against an unwanted intruder, or a desperate attempt to communicate its position to the mother.

The BEST order is:
A. III, II, IV, I, V   B. III, I, V, II, IV   C. I, V, IV, II, III   D. II, IV, I, V, III

6.
I. When two cats meet who are strangers, their first actions and gestures determine who the "dominant" cat will be, at least for the time being.
II. Unlike dogs, cats are typically a solitary animal species who avoid social interaction, but they do display specific social responses to each other upon meeting.
III. This is unlikely, however; before such a point of open hostility is reached, one of the cats will usually take the "submissive" position of crouching down while looking away from the other cat.
IV. If a cat desires dominance or sees the other cat as a threat to its territory, it will stare directly at the intruder with a lowered tail.
V. If the other cat responds with a similar gesture, or with the strong defensive posture of an arched back, laid-back ears and raised tail, a fight or chase is likely if neither cat gives in.

The BEST order is:
A. IV, II, I, V, III   B. I, II, IV, V, III   C. I, IV, V, III, II   D. II, I, IV, V, III

7.
I. A star or planet's gravitational force can best be explained in this way: anything passing through this "dent" in space will veer toward the star or planet as if it were rolling into a hole.
II. Objects that are massive or heavy, such as stars or planets, "sink" into this surface, creating a sort of dent or concavity in the surrounding space.
III. Black holes, the most massive objects known to exist in space, create dents so large and deep that the space surrounding them actually folds in on itself, preventing anything that falls in —even light —from ever escaping again.
IV. The sort of dent a star or planet makes depends on how massive it is; planets generally have weak gravitational pulls, but stars, which are larger and heavier, make a bigger "dent" that will attract more matter.
V. In outer space, the force of gravity works as if the surrounding space is a soft, flat surface.

The BEST order is:
A. III, V, II, I, IV   B. III, IV, I, V, II   C. V, II, I, IV, III   D. I, V, II, IV, III

8.
I. Eventually, the society of Kyoto gave the world one of its first and greatest novels when Japan's most promising writer, Lady Murasaki Shikibu, wrote her chronicle of Kyoto's society, *The Tale of Genji*, which preceded the first European novels by more than 500 years.
II. The society of Kyoto was dedicated to the pleasures of art; the courtiers experimented with new and colorful methods of sculpture, painting, writing, decorative gardening, and even making clothes.

III. Japanese culture began under the powerful authority of Chinese Buddhism, which influenced every aspect of Japanese life from religion to politics and art.
IV. This new, vibrant culture was so sophisticated that all the people in Kyoto's imperial court considered themselves poets, and the line between life and art hardly existed —lovers corresponded entirely through written verses, and even government officials communicated by writing poems to each other.
V. In the eighth century, when the emperor established the town of Kyoto as the capital of the Japanese empire, Japanese society began to develop its own distinctive style.

The BEST order is:
   A. V, II, IV, I, III   B. II, I, V, IV, III   C. V, III, IV, I, II   D. III, V, II, IV, I

9. I. Instead of wheels, the HSST uses two sets of magnets, one which sits on the track, and another that is carried by the train; these magnets generate an identical magnetic field which forces the two sets apart.
II. In the last few decades, railway travel has become less popular throughout the world, because it is much slower than travel by airplane, and not much less expensive.
III. The HSST's designers say that the train can take passengers from one town to another as quickly as a jet plane —while consuming less than half the energy.
IV. This repellent effect is strong enough to lift the entire train above the trackway, and the train, literally traveling on air, rockets along at speeds of up to 300 miles per hour.
V. The revolutionary technology of magnetic levitation, currently being tested by Japan's experimental HSST (High Speed Surface Transport), may yet bring passenger trains back from the dead.

The BEST order is:
   A. II, V, I, IV, III   B. II, I, IV, III, V   C. V, II, III, I, IV   D. V, I, III, IV, II

9.____

10. I. When European countries first began to colonize the African continent, their impression of the African people was of a vast group of loosely organized tribal societies, without any great centralized source of power or wealth.
II. The legend of Timbuktu persisted until the nineteenth century, when a French adventurer visited Timbuktu and found that raids by neighboring tribesmen had made the city a shadow of its former self.
III. In the fifteenth century, when the stories of travelers who had traveled Africa's Sudan region began circulating around Europe, this impression began to change.
IV. In 1470, an Italian merchant named Benedetto Dei traveled to Timbuktu and confirmed these rumors, describing a thriving metropolis where rich and poor people worshipped together in the city's many ornate mosques — there was even a university in Timbuktu, much like its European counterparts, where African scholars pursued their studies in the arts and sciences.

10.____

V. The travelers' legends told of an enormous city in the western Sudan, Timbuktu, where the streets were crowded with goods brought by faraway caravans, and where there was a stone palace as large as any in Europe.

The BEST order is:

A. III, V, I, IV, II   B. I, II, IV, III, V   C. I, III, V, IV II   D. II, I, III, IV, V

11.
I. Also, our reference points in sighting the moon make us believe that its size is changing; when the moon is rising through the trees, it seems huge, because our brains unconsciously compare the size of the moon with the size of the trees in the foreground.
II. To most people, the sky itself appears more distant at the horizon than directly overhead, and if the moon's size—which remains constant—is projected from the horizon, the apparent distance of the horizon makes the moon look bigger.
III. Up higher in the sky, the moon is set against tiny stars in the background, which will make the moon seem smaller.
IV. People often wonder why the moon becomes bigger when it approaches the horizon, but most scientists agree that this is a complicated optical illusion, produced by at least three factors.
V. The moon illusion may also be partially explained by a phenomenon that has nothing to do with errors in our perception—light that enters the earth's atmosphere is sometimes refracted, and so the atmosphere may act as a kind of magnifying glass for the moon's image.

The BEST order is:

A. IV, III, V, II, I   B. IV, II, I, III, V   C. V, II, I, III, IV   D. II, I, III, IV, V

11.____

12.
I. When the Native Americans were introduced to the horses used by white explorers, they were amazed at their new alternative—here was an animal that was strong and swift, would patiently carry a person or other loads on its back, and they later discovered, was right at home on the plains.
II. Before the arrival of European explorers to North America, the natives of the American plains used large dogs to carry their travois-long lodgepoles loaded with clothing, gear, and food.
III. These horses, it is now known, were not really strangers to North America; the very first horses originated here, on this continent, tens of thousands of years ago, and migrated into Asia across the Bering Land Bridge, a strip of land that used to link our continent with the Eastern world.
IV. At first, the natives knew so little about horses that at least one tribe tried to feed their new animals pieces of dried meat and animal fat, and were surprised when the horses turned their heads away and began to eat the grass of the prairie.
V. The American horse eventually became extinct, but its Asian cousins were reintroduced to the New World when the European explorers brought them to live among the Native Americans.

The BEST order is:

A. II, I, IV, III, V   B. II, IV, I, III, V   C. I, II, IV, III, V   D. I, III, V, II, IV

12.____

13. I. The dress worn by the dancer is believed to have been adorned in the past by shells which would strike each other as the dancer performed, creating a lovely sound.
    II. Today's jingle-dress is decorated with the tin lids of snuff cans, which are rolled into cones and sewn onto the dress,
    III. During the jingle-dress dance, the dancer must blend complicated footwork with a series of gentle hos that cause the cones to jingle in rhythm to a drumbeat.
    IV. When contemporary Native American tribes meet for a pow-wow, one of the most popular ceremonies to take place is the women's jingle-dress dance.
    V. Besides being more readily available than shells, the lids are thought by many dancers to create a softer, more subtle sound.
    The BEST order is:
    A. II, IV, V, I, III   B. IV, II, I, III, V   C. II, I, III, V, IV   D. IV, I, II, V, III

14. I. If a homeowner lives where seasonal climates are extreme, deciduous shade trees—which will drop their leaves in the winter and allow sunlight to pass through the windows—should be planted near the southern exposure in order to keep the house cool during the summer.
    II. This trajectory is shorter and lower in the sky than at any other time of year during the winter, when a house most requires heating; the northern-facing parts of a house do not receive any direct sunlight at all.
    III. In designing an energy-efficient house, especially in colder climates, it is important to remember that most of the house's windows should face south.
    IV. Though the sun always rises in the east and sets in the west, the sun of the northern hemisphere is permanently situated in the southern portion of the sky.
    V. The explanation for why so many architects and builders want this "southern exposure" is related to the path of the sun in the sky.
    The BEST order is:
    A. III, I, V, IV, II   B. III, V, IV, II, I   C. I, III, IV, II, V   D. I, II, V, IV, III

15. I. His journeying lasted twenty-four years and took him over an estimated 75,000 miles, a distance that would not be surpassed by anyone other than Magellan—who sailed around the world—for another six hundred years.
    II. Perhaps the most far-flung of these lesser-known travelers was Ibn Batuta, an African Moslem who left his birthplace of Tangier in the summer of 1325.
    III. Ibn Batuta traveled all over Africa and Asia, from Niger to Peking, and to the islands of Maldive and Indonesia.
    IV. However, a few explorers of the Eastern world logged enough miles and adventures to make Marco Polo's voyage look like an evening stroll.
    V. In America, the most well-known of the Old World's explorers are usually Europeans such as Marco Polo, the Italian who brought many elements of Chinese culture to the Western world.
    The BEST order is:
    A. V, IV, II, III, I   B. V, IV, III, II, I   C. III, II, I, IV, V   D. II, III, I, IV, V

16. I. In the rainforests of South America, a rare species of frog practices a reproductive method that is entirely different from this standard process.
    II. She will eventually carry each of the tadpoles up into the canopy and drop each into its own little pool, where it will be easy to locate and safe from most predators.
    III. After fertilization, the female of the species, who lives almost entirely on the forest floor, lays between 2 and 16 eggs among the leaf litter at the base of a tree, and stands watch over these eggs until they hatch.
    IV. Most frogs are pond-dwellers who are able to deposit hundreds of eggs in the water and then leave them alone, knowing that enough eggs have been laid to insure the survival of some of their offspring.
    V. Once the tadpoles emerge, the female backs in among them, and a tadpole will wriggle onto her back to be carried high into the forest canopy, where the female will deposit it in a little pool of water cupped in the leaf of a plant.
    The BEST order is:
    A. I, IV, III, II, V   B. I, III, V, II, IV   C. IV, III, II, V, I   D. IV, I, III, V, II

16._____

17. I. Eratosthenes had heard from travelers that at exactly noon on June 21, in the ancient city of Aswan, Egypt, the sun cast no shadow in a well, which meant that the sun must be directly overhead.
    II. He knew the sun always cast a shadow in Alexandria and so he figured that if he could measure the length of an Alexandria shadow at the time when there was no shadow in Aswan, he could calculate the angle of the sun, and therefore the circumference of the earth.
    III. The evidence for a round earth was not new in 1492; in fact, Eratosthenes, an Alexandrian geographer who lived nearly sixteen centuries before Columbus's voyage (275-195 B.C.), actually developed a method for calculating the circumference of the earth that is still in use today.
    IV. Eratosthenes's method was correct, but his result—28,700 miles—was about 15 percent too high, probably because of the inaccurate ancient methods of keeping time, and because Aswan was not due south of Alexandria, as Eratosthenes had believed.
    V. When Christopher Columbus sailed across the Atlantic Ocean for the first time in 1492, there were still some people in the world who ignored scientific evidence and believed that the earth was flat, rather than round.
    The BEST order is:
    A. I, II, V, III, IV   B. V, III, IV, I, II   C. V, III, I, II, IV   D. III, V, I, II, IV

17._____

18. I. The first name for the child is considered a trial naming, often impersonal and neutral, such as the Ngoni name *Chabwera*, meaning "it has arrived."
    II. This sort of name is not due to any parental indifference to the child, but is a kind of silent recognition of Africa's sometimes high infant death rate; most parents ease the pain of losing a child with the belief that it is not really a person until it has been given a final name.
    III. In many tribal African societies families often give two different names to their children, at different periods in time.
    IV. After the trial naming period has subsided and it is clear that the child will survive, the parents choose a final name for the child, an act that symbolically completes the act of birth.

18._____

V. In fact, some African first-given names are explicitly uncomplimentary, translating as "I am dead" or "I am ugly," in order to avoid the jealousy of ancestral spirits who might wish to take a child that is especially healthy or attractive.

The BEST order is:
A. III, I, II, V, IV B. III, IV, II, I, V C. IV, III, I, II, V D. IV, V, III, I, II

19. I. Though uncertain of the definite reasons for this behavior, scientists believe the birds digest the clay in order to counteract toxins contained in the seeds of certain fruits that are eaten by macaws.
   II. For example, all macaws flock to riverbanks at certain times of the year to eat the clay that is found in river mud.
   III. The macaws of South America are not only among the largest and most beautifully colored of the world's flying birds, but they are also one of the smartest.
   IV. It is believed that macaws are forced to resort to these toxic fruits during the dry season, when foods are more scarce.
   V. The macaw's intelligence has led to intense study by scientists, who have discovered some macaw behaviors that have not yet been explained.

The BEST order is:
A. III, IV, I, II, V B. III, V, II, I, IV C. V, II, I, IV, III D. IV, I, II, III, V

20. I. Although Maggie Kuhn has since passed away, the Gray Panthers are still waging a campaign to reinstate the historical view of the elderly as people whose experience allows them to make their greatest contribution in their later years.
   II. In 1972, an elderly woman named Maggie Kuhn responded to this sort of treatment by forming a group called the Gray Panthers, an organization of both old and young adults with the common goal of creating change.
   III. This attitude is reflected strongly in the way elderly people are treated by our society; many are forced into early retirement, or are placed in rest homes in which they are isolated from their communities.
   IV. Unlike most other cultures around the world, Americans tend to look upon old age with a sense of dread and sadness.
   V. Kuhn believed that when the elderly are forced to withdraw into lives that lack purpose, society loses one of its greatest resources: people who have a lifetime of experience and wisdom to offer their communities.

The BEST order is:
A. IV, III, II, V, I B. IV, II, I, III, V C. II, IV, III, V, I D. II, I, IV, III, V

21. I. The current theory among most anthropologists is that humans evolved from apes who lived in trees near the grasslands of Africa.
   II. Still, some anthropologists insist that such an invention was necessary for the survival of early humans, and point to the Kung Bushmen of central Africa as a society in which the sling is still used in this way.
   III. Two of these inventions—fire, and weapons such as spears and clubs—were obvious defenses against predators, and there is archaeological evidence to support the theory of their use.

IV. Once people had evolved enough to leave the safety of trees and walk upright, they needed the protection of several inventions in order to survive.
V. But another invention, a feather or fiber sling that allowed mothers to carry children while leaving their hands free to gather roots or berries, would certainly have decomposed and left behind no trace of itself.

The BEST order is:
A. I, II, III, V, IV   B. IV, I, II, III, V   C. I, IV, III, V, II   D. IV, III, V, II, I

22. I. The person holding the bird should keep it in hot water up to its neck, and the person cleaning should work a mild solution of dishwashing liquid into the bird's plumage, paying close attention to the head and neck.
II. When rinsing the bird, after all the oil has been removed, the running water should be directed against the lay of its feathers, until water begins to bead off the surface of the feathers—a sign that all the detergent has been rinsed out.
III. If you have rescued a sea bird from an oil spill and want to restore it to clean and normal living, you need a large sink, a constant supply of running hot water (a little over 100°F), and regular dishwashing liquid.
IV. This cleaning with detergent solution should be repeated as many times as it takes to remove all traces of oil from the bird's feathers, sometime over a period of several days.
V. But before you begin to clean the bird, you must find a partner because cleaning an oiled bird is a two-person job.

The BEST order is:
A. III, I, II, IV, V   B. III, V, I, IV, II   C. III, I, IV, V II   D. III, IV, V, I, II

23. I. The most difficult time of year for the Tsaatang is the spring calving, when the reindeer leave their wintering ground and rush to their accustomed calving place, without stopping by night or by day.
II. Reindeer travel in herds, and though some animals are tamed by the Tsaatang for riding or milking, the herds are allowed to roam free.
III. This journey is hard for the Tsaatang, who carry all their possessions with them, but once it's over it proves worthwhile; the Tsaatang can immediately begin to gather milk from reindeer cows who have given birth.
IV. The Tsaatang, a small tribe who live in the far northwest corner of Mongolia, practice a lifestyle that is completely dependent on the reindeer, their main resource for food, clothing, and transport.
V. The people must follow their yearly migrations, living in portable shelters that resemble Native American tepees.

The BEST order is:
A. I, III, II, V, IV   B. I, IV, II, V, III   C. IV, I, III, V, II   D. IV II, V, I, III

24. I. The Romans later improved this system by installing these heated pipe networks throughout walls and ceilings, supplying heat to even the uppermost floors of a building—a system that, to this day, hasn't been much improved.
II. Air-conditioning, the method by which humans control indoor temperatures, was practiced much earlier than most people think.

III. The earliest heating devices other than open fires were used in 350 B.C. by the ancient Greeks, who directed air that had been heated by underground fires into baked clay pipes that ran under the floor.
IV. Ironically, the first successful cooling system, patented in England in 1831, used fire as its main energy source—fires were lit in the attic of a building, creating an updraft of air that drew cool air into the building through ducts that had underground openings near the river Thames.
V. Cooling buildings was more of a challenge, and wasn't attempted until 1500: a water-based system, designed by Leonardo da Vinci, does not appear to have been successful, since it was never used again.
The BEST order is:
   A. III, V, IV, I, II   B. III, I, II, V, IV   C. II, III, I, V, IV   D. IV, II, III, I, V

25. I. Cold, dry air from Canada passes over the Rocky Mountains and sweeps down onto the plains, where it collides with warm, moist air from the waters of the Gulf of Mexico, and when the two air masses meet, the resulting disturbance sometimes forms a violent funnel cloud that strikes the earth and destroys virtually everything in its path.
II. Hurricanes, storms which are generally not this violent and last much longer, are usually given names by meteorologists, but this tradition cannot be applied to tornados, which have a life span measured in minutes and disappear in the same way as they are born—unnamed.
III. A tornado funnel forms rotating columns of air whose speed reaches three hundred miles an hour—a speed that can only be estimated, because no wind-measuring devices in the direct path of a storm have ever survived.
IV. The natural phenomena known as tornados occur primarily over the Midwestern grasslands of the United States.
V. It is here, meteorologists tell us, that conditions for the formation of tornados are sometimes perfect during the spring months.
The BEST order is:
   A. II, IV, V, I, III   B. II, III, I, V, IV   C. IV, V, I, III, II   D. IV, III, I, V, II

KEY (CORRECT ANSWERS)

1.	C		11.	B
2.	C		12.	A
3.	B		13.	D
4.	A		14.	B
5.	B		15.	A
6.	D		16.	D
7.	C		17.	C
8.	D		18.	A
9.	A		19.	B
10.	C		20.	A

21. C
22. B
23. D
24. C
25. C

PHILOSOPHY, PRINCIPLES, PRACTICES, AND TECHNICS OF SUPERVISION, ADMINISTRATION, MANAGEMENT, AND ORGANIZATION

TABLE OF CONTENTS

	Page
MEANING OF SUPERVISION	1
THE OLD AND THE NEW SUPERVISION	1
THE EIGHT (8) BASIC PRINCIPLES OF THE NEW SUPERVISION	1
I. Principle of Responsibility	1
II. Principle of Authority	2
III. Principle of Self-Growth	2
IV. Principle of Individual Worth	2
V. Principle of Creative Leadership	2
VI. Principle of Success and Failure	2
VII. Principle of Science	3
VIII. Principle of Cooperation	3
WHAT IS ADMINISTRATION?	3
I. Practices Commonly Classed as "Supervisory"	3
II. Practices Commonly Classed as "Administrative"	3
III. Practices Commonly Classed as Both "Supervisory" and "Administrative"	4
RESPONSIBILITIES OF THE SUPERVISOR	4
COMPETENCIES OF THE SUPERVISOR	4
THE PROFESSIONAL SUPERVISOR-EMPLOYEE RELATIONSHIP	4
MINI-TEXT IN SUPERVISION, ADMINISTRATION, MANAGEMENT, AND ORGANIZATION	5
I. Brief Highlights	5
A. Levels of Management	6
B. What the Supervisor Must Learn	6
C. A Definition of Supervision	6
D. Elements of the Team Concept	6
E. Principles of Organization	6
F. The Four Important Parts of Every Job	7
G. Principles of Delegation	7
H. Principles of Effective Communications	7
I. Principles of Work Improvement	7
J. Areas of Job Improvement	7
K. Seven Key Points in Making Improvements	8

	L.	Corrective Techniques for Job Improvement	8
	M.	A Planning Checklist	8
	N.	Five Characteristics of Good Directions	9
	O.	Types of Directions	9
	P.	Controls	9
	Q.	Orienting the New Employee	9
	R.	Checklist for Orienting New Employees	9
	S.	Principles of Learning	10
	T.	Causes of Poor Performance	10
	U.	Four Major Steps in On-the-Job Instructions	10
	V.	Employees Want Five Things	10
	W.	Some Don'ts in Regard to Praise	11
	X.	How to Gain Your Workers' Confidence	11
	Y.	Sources of Employee Problems	11
	Z.	The Supervisor's Key to Discipline	11
	AA.	Five Important Processes of Management	12
	BB.	When the Supervisor Fails to Plan	12
	CC.	Fourteen General Principles of Management	12
	DD.	Change	12

II. Brief Topical Summaries — 13
   A. Who/What is the Supervisor? — 13
   B. The Sociology of Work — 13
   C. Principles and Practices of Supervision — 14
   D. Dynamic Leadership — 14
   E. Processes for Solving Problems — 15
   F. Training for Results — 15
   G. Health, Safety, and Accident Prevention — 16
   H. Equal Employment Opportunity — 16
   I. Improving Communications — 16
   J. Self-Development — 17
   K. Teaching and Training — 17
     1. The Teaching Process — 17
       a. Preparation — 17
       b. Presentation — 18
       c. Summary — 18
       d. Application — 18
       e. Evaluation — 18
     2. Teaching Methods — 18
       a. Lecture — 18
       b. Discussion — 18
       c. Demonstration — 19
       d. Performance — 19
       e. Which Method to Use — 19

PHILOSOPHY, PRINCIPLES, PRACTICES, AND TECHNICS OF SUPERVISION, ADMINISTRATION, MANAGEMENT, AND ORGANIZATION

MEANING OF SUPERVISION

The extension of the democratic philosophy has been accompanied by an extension in the scope of supervision. Modern leaders and supervisors no longer think of supervision in the narrow sense of being confined chiefly to visiting employees, supplying materials, or rating the staff. They regard supervision as being intimately related to al the concerned agencies of society, they speak of the supervisor's function in terms of "growth," rather than the "improvement" of employees.

This modern concept of supervision may be defined as follows: Supervision is leadership and the development of leadership within groups which are cooperatively engaged in inspection, research, training, guidance, and evaluation.

THE OLD AND THE NEW SUPERVISION

TRADITIONAL
1. Inspection
2. Focused on the employee
3. Visitation
4. Random and haphazard
5. Imposed and authoritarian
6. One person usually

MODERN
1. Study and analysis
2. Focused on aims, materials, methods, supervisors, employees, environment
3. Demonstrations, intervisitation, workshops, directed reading, bulletins, etc.
4. Definitely organized and planned (scientific)
5. Cooperative and democratic
6. Many persons involved (creative)

THE EIGHT (8) BASIC PRINCIPLES OF THE NEW SUPERVISION

I. Principle of Responsibility
   Authority to act and responsibility for acting must be joined.
   A. If you give responsibility, give authority.
   B. Define employee duties clearly.
   C. Protect employees from criticism by others.
   D. Recognize the rights as well as obligations of employees.
   E. Achieve the aims of a democratic society insofar as it is possible within the area of your work.
   F. Establish a situation favorable to training and learning.
   G. Accept ultimate responsibility for everything done in your section, unit, office, division, department.
   H. Good administration and good supervision are inseparable.

II. Principle of Authority
   The success of the supervisor is measured by the extent to which the power of authority is not used.
   A. Exercise simplicity and informality in supervision
   B. Use the simplest machinery of supervision
   C. If it is good for the organization as a whole, it is probably justified.
   D. Seldom be arbitrary or authoritative.
   E. Do not base your work on the power of position or of personality.
   F. Permit and encourage the free expression of opinions.

III. Principle of Self-Growth
   The success of the supervisor is measured by the extent to which, and the speed with which, he is no longer needed.
   A. Base criticism on principles, not on specifics.
   B. Point out higher activities to employees.
   C. Train for self-thinking by employees to meet new situations.
   D. Stimulate initiative, self-reliance, and individual responsibility
   E. Concentrate on stimulating the growth of employees rather than on removing defects.

IV. Principle of Individual Worth
   Respect for the individual is a paramount consideration in supervision.
   A. Be human and sympathetic in dealing with employees.
   B. Don't nag about things to be done.
   C. Recognize the individual differences among employees and seek opportunities to permit best expression of each personality.

V. Principle of Creative Leadership
   The best supervision is that which is not apparent to the employee.
   A. Stimulate, don't drive employees to creative action.
   B. Emphasize doing good things.
   C. Encourage employees to do what they do best.
   D. Do not be too greatly concerned with details of subject or method.
   E. Do not be concerned exclusively with immediate problems and activities.
   F. Reveal higher activities and make them both desired and maximally possible.
   G. Determine procedures in the light of each situation but see that these are derived from a sound basic philosophy.
   H. Aid, inspire, and lead so as to liberate the creative spirit latent in all good employees.

VI. Principle of Success and Failure
   There are no unsuccessful employees, only unsuccessful supervisors who have failed to give proper leadership.
   A. Adapt suggestions to the capacities, attitudes, and prejudices of employees.
   B. Be gradual, be progressive, be persistent.
   C. Help the employee find the general principle; have the employee apply his own problem to the general principle.
   D. Give adequate appreciation for good work and honest effort.
   E. Anticipate employee difficulties and help to prevent them.
   F. Encourage employees to do the desirable things they will do anyway.
   G. Judge your supervision by the results it secures.

VII. Principle of Science
Successful supervision is scientific, objective, and experimental. It is based on facts, not on prejudices.
- A. Be cumulative in results.
- B. Never divorce your suggestions from the goals of training.
- C. Don't be impatient of results.
- D. Keep all matters on a professional, not a personal, level.
- E. Do not be concerned exclusively with immediate problems and activities.
- F. Use objective means of determining achievement and rating where possible.

VIII. Principle of Cooperation
Supervision is a cooperative enterprise between supervisor and employee.
- A. Begin with conditions as they are.
- B. Ask opinions of all involved when formulating policies.
- C. Organization is as good as its weakest link.
- D. Let employees help to determine policies and department programs.
- E. Be approachable and accessible—physically and mentally.
- F. Develop pleasant social relationships.

WHAT IS ADMINISTRATION

Administration is concerned with providing the environment, the material facilities, and the operational procedures that will promote the maximum growth and development of supervisors and employees. (Organization is an aspect and a concomitant of administration.)

There is no sharp line of demarcation between supervision and administration; these functions are intimately interrelated and, often, overlapping. They are complementary activities.

I. Practices Commonly Classed as "Supervisory"
- A. Conducting employees' conferences
- B. Visiting sections, units, offices, divisions, departments
- C. Arranging for demonstrations
- D. Examining plans
- E. Suggesting professional reading
- F. Interpreting bulletins
- G. Recommending in-service training courses
- H. Encouraging experimentation
- I. Appraising employee morale
- J. Providing for intervisitation

II. Practices Commonly Classified as "Administrative"
- A. Management of the office
- B. Arrangement of schedules for extra duties
- C. Assignment of rooms or areas
- D. Distribution of supplies
- E. Keeping records and reports
- F. Care of audio-visual materials
- G. Keeping inventory records
- H. Checking record cards and books

I. Programming special activities
　　　J. Checking on the attendance and punctuality of employees

III. Practices Commonly Classified as Both "Supervisory" and "Administrative"
　　A. Program construction
　　B. Testing or evaluating outcomes
　　C. Personnel accounting
　　D. Ordering instructional materials

RESPONSIBILITIES OF THE SUPERVISOR

A person employed in a supervisory capacity must constantly be able to improve his own efficiency and ability. He represent the employer to the employees and only continuous self-examination can make him a capable supervisor.

Leadership and training are the supervisor's responsibility. An efficient working unit is one in which the employees work with the supervisor. It is his job to bring out the best in his employees. He must always be relaxed, courteous, and calm in his association with his employees. Their feelings are important, and a harsh attitude does not develop the most efficient employees.

COMPETENCES OF THE SUPERVISOR

　　I. Complete knowledge of the duties and responsibilities of his position.
　　II. To be able to organize a job, plan ahead, and carry through.
　　III. To have self-confidence and initiative.
　　IV. To be able to handle the unexpected situation and make quick decisions.
　　V. To be able to properly train subordinates in the positions they are best suited for.
　　VI. To be able to keep good human relations among his subordinates.
　　VII. To be able to keep good human relations between his subordinates and himself and to earn their respect and trust.

THE PROFESSIONAL SUPERVISOR-EMPLOYEE RELATIONSHIP

There are two kinds of efficiency: one kind is only apparent and is produced in organizations through the exercise of mere discipline; this is but a simulation of the second, or true, efficiency which springs from spontaneous cooperation. If you are a manager, no matter how great or small your responsibility, it is your job, in the final analysis, to create and develop this involuntary cooperation among the people whom you supervise. For, no matter how powerful a combination of money, machines, and materials a company may have, this is a dead and sterile thing without a team of willing, thinking, and articulate people to guide it.

The following 21 points are presented as indicative of the exemplary basic relationship that should exist between supervisor and employee:

1. Each person wants to be liked and respected by his fellow employee and wants to be treated with consideration and respect by his superior.
2. The most competent employee will make an error. However, in a unit where good relations exist between the supervisor and his employees, tenseness and fear do not exist. Thus, errors are not hidden or covered up, and the efficiency of a unit is not impaired.

3. Subordinates resent rules, regulations, or orders that are unreasonable or unexplained.
4. Subordinates are quick to resent unfairness, harshness, injustices, and favoritism.
5. An employee will accept responsibility if he knows that he will be complimented for a job well done, and not too harshly chastised for failure; that his supervisor will check the cause of the failure, and, if it was the supervisor's fault, he will assume the blame therefore. If it was the employee's fault, his supervisor will explain the correct method or means of handling the responsibility.
6. An employee wants to receive credit for a suggestion he has made, that is used. If a suggestion cannot be used, the employee is entitled to an explanation. The supervisor should not say "no" and close the subject.
7. Fear and worry slow up a worker's ability. Poor working environment can impair his physical and mental health. A good supervisor avoids forceful methods, threats, and arguments to get a job done.
8. A forceful supervisor is able to train his employees individually and as a team, and is able to motivate them in the proper channels.
9. A mature supervisor is able to properly evaluate his subordinates and to keep them happy and satisfied.
10. A sensitive supervisor will never patronize his subordinates.
11. A worthy supervisor will respect his employees' confidences.
12. Definite and clear-cut responsibilities should be assigned to each executive.
13. Responsibility should always be coupled with corresponding authority.
14. No change should be made in the scope or responsibilities of a position without a definite understanding to that effect on the part of all persons concerned.
15. No executive or employee, occupying a single position in the organization, should be subject to definite orders from more than one source.
16. Orders should never be given to subordinates over the head of a responsible executive. Rather than do this, the officer in question should be supplanted.
17. Criticisms of subordinates should, whoever possible, be made privately, and in no case should a subordinate be criticized in the presence of executives or employees of equal or lower rank.
18. No dispute or difference between executives or employees as to authority or responsibilities should be considered too trivial for prompt and careful adjudication.
19. Promotions, wage changes, and disciplinary action should always be approved by the executive immediately superior to the one directly responsible.
20. No executive or employee should ever be required, or expected, to be at the same time an assistant to, and critic of, another.
21. Any executive whose work is subject to regular inspection should, wherever practicable, be given the assistance and facilities necessary to enable him to maintain an independent check of the quality of his work.

MINI-TEXT IN SUPERVISION, ADMINISTRATION, MANAGEMENT, AND ORGANIZATION

I. Brief Highlights

Listed concisely and sequentially are major headings and important data in the field for quick recall and review.

A. Levels of Management
Any organization of some size has several levels of management. In terms of a ladder, the levels are:

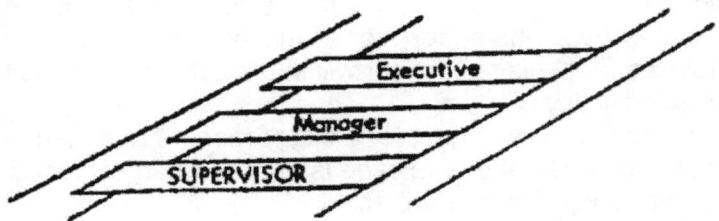

The first level is very important because it is the beginning point of management leadership.

B. What the Supervisor Must Learn
A supervisor must learn to:
1. Deal with people and their differences
2. Get the job done through people
3. Recognize the problems when they exist
4. Overcome obstacles to good performance
5. Evaluate the performance of people
6. Check his own performance in terms of accomplishment

C. A Definition of Supervisor
The term supervisor means any individual having authority, in the interests of the employer, to hire, transfer, suspend, lay-off, recall, promote, discharge, assign, reward, or discipline other employees or responsibility to direct them, or to adjust their grievances, or effectively to recommend such action, if, in connection with the foregoing, exercise of such authority is not of a merely routine or clerical nature but requires the use of independent judgment.

D. Elements of the Team Concept
What is involved in teamwork? The component parts are:
1. Members
2. A leader
3. Goals
4. Plans
5. Cooperation
6. Spirit

E. Principles of Organization
1. A team member must know what his job is.
2. Be sure that the nature and scope of a job are understood.
3. Authority and responsibility should be carefully spelled out.
4. A supervisor should be permitted to make the maximum number of decisions affecting his employees.
5. Employees should report to only one supervisor.
6. A supervisor should direct only as many employees as he can handle effectively.
7. An organization plan should be flexible.

8. Inspection and performance of work should be separate.
9. Organizational problems should receive immediate attention.
10. Assign work in line with ability and experience.

F. The Four Important Parts of Every Job
1. Inherent in every job is the *accountability* for results.
2. A second set of factors in every job is *responsibilities*.
3. Along with duties and responsibilities one must have the *authority* to act within certain limits without obtaining permission to proceed.
4. No job exists in a vacuum. The supervisor is surrounded by key *relationships*.

G. Principles of Delegation
Where work is delegated for the first time, the supervisor should think in terms of these questions:
1. Who is best qualified to do this?
2. Can an employee improve his abilities by doing this?
3. How long should an employee spend on this?
4. Are there any special problems for which he will need guidance?
5. How broad a delegation can I make?

H. Principles of Effective Communications
1. Determine the media.
2. To whom directed?
3. Identification and source authority.
4. Is communication understood?

I. Principles of Work Improvement
1. Most people usually do only the work which is assigned to them.
2. Workers are likely to fit assigned work into the time available to perform it.
3. A good workload usually stimulates output.
4. People usually do their best work when they know that results will be reviewed or inspected.
5. Employees usually feel that someone else is responsible for conditions of work, workplace layout, job methods, type of tools/equipment, and other such factors.
6. Employees are usually defensive about their job security.
7. Employees have natural resistance to change.
8. Employees can support or destroy a supervisor.
9. A supervisor usually earns the respect of his people through his personal example of diligence and efficiency.

J. Areas of Job Improvement
The areas of job improvement are quite numerous, but the most common ones which a supervisor can identify and utilize are:
1. Departmental layout
2. Flow of work
3. Workplace layout
4. Utilization of manpower
5. Work methods
6. Materials handling

7. Utilization
8. Motion economy

K. Seven Key Points in Making Improvements
1. Select the job to be improved
2. Study how it is being done now
3. Question the present method
4. Determine actions to be taken
5. Chart proposed method
6. Get approval and apply
7. Solicit worker participation

I. Corrective Techniques of Job Improvement
Specific Problems
1. Size of workload
2. Inability to meet schedules
3. Strain and fatigue
4. Improper use of men and skills
5. Waste, poor quality, unsafe conditions
6. Bottleneck conditions that hinder output
7. Poor utilization of equipment and machine
8. Efficiency and productivity of labor

General Improvement
1. Departmental layout
2. Flow of work
3. Work plan layout
4. Utilization of manpower
5. Work methods
6. Materials handling
7. Utilization of equipment
8. Motion economy

Corrective Techniques
1. Study with scale model
2. Flow chart study
3. Motion analysis
4. Comparison of units produced to standard allowance
5. Methods analysis
6. Flow chart and equipment study
7. Down time vs. running time
8. Motion analysis

M. A Planning Checklist
1. Objectives
2. Controls
3. Delegations
4. Communications
5. Resources
6. Manpower

7. Equipment
8. Supplies and materials
9. Utilization of time
10. Safety
11. Money
12. Work
13. Timing of improvements

N. Five Characteristics of Good Directions
In order to get results, directions must be:
1. Possible of accomplishment
2. Agreeable with worker interests
3. Related to mission
4. Planned and complete
5. Unmistakably clear

O. Types of Directions
1. Demands or direct orders
2. Requests
3. Suggestion or implication
4. volunteering

P. Controls
A typical listing of the overall areas in which the supervisor should establish controls might be:
1. Manpower
2. Materials
3. Quality of work
4. Quantity of work
5. Time
6. Space
7. Money
8. Methods

Q. Orienting the New Employee
1. Prepare for him
2. Welcome the new employee
3. Orientation for the job
4. Follow-up

R. Checklist for Orienting New Employees

	Yes	No
1. Do you appreciate the feelings of new employees when they first report for work?	___	___
2. Are you aware of the fact that the new employee must make a big adjustment to his job?	___	___
3. Have you given him good reasons for liking the job and the organization?	___	___
4. Have you prepared for his first day on the job?	___	___
5. Did you welcome him cordially and make him feel needed?	___	___

		Yes	No

6. Did you establish rapport with him so that he feels free to talk and discuss matters with you? ___ ___
7. Did you explain his job to him and his relationship to you? ___ ___
8. Does he know that his work will be evaluated periodically on a basis that is fair and objective? ___ ___
9. Did you introduce him to his fellow workers in such a way that they are likely to accept him? ___ ___
10. Does he know what employee benefits he will receive? ___ ___
11. Does he understand the importance of being on the job and what to do if he must leave his duty station? ___ ___
12. Has he been impressed with the importance of accident prevention and safe practice? ___ ___
13. Does he generally know his way around the department? ___ ___
14. Is he under the guidance of a sponsor who will teach the right way of doing things? ___ ___
15. Do you plan to follow-up so that he will continue to adjust successfully to his job? ___ ___

S. Principles of Learning
 1. Motivation
 2. Demonstration or explanation
 3. Practice

T. Causes of Poor Performance
 1. Improper training for job
 2. Wrong tools
 3. Inadequate directions
 4. Lack of supervisory follow-up
 5. Poor communications
 6. Lack of standards of performance
 7. Wrong work habits
 8. Low morale
 9. Other

U. Four Major Steps in On-The-Job Instruction
 1. Prepare the worker
 2. Present the operation
 3. Tryout performance
 4. Follow-up

V. Employees Want Five Things
 1. Security
 2. Opportunity
 3. Recognition
 4. Inclusion
 5. Expression

W. Some Don'ts in Regard to Praise
1. Don't praise a person for something he hasn't done.
2. Don't praise a person unless you can be sincere.
3. Don't be sparing in praise just because your superior withholds it from you.
4. Don't let too much time elapse between good performance and recognition of it

X. How to Gain Your Workers' Confidence
Methods of developing confidence include such things as:
1. Knowing the interests, habits, hobbies of employees
2. Admitting your own inadequacies
3. Sharing and telling of confidence in others
4. Supporting people when they are in trouble
5. Delegating matters that can be well handled
6. Being frank and straightforward about problems and working conditions
7. Encouraging others to bring their problems to you
8. Taking action on problems which impede worker progress

Y. Sources of Employee Problems
On-the-job causes might be such things as:
1. A feeling that favoritism is exercised in assignments
2. Assignment of overtime
3. An undue amount of supervision
4. Changing methods or systems
5. Stealing of ideas or trade secrets
6. Lack of interest in job
7. Threat of reduction in force
8. Ignorance or lack of communications
9. Poor equipment
10. Lack of knowing how supervisor feels toward employee
11. Shift assignments

Off-the-job problems might have to do with:
1. Health
2. Finances
3. Housing
4. Family

Z. The Supervisor's Key to Discipline
There are several key points about discipline which the supervisor should keep in mind:
1. Job discipline is one of the disciplines of life and is directed by the supervisor.
2. It is more important to correct an employee fault than to fix blame for it.
3. Employee performance is affected by problems both on the job and off.
4. Sudden or abrupt changes in behavior can be indications of important employee problems.
5. Problems should be dealt with as soon as possible after they are identified.
6. The attitude of the supervisor may have more to do with solving problems than the techniques of problem solving.
7. Correction of employee behavior should be resorted to only after the supervisor is sure that training or counseling will not be helpful.

8. Be sure to document your disciplinary actions.
9. Make sure that you are disciplining on the basis of facts rather than personal feelings.
10. Take each disciplinary step in order, being careful not to make snap judgments, or decisions based on impatience.

AA. Five Important Processes of Management
1. Planning
2. Organizing
3. Scheduling
4. Controlling
5. Motivating

BB. When the Supervisor Fails to Plan
1. Supervisor creates impression of not knowing his job
2. May lead to excessive overtime
3. Job runs itself—supervisor lacks control
4. Deadlines and appointments missed
5. Parts of the work go undone
6. Work interrupted by emergencies
7. Sets a bad example
8. Uneven workload creates peaks and valleys
9. Too much time on minor details at expense of more important tasks

CC. Fourteen General Principles of Management
1. Division of work
2. Authority and responsibility
3. Discipline
4. Unity of command
5. Unity of direction
6. Subordination of individual interest to general interest
7. Remuneration of personnel
8. Centralization
9. Scalar chain
10. Order
11. Equity
12. Stability of tenure of personnel
13. Initiative
14. Esprit de corps

DD. Change

Bringing about change is perhaps attempted more often, and yet less well understood, than anything else the supervisor does. How do people generally react to change? (People tend to resist change that is imposed upon them by other individuals or circumstances.

Change is characteristic of every situation. It is a part of every real endeavor where the efforts of people are concerned.

13

1. Why do people resist change?
   People may resist change because of:
   a. Fear of the unknown
   b. Implied criticism
   c. Unpleasant experiences in the past
   d. Fear of loss of status
   e. Threat to the ego
   f. Fear of loss of economic stability

2. How can we best overcome the resistance to change?
   In initiating change, take these steps:
   a. Get ready to sell
   b. Identify sources of help
   c. Anticipate objections
   d. Sell benefits
   e. Listen in depth
   f. Follow up

II. Brief Topical Summaries

  A. Who/What is the Supervisor?
   1. The supervisor is often called the "highest level employee and the lowest level manager."
   2. A supervisor is a member of both management and the work group. He acts as a bridge between the two.
   3. Most problems in supervision are in the area of human relations, or people problems.
   4. Employees expect: Respect, opportunity to learn and to advance, and a sense of belonging, and so forth.
   5. Supervisors are responsible for directing people and organizing work. Planning is of paramount importance.
   6. A position description is a set of duties and responsibilities inherent to a given position.
   7. It is important to keep the position description up-to-date and to provide each employee with his own copy.

  B. The Sociology of Work
   1. People are alike in many ways; however, each individual is unique.
   2. The supervisor is challenged in getting to know employee differences. Acquiring skills in evaluating individuals is an asset.
   3. Maintaining meaningful working relationships in the organization is of great importance.
   4. The supervisor has an obligation to help individuals to develop to their fullest potential.
   5. Job rotation on a planned basis helps to build versatility and to maintain interest and enthusiasm in work groups.
   6. Cross training (job rotation) provides backup skills.

7. The supervisor can help reduce tension by maintaining a sense of humor, providing guidance to employees, and by making reasonable and timely decisions. Employees respond favorably to working under reasonably predictable circumstances.
8. Change is characteristic of all managerial behavior. The supervisor must adjust to changes in procedures, new methods, technological changes, and to a number of new and sometimes challenging situations.
9. To overcome the natural tendency for people to resist change, the supervisor should become more skillful in initiating change.

C. Principles and Practices of Supervision
1. Employees should be required to answer to only one superior.
2. A supervisor can effectively direct only a limited number of employees, depending upon the complexity, variety, and proximity of the jobs involved.
3. The organizational chart presents the organization in graphic form. It reflects lines of authority and responsibility as well as interrelationships of units within the organization.
4. Distribution of work can be improved through an analysis using the "Work Distribution Chart."
5. The "Work Distribution Chart" reflects the division of work within a unit in understandable form.
6. When related tasks are given to an employee, he has a better chance of increasing his skills through training.
7. The individual who is given the responsibility for tasks must also be given the appropriate authority to insure adequate results.
8. The supervisor should delegate repetitive, routine work. Preparation of recurring reports, maintaining leave and attendance records are some examples.
9. Good discipline is essential to good task performance. Discipline is reflected in the actions of employees on the job in the absence of supervision.
10. Disciplinary action may have to be taken when the positive aspects of discipline have failed. Reprimand, warning, and suspension are examples of disciplinary action.
11. If a situation calls for a reprimand, be sure it is deserved and remember it is to be done in private.

D. Dynamic Leadership
1. A style is a personal method or manner of exerting influence.
2. Authoritarian leaders often see themselves as the source of power and authority.
3. The democratic leader often perceives the group as the source of authority and power.
4. Supervisors tend to do better when using the pattern of leadership that is most natural for them.
5. Social scientists suggest that the effective supervisor use the leadership style that best fits the problem or circumstances involved.
6. All four styles—telling, selling, consulting, joining—have their place. Using one does not preclude using the other at another time.

7. The theory X point of view assumes that the average person dislikes work, will avoid it whenever possible, and must be coerced to achieve organizational objectives.
8. The theory Y point of view assumes that the average person considers work to be a natural as play, and, when the individual is committed, he requires little supervision or direction to accomplish desired objectives.
9. The leader's basic assumptions concerning human behavior and human nature affect his actions, decisions, and other managerial practices.
10. Dissatisfaction among employees is often present, but difficult to isolate. The supervisor should seek to weaken dissatisfaction by keeping promises, being sincere and considerate, keeping employees informed, and so forth.
11. Constructive suggestions should be encouraged during the natural progress of the work.

E. Processes for Solving Problems
1. People find their daily tasks more meaningful and satisfying when they can improve them.
2. The causes of problems, or the key factors, are often hidden in the background. Ability to solve problems often involves the ability to isolate them from their backgrounds. There is some substance to the cliché that some persons "can't see the forest for the trees."
3. New procedures are often developed from old ones. Problems should be broken down into manageable parts. New ideas can be adapted from old one.
4. People think differently in problem-solving situations. Using a logical, patterned approach is often useful. One approach found to be useful includes these steps:
    a. Define the problem
    b. Establish objectives
    c. Get the facts
    d. Weigh and decide
    e. Take action
    f. Evaluate action

F. Training for Results
1. Participants respond best when they feel training is important to them.
2. The supervisor has responsibility for the training and development of those who report to him.
3. When training is delegated to others, great care must be exercised to insure the trainer has knowledge, aptitude, and interest for his work as a trainer.
4. Training (learning) of some type goes on continually. The most successful supervisor makes certain the learning contributes in a productive manner to operational goals.
5. New employees are particularly susceptible to training. Older employees facing new job situations require specific training, as well as having need for development and growth opportunities.
6. Training needs require continuous monitoring.
7. The training officer of an agency is a professional with a responsibility to assist supervisors in solving training problems.

8. Many of the self-development steps important to the supervisor's own growth are equally important to the development of peers and subordinates. Knowledge of these is important when the supervisor consults with others on development and growth opportunities.

G. Health, Safety, and Accident Prevention
1. Management-minded supervisors take appropriate measures to assist employees in maintaining health and in assuring safe practices in the work environment.
2. Effective safety training and practices help to avoid injury and accidents.
3. Safety should be a management goal. All infractions of safety which are observed should be corrected without exception.
4. Employees' safety attitude, training and instruction, provision of safe tools and equipment, supervision, and leadership are considered highly important factors which contribute to safety and which can be influenced directly by supervisors.
5. When accidents do occur, they should be investigated promptly for very important reasons, including the fact that information which is gained can be used to prevent accidents in the future.

H. Equal Employment Opportunity
1. The supervisor should endeavor to treat all employees fairly, without regard to religion, race, sex, or national origin.
2. Groups tend to reflect the attitude of the leader. Prejudice can be detected even in very subtle form. Supervisors must strive to create a feeling of mutual respect and confidence in every employee.
3. Complete utilization of all human resources is a national goal. Equitable consideration should be accorded women in the work force, minority-group members, the physically and mentally handicapped, and the older employee. The important question is: "Who can do the job?"
4. Training opportunities, recognition for performance, overtime assignments, promotional opportunities, and all other personnel actions are to be handled on an equitable basis.

I. Improving Communications
1. Communications is achieving understanding between the sender and the receiver of a message. It also means sharing information—the creation of understanding.
2. Communication is basic to all human activity. Words are means of conveying meanings; however, real meanings are in people.
3. There are very practical differences in the effectiveness of one-way, impersonal, and two-way communications. Words spoken face-to-face are better understood. Telephone conversations are effective, but lack the rapport of person-to-person exchanges. The whole person communicates.
4. Cooperation and communication in an organization go hand in hand. When there is a mutual respect between people, spelling out rules and procedures for communicating is unnecessary.
5. There are several barriers to effective communications. These include failure to listen with respect and understanding, lack of skill in feedback, and misinterpreting the meanings of words used by the speaker. It is also common

practice to listen to what we want to hear, and tune out things we do not want to hear.
6. Communication is management's chief problem. The supervisor should accept the challenge to communicate more effectively and to improve interagency and intra-agency communications.
7. The supervisor may often plan for and conduct meetings. The planning phase is critical and may determine the success or the failure of a meeting.
8. Speaking before groups usually requires extra effort. Stage fright may never disappear completely, but it can be controlled.

J. Self-Development
1. Every employee is responsible for his own self-development.
2. Toastmaster and toastmistress clubs offer opportunities to improve skills in oral communications.
3. Planning for one's own self-development is of vital importance. Supervisors know their own strengths and limitations better than anyone else.
4. Many opportunities are open to aid the supervisor in his developmental efforts, including job assignments; training opportunities, both governmental and non-governmental—to include universities and professional conferences and seminars.
5. Programmed instruction offers a means of studying at one's own rate.
6. Where difficulties may arise from a supervisor's being away from his work for training, he may participate in televised home study or correspondence courses to meet his self-development needs.

K. Teaching and Training
1. The Teaching Process
Teaching is encouraging and guiding the learning activities of students toward established goals. In most cases this process consists of five steps: preparation, presentation, summarization, evaluation, and application.

   a. Preparation
   Preparation is two-fold in nature; that of the supervisor and the employee. Preparation by the supervisor is absolutely essential to success. He must know what, when, where, how, and whom he will teach. Some of the factors that should be considered are:
   1) The objectives
   2) The materials needed
   3) The methods to be used
   4) Employee participation
   5) Employee interest
   6) Training aids
   7) Evaluation
   8) Summarization

   Employee preparation consists in preparing the employee to receive the material. Probably the most important single factor in the preparation of the employee is arousing and maintaining his interest. He must know the objectives of the training, why he is there, how the material can be used, and its importance to him.

b. Presentation
In presentation, have a carefully designed plan and follow it. The plan should be accurate and complete, yet flexible enough to meet situations as they arise. The method of presentation will be determined by the particular situation and objectives.

c. Summary
A summary should be made at the end of every training unit and program. In addition, there may be internal summaries depending on the nature of the material being taught. The important thing is that the trainee must always be able to understand how each part of the new material relates to the whole.

d. Application
The supervisor must arrange work so the employee will be given a chance to apply new knowledge or skills while the material is still clear in his mind and interest is high. The trainee does not really know whether he has learned the material until he has been given a chance to apply it. If the material is not applied, it loses most of its value.

e. Evaluation
The purpose of all training is to promote learning. To determine whether the training has been a success or failure, the supervisor must evaluate this learning.
In the broadest sense, evaluation includes all the devices, methods, skills, and techniques used by the supervisor to keep himself and the employees informed as to their progress toward the objectives they are pursuing. The extent to which the employee has mastered the knowledge, skills, and abilities, or changed his attitudes, as determined by the program objectives, is the extent to which instruction has succeeded or failed.
Evaluation should not be confined to the end of the lesson, day, or program but should be used continuously. We shall note later the way this relates to the rest of the teaching process.

2. Teaching Methods
A teaching method is a pattern of identifiable student and instructor activity used in presenting training material.
All supervisors are faced with the problem of deciding which method should be used at a given time.

a. Lecture
The lecture is direct oral presentation of material by the supervisor. The present trend is to place less emphasis on the trainer's activity and more on that of the trainee.

b. Discussion
Teaching by discussion or conference involves using questions and other techniques to arouse interest and focus attention upon certain areas, and by doing so creating a learning situation. This can be one of the most

valuable methods because it gives the employees an opportunity to express their ideas and pool their knowledge.

    c. Demonstration
The demonstration is used to teach how something works or how to do something. It can be used to show a principle or what the results of a series of actions will be. A well-staged demonstration is particularly effective because it shows proper methods of performance in a realistic manner.

    d. Performance
Performance is one of the most fundamental of all learning techniques or teaching methods. The trainee may be able to tell how a specific operation should be performed but he cannot be sure he knows how to perform the operation until he has done so.
As with all methods, there are certain advantages and disadvantages to each method.

    e. Which Method to Use
Moreover, there are other methods and techniques of teaching. It is difficult to use any method without other methods entering into it. In any learning situation, a combination of methods is usually more effective than any one method alone.

Finally, evaluation must be integrated into the other aspects of the teaching-learning process.

It must be used in the motivation of the trainees; it must be used to assist in developing understanding during the training; and it must be related to employee application of the results of training.

This is distinctly the role of the supervisor.

COURTROOM TERMS

A/K/A: Acronym that stands for "also known as" and introduces any alternative or assumed names or aliases of an individual. A term to indicate another name by which a person is known.

Arraignment: The bringing of a defendant before the court to answer the matters charged against him in an indictment or information. The defendant is read the charges and must respond with his plea.

Arrest: Deprivation of one's liberty by legal authority.

Bail: An amount of money set by the court to procure the release of a person from legal custody; this money is to be forfeited if the defendant fails to appear for trial.

Beyond a Reasonable Doubt: The standard of proof required for a finding of guilty in a criminal matter. Satisfied to a moral certainty. This is a higher standard of proof than that required in a civil matter (preponderance of the evidence).

Co-Defendant: Any additional defendant or respondent in the same case.

Confession: A voluntary statement made by a person charged with a crime wherein said person acknowledges his/her guilt of the offense charged and discloses participation in the act.

Controlled Dangerous Substance: That group of legally designated drugs, which, by statute, it is illegal to possess or distribute.

Criminal complaint: The initial written notice to a defendant that he/she is being charged with a public offense.

Due Process of Law: The exercise of the powers of the government with the safeguards for the protection of individual rights as set forth in the constitution, statutes, and common case law.

Felony: A crime of a more serious nature than a misdemeanor, the exact nature of which is defined by state statute and which is punishable by a term of imprisonment exceeding one year or by death.

Grand Jury: A jury of inquiry whose duty is to receive complaints and accusations in criminal cases, hear the evidence presented on the part of the state, and determine whether to indict (see "indictment" below).

Impeach: As used in the Law of Evidence, to call into question the truthfulness of a witness, by means of introducing evidence to discredit him or her.

Indictment: A written accusation presented by a grand jury after having been presented with evidence, charging that a person named therein has done some act, or has been guilty of some omission that by law is a public offense.

Miranda Warnings: The compulsory advisement of a person's rights prior to any custodial interrogation; these include: a) the right to remain silent; b) that any statement made may be used against him/her; c) the right to an attorney; d) the appointment of counsel if the accused cannot afford his or her own attorney. Unless these rights are given, any evidence obtained in an interrogation cannot be used in the individual's trial against him/her.

Misdemeanor: Offense lower than felony and generally punishable by a fine or imprisonment other than in a penitentiary.

Motion to Quash: Application to the court to set aside the complaint, indictment or subpoena due to a lack of probable cause to arrest the defendant, or in matters heard by a grand jury, due to evidence not properly presented to the grand jury.

Motion to Sever: Application to the court made when there are two defendants charged with the same crimes or who acted jointly in the commission of a crime, when their attorneys feel it would be in their best interest if they had separate trials.

Motion to Suppress Evidence: Application to the court to prevent evidence from being presented at trial when said evidence has been obtained by illegal means. It applies to physical evidence, statements made by defendant when not advised by counsel or through wiretapping, prior convictions, etc..

Parole: A conditional release from custody at the discretion of the paroling authority prior to his or her completing the prison sentence imposed. During said release the offender is required to observe conditions of this status under the supervision of a parole agency.

Plea: A defendant's formal answer in court to the charges contained in a charging document.

Guilty: A plea by the defendant in which he acknowledges guilt either of the offense charged or of a less serious offense pursuant to an agreement with the prosecuting attorney. It should be understood, however, that the court may not be obliged to recognize this.

Nolo Contendere: A plea that is admissible in some jurisdictions, in which the defendant states that he does not contest the charges against him. Also called "no contest", this plea has the same effect as a guilty plea, except that it cannot be used against the defendant in civil actions arising out of the same incident which gave rise to the criminal charges.

Not Guilty: A plea of innocence by the defendant.

Not Guilty by Reason of Insanity: A plea that is sometimes entered in conjunction with the "not guilty" plea.

Double Jeopardy: A plea entered by a defendant who has been tried for an offense wherein he asserts that he cannot be tried a second time for said offense, unless he successfully secured a new trial after an appeal, or after a motion for a new trial was granted by the trial court.

Police Report: The official report made by any police officer involved with the incident or appearing after the incident, setting forth the officer's observations and statements of parties and witnesses. It can be used as evidence in a trial.

Pre-Trial Intervention: Utilized in some states when a defendant is accused of a first offense, to divert the defendant from the criminal justice system.

Probation: To allow a person convicted of a minor offense to go at large, under a suspension of sentence, during good behavior, and generally under the supervision of a probation officer.

Prosecutor: The attorney who prosecutes defendants for crimes, in the name of the government.

Search Warrant: A written order, issued by the court, directing the police to search a specified location for particular personal property (stolen or illegally possessed).

Speedy Trial: Mandate by the government that all criminal trials must take place within a specified time after arrest.

Writ of Habeas Corpus: A mandate issued from a court requiring that an individual be brought before the court.

GLOSSARY OF LEGAL TERMS

TABLE OF CONTENTS

	Page
Action ... Affiant	1
Affidavit ... At Bar	2
At Issue ... Burden of Proof	3
Business ... Commute	4
Complainant ... Conviction	5
Cooperative ... Demur (v.)	6
Demurrage ... Endorsement	7
Enjoin ... Facsimile	8
Factor ... Guilty	9
Habeas Corpus ... Incumbrance	10
Indemnify ... Laches	11
Landlord and Tenant ... Malice	12
Mandamus ... Obiter Dictum	13
Object (v.) ... Perjury	14
Perpetuity ... Proclamation	15
Proffered Evidence ... Referee	16
Referendum ... Stare Decisis	17
State ... Term	18
Testamentary ... Warrant (Warranty) (v.)	19
Warrant (n.) ... Zoning	20

GLOSSARY OF LEGAL TERMS

A

ACTION - "Action" includes a civil action and a criminal action.
A FORTIORI - A term meaning you can reason one thing from the existence of certain facts.
A POSTERIORI - From what goes after; from effect to cause.
A PRIORI - From what goes before; from cause to effect.
AB INITIO - From the beginning.
ABATE - To diminish or put an end to.
ABET - To encourage the commission of a crime.
ABEYANCE - Suspension, temporary suppression.
ABIDE - To accept the consequences of.
ABJURE - To renounce; give up.
ABRIDGE - To reduce; contract; diminish.
ABROGATE - To annul, repeal, or destroy.
ABSCOND - To hide or absent oneself to avoid legal action.
ABSTRACT - A summary.
ABUT - To border on, to touch.
ACCESS - Approach; in real property law it means the right of the owner of property to the use of the highway or road next to his land, without obstruction by intervening property owners.
ACCESSORY - In criminal law, it means the person who contributes or aids in the commission of a crime.
ACCOMMODATED PARTY - One to whom credit is extended on the strength of another person signing a commercial paper.
ACCOMMODATION PAPER - A commercial paper to which the accommodating party has put his name.
ACCOMPLICE - In criminal law, it means a person who together with the principal offender commits a crime.
ACCORD - An agreement to accept something different or less than that to which one is entitled, which extinguishes the entire obligation.
ACCOUNT - A statement of mutual demands in the nature of debt and credit between parties.
ACCRETION - The act of adding to a thing; in real property law, it means gradual accumulation of land by natural causes.
ACCRUE - To grow to; to be added to.
ACKNOWLEDGMENT - The act of going before an official authorized to take acknowledgments, and acknowledging an act as one's own.
ACQUIESCENCE - A silent appearance of consent.
ACQUIT - To legally determine the innocence of one charged with a crime.
AD INFINITUM - Indefinitely.
AD LITEM - For the suit.
AD VALOREM - According to value.
ADJECTIVE LAW - Rules of procedure.
ADJUDICATION - The judgment given in a case.
ADMIRALTY - Court having jurisdiction over maritime cases.
ADULT - Sixteen years old or over (in criminal law).
ADVANCE - In commercial law, it means to pay money or render other value before it is due.
ADVERSE - Opposed; contrary.
ADVOCATE - (v.) To speak in favor of;
(n.) One who assists, defends, or pleads for another.
AFFIANT - A person who makes and signs an affidavit.

AFFIDAVIT - A written and sworn to declaration of facts, voluntarily made.

AFFINITY - The relationship between persons through marriage with the kindred of each other; distinguished from consanguinity, which is the relationship by blood.

AFFIRM - To ratify; also when an appellate court affirms a judgment, decree, or order, it means that it is valid and right and must stand as rendered in the lower court.

AFOREMENTIONED; AFORESAID - Before or already said.

AGENT - One who represents and acts for another.

AID AND COMFORT - To help; encourage.

ALIAS - A name not one's true name.

ALIBI - A claim of not being present at a certain place at a certain time.

ALLEGE - To assert.

ALLOTMENT - A share or portion.

AMBIGUITY - Uncertainty; capable of being understood in more than one way.

AMENDMENT - Any language made or proposed as a change in some principal writing.

AMICUS CURIAE - A friend of the court; one who has an interest in a case, although not a party in the case, who volunteers advice upon matters of law to the judge. For example, a brief amicus curiae.

AMORTIZATION - To provide for a gradual extinction of (a future obligation) in advance of maturity, especially, by periodical contributions to a sinking fund which will be adequate to discharge a debt or make a replacement when it becomes necessary.

ANCILLARY - Aiding, auxiliary.

ANNOTATION - A note added by way of comment or explanation.

ANSWER - A written statement made by a defendant setting forth the grounds of his defense.

ANTE - Before.

ANTE MORTEM - Before death.

APPEAL - The removal of a case from a lower court to one of superior jurisdiction for the purpose of obtaining a review.

APPEARANCE - Coming into court as a party to a suit.

APPELLANT - The party who takes an appeal from one court or jurisdiction to another (appellate) court for review.

APPELLEE - The party against whom an appeal is taken.

APPROPRIATE - To make a thing one's own.

APPROPRIATION - Prescribing the destination of a thing; the act of the legislature designating a particular fund, to be applied to some object of government expenditure.

APPURTENANT - Belonging to; accessory or incident to.

ARBITER - One who decides a dispute; a referee.

ARBITRARY - Unreasoned; not governed by any fixed rules or standard.

ARGUENDO - By way of argument.

ARRAIGN - To call the prisoner before the court to answer to a charge.

ASSENT - A declaration of willingness to do something in compliance with a request.

ASSERT - Declare.

ASSESS - To fix the rate or amount.

ASSIGN - To transfer; to appoint; to select for a particular purpose.

ASSIGNEE - One who receives an assignment.

ASSIGNOR - One who makes an assignment.

AT BAR - Before the court.

AT ISSUE - When parties in an action come to a point where one asserts something and the other denies it.
ATTACH - Seize property by court order and sometimes arrest a person.
ATTEST - To witness a will, etc.; act of attestation.
AVERMENT - A positive statement of facts.

B

BAIL - To obtain the release of a person from legal custody by giving security and promising that he shall appear in court; to deliver (goods, etc.) in trust to a person for a special purpose.
BAILEE - One to whom personal property is delivered under a contract of bailment.
BAILMENT - Delivery of personal property to another to be held for a certain purpose and to be returned when the purpose is accomplished.
BAILOR - The party who delivers goods to another, under a contract of bailment.
BANC (OR BANK) - Bench; the place where a court sits permanently or regularly; also the assembly of all the judges of a court.
BANKRUPT - An insolvent person, technically, one declared to be bankrupt after a bankruptcy proceeding.
BAR - The legal profession.
BARRATRY - Exciting groundless judicial proceedings.
BARTER - A contract by which parties exchange goods for other goods.
BATTERY - Illegal interfering with another's person.
BEARER - In commercial law, it means the person in possession of a commercial paper which is payable to the bearer.
BENCH - The court itself or the judge.
BENEFICIARY - A person benefiting under a will, trust, or agreement.
BEST EVIDENCE RULE, THE - Except as otherwise provided by statute, no evidence other than the writing itself is admissible to prove the content of a writing. This section shall be known and may be cited as the best evidence rule.
BEQUEST - A gift of personal property under a will.
BILL - A formal written statement of complaint to a court of justice; also, a draft of an act of the legislature before it becomes a law; also, accounts for goods sold, services rendered, or work done.
BONA FIDE - In or with good faith; honestly.
BOND - An instrument by which the maker promises to pay a sum of money to another, usually providing that upon performances of a certain condition the obligation shall be void.
BOYCOTT - A plan to prevent the carrying on of a business by wrongful means.
BREACH - The breaking or violating of a law, or the failure to carry out a duty.
BRIEF - A written document, prepared by a lawyer to serve as the basis of an argument upon a case in court, usually an appellate court.
BURDEN OF PRODUCING EVIDENCE - The obligation of a party to introduce evidence sufficient to avoid a ruling against him on the issue.
BURDEN OF PROOF - The obligation of a party to establish by evidence a requisite degree of belief concerning a fact in the mind of the trier of fact or the court. The burden of proof may require a party to raise a reasonable doubt concerning the existence of nonexistence of a fact or that he establish the existence or nonexistence of a fact by a preponderance of the evidence, by clear and convincing proof, or by proof beyond a reasonable doubt.

Except as otherwise provided by law, the burden of proof requires proof by a preponderance of the evidence.

BUSINESS, A - Shall include every kind of business, profession, occupation, calling or operation of institutions, whether carried on for profit or not.

BY-LAWS - Regulations, ordinances, or rules enacted by a corporation, association, etc., for its own government.

C

CANON - A doctrine; also, a law or rule, of a church or association in particular.

CAPIAS - An order to arrest.

CAPTION - In a pleading, deposition or other paper connected with a case in court, it is the heading or introductory clause which shows the names of the parties, name of the court, number of the case on the docket or calendar, etc.

CARRIER - A person or corporation undertaking to transport persons or property.

CASE - A general term for an action, cause, suit, or controversy before a judicial body.

CAUSE - A suit, litigation or action before a court.

CAVEAT EMPTOR - Let the buyer beware. This term expresses the rule that the purchaser of an article must examine, judge, and test it for himself, being bound to discover any obvious defects or imperfections.

CERTIFICATE - A written representation that some legal formality has been complied with.

CERTIORARI - To be informed of; the name of a writ issued by a superior court directing the lower court to send up to the former the record and proceedings of a case.

CHANGE OF VENUE - To remove place of trial from one place to another.

CHARGE - An obligation or duty; a formal complaint; an instruction of the court to the jury upon a case.

CHARTER - (n.) The authority by virtue of which an organized body acts;
(v.) in mercantile law, it means to hire or lease a vehicle or vessel for transportation.

CHATTEL - An article of personal property.

CHATTEL MORTGAGE - A mortgage on personal property.

CIRCUIT - A division of the country, for the administration of justice; a geographical area served by a court.

CITATION - The act of the court by which a person is summoned or cited; also, a reference to legal authority.

CIVIL (ACTIONS) - It indicates the private rights and remedies of individuals in contrast to the word "criminal" (actions) which relates to prosecution for violation of laws.

CLAIM (n.) - Any demand held or asserted as of right.

CODICIL - An addition to a will.

CODIFY - To arrange the laws of a country into a code.

COGNIZANCE - Notice or knowledge.

COLLATERAL - By the side; accompanying; an article or thing given to secure performance of a promise.

COMITY - Courtesy; the practice by which one court follows the decision of another court on the same question.

COMMIT - To perform, as an act; to perpetrate, as a crime; to send a person to prison.

COMMON LAW - As distinguished from law created by the enactment of the legislature (called statutory law), it relates to those principles and rules of action which derive their authority solely from usages and customs of immemorial antiquity, particularly with reference to the ancient unwritten law of England. The written pronouncements of the common law are found in court decisions.

COMMUTE - Change punishment to one less severe.

COMPLAINANT - One who applies to the court for legal redress.
COMPLAINT - The pleading of a plaintiff in a civil action; or a charge that a person has committed a specified offense.
COMPROMISE - An arrangement for settling a dispute by agreement.
CONCUR - To agree, consent.
CONCURRENT - Running together, at the same time.
CONDEMNATION - Taking private property for public use on payment therefor.
CONDITION - Mode or state of being; a qualification or restriction.
CONDUCT - Active and passive behavior; both verbal and nonverbal.
CONFESSION - Voluntary statement of guilt of crime.
CONFIDENTIAL COMMUNICATION BETWEEN CLIENT AND LAWYER - Information transmitted between a client and his lawyer in the course of that relationship and in confidence by a means which, so far as the client is aware, discloses the information to no third persons other than those who are present to further the interest of the client in the consultation or those to whom disclosure is reasonably necessary for the transmission of the information or the accomplishment of the purpose for which the lawyer is consulted, and includes a legal opinion formed and the advice given by the lawyer in the course of that relationship.
CONFRONTATION - Witness testifying in presence of defendant.
CONSANGUINITY - Blood relationship.
CONSIGN - To give in charge; commit; entrust; to send or transmit goods to a merchant, factor, or agent for sale.
CONSIGNEE - One to whom a consignment is made.
CONSIGNOR - One who sends or makes a consignment.
CONSPIRACY - In criminal law, it means an agreement between two or more persons to commit an unlawful act.
CONSPIRATORS - Persons involved in a conspiracy.
CONSTITUTION - The fundamental law of a nation or state.
CONSTRUCTION OF GENDERS - The masculine gender includes the feminine and neuter.
CONSTRUCTION OF SINGULAR AND PLURAL - The singular number includes the plural; and the plural, the singular.
CONSTRUCTION OF TENSES - The present tense includes the past and future tenses; and the future, the present.
CONSTRUCTIVE - An act or condition assumed from other parts or conditions.
CONSTRUE - To ascertain the meaning of language.
CONSUMMATE - To complete.
CONTIGUOUS - Adjoining; touching; bounded by.
CONTINGENT - Possible, but not assured; dependent upon some condition.
CONTINUANCE - The adjournment or postponement of an action pending in a court.
CONTRA - Against, opposed to; contrary.
CONTRACT - An agreement between two or more persons to do or not to do a particular thing.
CONTROVERT - To dispute, deny.
CONVERSION - Dealing with the personal property of another as if it were one's own, without right.
CONVEYANCE - An instrument transferring title to land.
CONVICTION - Generally, the result of a criminal trial which ends in a judgment or sentence that the defendant is guilty as charged.

COOPERATIVE - A cooperative is a voluntary organization of persons with a common interest, formed and operated along democratic lines for the purpose of supplying services at cost to its members and other patrons, who contribute both capital and business.
CORPUS DELICTI - The body of a crime; the crime itself.
CORROBORATE - To strengthen; to add weight by additional evidence.
COUNTERCLAIM - A claim presented by a defendant in opposition to or deduction from the claim of the plaintiff.
COUNTY - Political subdivision of a state.
COVENANT - Agreement.
CREDIBLE - Worthy of belief.
CREDITOR - A person to whom a debt is owing by another person, called the "debtor."
CRIMINAL ACTION - Includes criminal proceedings.
CRIMINAL INFORMATION - Same as complaint.
CRITERION (sing.)
CRITERIA (plural) - A means or tests for judging; a standard or standards.
CROSS-EXAMINATION - Examination of a witness by a party other than the direct examiner upon a matter that is within the scope of the direct examination of the witness.
CULPABLE - Blamable.
CY-PRES - As near as (possible). The rule of *cy-pres* is a rule for the construction of instruments in equity by which the intention of the party is carried out *as near as may be*, when it would be impossible or illegal to give it literal effect.

D

DAMAGES - A monetary compensation, which may be recovered in the courts by any person who has suffered loss, or injury, whether to his person, property or rights through the unlawful act or omission or negligence of another.
DECLARANT - A person who makes a statement.
DE FACTO - In fact; actually but without legal authority.
DE JURE - Of right; legitimate; lawful.
DE MINIMIS - Very small or trifling.
DE NOVO - Anew; afresh; a second time.
DEBT - A specified sum of money owing to one person from another, including not only the obligation of the debtor to pay, but the right of the creditor to receive and enforce payment.
DECEDENT - A dead person.
DECISION - A judgment or decree pronounced by a court in determination of a case.
DECREE - An order of the court, determining the rights of all parties to a suit.
DEED - A writing containing a contract sealed and delivered; particularly to convey real property.
DEFALCATION - Misappropriation of funds.
DEFAMATION - Injuring one's reputation by false statements.
DEFAULT - The failure to fulfill a duty, observe a promise, discharge an obligation, or perform an agreement.
DEFENDANT - The person defending or denying; the party against whom relief or recovery is sought in an action or suit.
DEFRAUD - To practice fraud; to cheat or trick.
DELEGATE (v.)- To entrust to the care or management of another.
DELICTUS - A crime.
DEMUR (v.) - To dispute the sufficiency in law of the pleading of the other side.

DEMURRAGE - In maritime law, it means, the sum fixed or allowed as remuneration to the owners of a ship for the detention of their vessel beyond the number of days allowed for loading and unloading or for sailing; also used in railroad terminology.
DENIAL - A form of pleading; refusing to admit the truth of a statement, charge, etc.
DEPONENT - One who gives testimony under oath reduced to writing.
DEPOSITION - Testimony given under oath outside of court for use in court or for the purpose of obtaining information in preparation for trial of a case.
DETERIORATION - A degeneration such as from decay, corrosion or disintegration.
DETRIMENT - Any loss or harm to person or property.
DEVIATION - A turning aside.
DEVISE - A gift of real property by the last will and testament of the donor.
DICTUM (sing.)
DICTA (plural) - Any statements made by the court in an opinion concerning some rule of law not necessarily involved nor essential to the determination of the case.
DIRECT EVIDENCE - Evidence that directly proves a fact, without an inference or presumption, and which in itself if true, conclusively establishes that fact.
DIRECT EXAMINATION - The first examination of a witness upon a matter that is not within the scope of a previous examination of the witness.
DISAFFIRM - To repudiate.
DISMISS - In an action or suit, it means to dispose of the case without any further consideration or hearing.
DISSENT - To denote disagreement of one or more judges of a court with the decision passed by the majority upon a case before them.
DOCKET (n.) - A formal record, entered in brief, of the proceedings in a court.
DOCTRINE - A rule, principle, theory of law.
DOMICILE - That place where a man has his true, fixed and permanent home to which whenever he is absent he has the intention of returning.
DRAFT (n.) - A commercial paper ordering payment of money drawn by one person on another.
DRAWEE - The person who is requested to pay the money.
DRAWER - The person who draws the commercial paper and addresses it to the drawee.
DUPLICATE - A counterpart produced by the same impression as the original enlargements and miniatures, or by mechanical or electronic re-recording, or by chemical reproduction, or by other equivalent technique which accurately reproduces the original.
DURESS - Use of force to compel performance or non-performance of an act.

E

EASEMENT - A liberty, privilege, or advantage without profit, in the lands of another.
EGRESS - Act or right of going out or leaving; emergence.
EIUSDEM GENERIS - Of the same kind, class or nature. A rule used in the construction of language in a legal document.
EMBEZZLEMENT - To steal; to appropriate fraudulently to one's own use property entrusted to one's care.
EMBRACERY - Unlawful attempt to influence jurors, etc., but not by offering value.
EMINENT DOMAIN - The right of a state to take private property for public use.
ENACT - To make into a law.
ENDORSEMENT - Act of writing one's name on the back of a note, bill or similar written instrument.

ENJOIN - To require a person, by writ of injunction from a court of equity, to perform or to abstain or desist from some act.
ENTIRETY - The whole; that which the law considers as one whole, and not capable of being divided into parts.
ENTRAPMENT - Inducing one to commit a crime so as to arrest him.
ENUMERATED - Mentioned specifically; designated.
ENURE - To operate or take effect.
EQUITY - In its broadest sense, this term denotes the spirit and the habit of fairness, justness, and right dealing which regulate the conduct of men.
ERROR - A mistake of law, or the false or irregular application of law as will nullify the judicial proceedings.
ESCROW - A deed, bond or other written engagement, delivered to a third person, to be delivered by him only upon the performance or fulfillment of some condition.
ESTATE - The interest which any one has in lands, or in any other subject of property.
ESTOP - To stop, bar, or impede.
ESTOPPEL - A rule of law which prevents a man from alleging or denying a fact, because of his own previous act.
ET AL. (alii) - And others.
ET SEQ. (sequential) - And the following.
ET UX. (uxor) - And wife.
EVIDENCE - Testimony, writings, material objects, or other things presented to the senses that are offered to prove the existence or non-existence of a fact.
    Means from which inferences may be drawn as a basis of proof in duly constituted judicial or fact finding tribunals, and includes testimony in the form of opinion and hearsay.
EX CONTRACTU
EX DELICTO - In law, rights and causes of action are divided into two classes, those arising *ex contractu* (from a contract) and those arising *ex delicto* (from a delict or tort).
EX OFFICIO - From office; by virtue of the office.
EX PARTE - On one side only; by or for one.
EX POST FACTO - After the fact.
EX POST FACTO LAW - A law passed after an act was done which retroactively makes such act a crime.
EX REL. (relations) - Upon relation or information.
EXCEPTION - An objection upon a matter of law to a decision made, either before or after judgment by a court.
EXECUTOR (male)
EXECUTRIX (female) - A person who has been appointed by will to execute the will.
EXECUTORY - That which is yet to be executed or performed.
EXEMPT - To release from some liability to which others are subject.
EXONERATION - The removal of a burden, charge or duty.
EXTRADITION - Surrender of a fugitive from one nation to another.

F

F.A.S.- "Free alongside ship"; delivery at dock for ship named.
F.O.B.- "Free on board"; seller will deliver to car, truck, vessel, or other conveyance by which goods are to be transported, without expense or risk of loss to the buyer or consignee.
FABRICATE - To construct; to invent a false story.
FACSIMILE - An exact or accurate copy of an original instrument.

FACTOR - A commercial agent.
FEASANCE - The doing of an act.
FELONIOUS - Criminal, malicious.
FELONY - Generally, a criminal offense that may be punished by death or imprisonment for more than one year as differentiated from a misdemeanor.
FEME SOLE - A single woman.
FIDUCIARY - A person who is invested with rights and powers to be exercised for the benefit of another person.
FIERI FACIAS - A writ of execution commanding the sheriff to levy and collect the amount of a judgment from the goods and chattels of the judgment debtor.
FINDING OF FACT - Determination from proof or judicial notice of the existence of a fact. A ruling implies a supporting finding of fact; no separate or formal finding is required unless required by a statute of this state.
FISCAL - Relating to accounts or the management of revenue.
FORECLOSURE (sale) - A sale of mortgaged property to obtain satisfaction of the mortgage out of the sale proceeds.
FORFEITURE - A penalty, a fine.
FORGERY - Fabricating or producing falsely, counterfeited.
FORTUITOUS - Accidental.
FORUM - A court of justice; a place of jurisdiction.
FRAUD - Deception; trickery.
FREEHOLDER - One who owns real property.
FUNGIBLE - Of such kind or nature that one specimen or part may be used in the place of another.

G

GARNISHEE - Person garnished.
GARNISHMENT - A legal process to reach the money or effects of a defendant, in the possession or control of a third person.
GRAND JURY - Not less than 16, not more than 23 citizens of a county sworn to inquire into crimes committed or triable in the county.
GRANT - To agree to; convey, especially real property.
GRANTEE - The person to whom a grant is made.
GRANTOR - The person by whom a grant is made.
GRATUITOUS - Given without a return, compensation or consideration.
GRAVAMEN - The grievance complained of or the substantial cause of a criminal action.
GUARANTY (n.) - A promise to answer for the payment of some debt, or the performance of some duty, in case of the failure of another person, who, in the first instance, is liable for such payment or performance.
GUARDIAN - The person, committee, or other representative authorized by law to protect the person or estate or both of an incompetent (or of a *sui juris* person having a guardian) and to act for him in matters affecting his person or property or both. An incompetent is a person under disability imposed by law.
GUILTY - Establishment of the fact that one has committed a breach of conduct; especially, a violation of law.

H

HABEAS CORPUS - You have the body; the name given to a variety of writs, having for their object to bring a party before a court or judge for decision as to whether such person is being lawfully held prisoner.
HABENDUM - In conveyancing; it is the clause in a deed conveying land which defines the extent of ownership to be held by the grantee.
HEARING - A proceeding whereby the arguments of the interested parties are heared.
HEARSAY - A type of testimony given by a witness who relates, not what he knows personally, but what others have told hi, or what he has heard said by others.
HEARSAY RULE, THE - (a) "Hearsay evidence" is evidence of a statement that was made other than by a witness while testifying at the hearing and that is offered to prove the truth of the matter stated; (b) Except as provided by law, hearsay evidence is inadmissible; (c) This section shall be known and may be cited as the hearsay rule.
HEIR - Generally, one who inherits property, real or personal.
HOLDER OF THE PRIVILEGE - (a) The client when he has no guardian or conservator; (b) A guardian or conservator of the client when the client has a guardian or conservator; (c) The personal representative of the client if the client is dead; (d) A successor, assign, trustee in dissolution, or any similar representative of a firm, association, organization, partnership, business trust, corporation, or public entity that is no longer in existence.
HUNG JURY - One so divided that they can't agree on a verdict.
HUSBAND-WIFE PRIVILEGE - An accused in a criminal proceeding has a privilege to prevent his spouse from testifying against him.
HYPOTHECATE - To pledge a thing without delivering it to the pledgee.
HYPOTHESIS - A supposition, assumption, or toehry.

I

I.E. (id est) - That is.
IB., OR IBID.(ibidem) - In the same place; used to refer to a legal reference previously cited to avoid repeating the entire citation.
ILLICIT - Prohibited; unlawful.
ILLUSORY - Deceiving by false appearance.
IMMUNITY - Exemption.
IMPEACH - To accuse, to dispute.
IMPEDIMENTS - Disabilities, or hindrances.
IMPLEAD - To sue or prosecute by due course of law.
IMPUTED - Attributed or charged to.
IN LOCO PARENTIS - In place of parent, a guardian.
IN TOTO - In the whole; completely.
INCHOATE - Imperfect; unfinished.
INCOMMUNICADO - Denial of the right of a prisoner to communicate with friends or relatives.
INCOMPETENT - One who is incapable of caring for his own affairs because he is mentally deficient or undeveloped.
INCRIMINATION - A matter will incriminate a person if it constitutes, or forms an essential part of, or, taken in connection with other matters disclosed, is a basis for a reasonable inference of such a violation of the laws of this State as to subject him to liability to punishment therefor, unless he has become for any reason permanently immune from punishment for such violation.
INCUMBRANCE - Generally a claim, lien, charge or liability attached to and binding real property.

INDEMNIFY - To secure against loss or damage; also, to make reimbursement to one for a loss already incurred by him.
INDEMNITY - An agreement to reimburse another person in case of an anticipated loss falling upon him.
INDICIA - Signs; indications.
INDICTMENT - An accusation in writing found and presented by a grand jury charging that a person has committed a crime.
INDORSE - To write a name on the back of a legal paper or document, generally, a negotiable instrument
INDUCEMENT - Cause or reason why a thing is done or that which incites the person to do the act or commit a crime; the motive for the criminal act.
INFANT - In civil cases one under 21 years of age.
INFORMATION - A formal accusation of crime made by a prosecuting attorney.
INFRA - Below, under; this word occurring by itself in a publication refers the reader to a future part of the publication.
INGRESS - The act of going into.
INJUNCTION - A writ or order by the court requiring a person, generally, to do or to refrain from doing an act.
INSOLVENT - The condition of a person who is unable to pay his debts.
INSTRUCTION - A direction given by the judge to the jury concerning the law of the case.
INTERIM - In the meantime; time intervening.
INTERLOCUTORY - Temporary, not final; something intervening between the commencement and the end of a suit which decides some point or matter, but is not a final decision of the whole controversy.
INTERROGATORIES - A series of formal written questions used in the examination of a party or a witness usually prior to a trial.
INTESTATE - A person who dies without a will.
INURE - To result, to take effect.
IPSO FACTO - By the fact iself; by the mere fact.
ISSUE (n.) The disputed point or question in a case,

J

JEOPARDY - Danger, hazard, peril.
JOINDER - Joining; uniting with another person in some legal steps or proceeding.
JOINT - United; combined.
JUDGE - Member or members or representative or representatives of a court conducting a trial or hearing at which evidence is introduced.
JUDGMENT - The official decision of a court of justice.
JUDICIAL OR JUDICIARY - Relating to or connected with the administration of justice.
JURAT - The clause written at the foot of an affidavit, stating when, where and before whom such affidavit was sworn.
JURISDICTION - The authority to hear and determine controversies between parties.
JURISPRUDENCE - The philosophy of law.
JURY - A body of persons legally selected to inquire into any matter of fact, and to render their verdict according to the evidence.

L

LACHES - The failure to diligently assert a right, which results in a refusal to allow relief.

LANDLORD AND TENANT - A phrase used to denote the legal relation existing between the owner and occupant of real estate.

LARCENY - Stealing personal property belonging to another.

LATENT - Hidden; that which does not appear on the face of a thing.

LAW - Includes constitutional, statutory, and decisional law.

LAWYER-CLIENT PRIVILEGE - (1) A "client" is a person, public officer, or corporation, association, or other organization or entity, either public or private, who is rendered professional legal services by a lawyer, or who consults a lawyer with a view to obtaining professional legal services from him; (2) A "lawyer" is a person authorized, or reasonably believed by the client to be authorized, to practice law in any state or nation; (3) A "representative of the lawyer" is one employed to assist the lawyer in the rendition of professional legal services; (4) A communication is "confidential" if not intended to be disclosed to third persons other than those to whom disclosure is in furtherance of the rendition of professional legal services to the client or those reasonably necessary for the transmission of the communication.

General rule of privilege - A client has a privilege to refuse to disclose and to prevent any other person from disclosing confidential communications made for the purpose of facilitating the rendition of professional legal services to the client, (1) between himself or his representative and his lawyer or his lawyer's representative, or (2) between his lawyer and the lawyer's representative, or (3) by him or his lawyer to a lawyer representing another in a matter of common interest, or (4) between representatives of the client or between the client and a representative of the client, or (5) between lawyers representing the client.

LEADING QUESTION - Question that suggests to the witness the answer that the examining party desires.

LEASE - A contract by which one conveys real estate for a limited time usually for a specified rent; personal property also may be leased.

LEGISLATION - The act of enacting laws.

LEGITIMATE - Lawful.

LESSEE - One to whom a lease is given.

LESSOR - One who grants a lease

LEVY - A collecting or exacting by authority.

LIABLE - Responsible; bound or obligated in law or equity.

LIBEL (v.) - To defame or injure a person's reputation by a published writing.

(n.) - The initial pleading on the part of the plaintiff in an admiralty proceeding.

LIEN - A hold or claim which one person has upon the property of another as a security for some debt or charge.

LIQUIDATED - Fixed; settled.

LIS PENDENS - A pending civil or criminal action.

LITERAL - According to the language.

LITIGANT - A party to a lawsuit.

LITATION - A judicial controversy.

LOCUS - A place.

LOCUS DELICTI - Place of the crime.

LOCUS POENITENTIAE - The abandoning or giving up of one's intention to commit some crime before it is fully completed or abandoning a conspiracy before its purpose is accomplished.

M

MALFEASANCE - To do a wrongful act.

MALICE - The doing of a wrongful act Intentionally without just cause or excuse.

MANDAMUS - The name of a writ issued by a court to enforce the performance of some public duty.
MANDATORY (adj.) Containing a command.
MARITIME - Pertaining to the sea or to commerce thereon.
MARSHALING - Arranging or disposing of in order.
MAXIM - An established principle or proposition.
MINISTERIAL - That which involves obedience to instruction, but demands no special discretion, judgment or skill.
MISAPPROPRIATE - Dealing fraudulently with property entrusted to one.
MISDEMEANOR - A crime less than a felony and punishable by a fine or imprisonment for less than one year.
MISFEASANCE - Improper performance of a lawful act.
MISREPRESENTATION - An untrue representation of facts.
MITIGATE - To make or become less severe, harsh.
MITTIMUS - A warrant of commitment to prison.
MOOT (adj.) Unsettled, undecided, not necessary to be decided.
MORTGAGE - A conveyance of property upon condition, as security for the payment of a debt or the performance of a duty, and to become void upon payment or performance according to the stipulated terms.
MORTGAGEE - A person to whom property is mortgaged.
MORTGAGOR - One who gives a mortgage.
MOTION - In legal proceedings, a "motion" is an application, either written or oral, addressed to the court by a party to an action or a suit requesting the ruling of the court on a matter of law.
MUTUALITY - Reciprocation.

N

NEGLIGENCE - The failure to exercise that degree of care which an ordinarily prudent person would exercise under like circumstances.
NEGOTIABLE (instrument) - Any instrument obligating the payment of money which is transferable from one person to another by endorsement and delivery or by delivery only.
NEGOTIATE - To transact business; to transfer a negotiable instrument; to seek agreement for the amicable disposition of a controversy or case.
NOLLE PROSEQUI - A formal entry upon the record, by the plaintiff in a civil suit or the prosecuting officer in a criminal action, by which he declares that he "will no further prosecute" the case.
NOLO CONTENDERE - The name of a plea in a criminal action, having the same effect as a plea of guilty; but not constituting a direct admission of guilt.
NOMINAL - Not real or substantial.
NOMINAL DAMAGES - Award of a trifling sum where no substantial injury is proved to have been sustained.
NONFEASANCE - Neglect of duty.
NOVATION - The substitution of a new debt or obligation for an existing one.
NUNC PRO TUNC - A phrase applied to acts allowed to be done after the time when they should be done, with a retroactive effect.("Now for then.")

O

OATH - Oath includes affirmation or declaration under penalty of perjury.
OBITER DICTUM - Opinion expressed by a court on a matter not essentially involved in a case and hence not a decision; also called dicta, if plural.

OBJECT (v.) - To oppose as improper or illegal and referring the question of its propriety or legality to the court.

OBLIGATION - A legal duty, by which a person is bound to do or not to do a certain thing.

OBLIGEE - The person to whom an obligation is owed.

OBLIGOR - The person who is to perform the obligation.

OFFER (v.) - To present for acceptance or rejection.

(n.) - A proposal to do a thing, usually a proposal to make a contract.

OFFICIAL INFORMATION - Information within the custody or control of a department or agency of the government the disclosure of which is shown to be contrary to the public interest.

OFFSET - A deduction.

ONUS PROBANDI - Burden of proof.

OPINION - The statement by a judge of the decision reached in a case, giving the law as applied to the case and giving reasons for the judgment; also a belief or view.

OPTION - The exercise of the power of choice; also a privilege existing in one person, for which he has paid money, which gives him the right to buy or sell real or personal property at a given price within a specified time.

ORDER - A rule or regulation; every direction of a court or judge made or entered in writing but not including a judgment.

ORDINANCE - Generally, a rule established by authority; also commonly used to designate the legislative acts of a municipal corporation.

ORIGINAL - Writing or recording itself or any counterpart intended to have the same effect by a person executing or issuing it. An "original" of a photograph includes the negative or any print therefrom. If data are stored in a computer or similar device, any printout or other output readable by sight, shown to reflect the data accurately, is an "original."

OVERT - Open, manifest.

P

PANEL - A group of jurors selected to serve during a term of the court.

PARENS PATRIAE - Sovereign power of a state to protect or be a guardian over children and incompetents.

PAROL - Oral or verbal.

PAROLE - To release one in prison before the expiration of his sentence, conditionally.

PARITY - Equality in purchasing power between the farmer and other segments of the economy.

PARTITION - A legal division of real or personal property between one or more owners.

PARTNERSHIP - An association of two or more persons to carry on as co-owners a business for profit.

PATENT (adj.) - Evident.

(n.) - A grant of some privilege, property, or authority, made by the government or sovereign of a country to one or more individuals.

PECULATION - Stealing.

PECUNIARY - Monetary.

PENULTIMATE - Next to the last.

PER CURIAM - A phrase used in the report of a decision to distinguish an opinion of the whole court from an opinion written by any one judge.

PER SE - In itself; taken alone.

PERCEIVE - To acquire knowledge through one's senses.

PEREMPTORY - Imperative; absolute.

PERJURY - To lie or state falsely under oath.

PERPETUITY - Perpetual existence; also the quality or condition of an estate limited so that it will not take effect or vest within the period fixed by law.
PERSON - Includes a natural person, firm, association, organization, partnership, business trust, corporation, or public entity.
PERSONAL PROPERTY - Includes money, goods, chattels, things in action, and evidences of debt.
PERSONALTY - Short term for personal property.
PETITION - An application in writing for an order of the court, stating the circumstances upon which it is founded and requesting any order or other relief from a court.
PLAINTIFF - A person who brings a court action.
PLEA - A pleading in a suit or action.
PLEADINGS - Formal allegations made by the parties of their respective claims and defenses, for the judgment of the court.
PLEDGE - A deposit of personal property as a security for the performance of an act.
PLEDGEE - The party to whom goods are delivered in pledge.
PLEDGOR - The party delivering goods in pledge.
PLENARY - Full; complete.
POLICE POWER - Inherent power of the state or its political subdivisions to enact laws within constitutional limits to promote the general welfare of society or the community.
POLLING THE JURY - Call the names of persons on a jury and requiring each juror to declare what his verdict is before it is legally recorded.
POST MORTEM - After death.
POWER OF ATTORNEY - A writing authorizing one to act for another.
PRECEPT - An order, warrant, or writ issued to an officer or body of officers, commanding him or them to do some act within the scope of his or their powers.
PRELIMINARY FACT - Fact upon the existence or nonexistence of which depends the admissibility or inadmissibility of evidence. The phrase "the admissibility or inadmissibility of evidence" includes the qualification or disqualification of a person to be a witness and the existence or nonexistence of a privilege.
PREPONDERANCE - Outweighing.
PRESENTMENT - A report by a grand jury on something they have investigated on their own knowledge.
PRESUMPTION - An assumption of fact resulting from a rule of law which requires such fact to be assumed from another fact or group of facts found or otherwise established in the action.
PRIMA FACUE - At first sight.
PRIMA FACIE CASE - A case where the evidence is very patent against the defendant.
PRINCIPAL - The source of authority or rights; a person primarily liable as differentiated from "principle" as a primary or basic doctrine.
PRO AND CON - For and against.
PRO RATA - Proportionally.
PROBATE - Relating to proof, especially to the proof of wills.
PROBATIVE - Tending to prove.
PROCEDURE - In law, this term generally denotes rules which are established by the Federal, State, or local Governments regarding the types of pleading and courtroom practice which must be followed by the parties involved in a criminal or civil case.
PROCLAMATION - A public notice by an official of some order, intended action, or state of facts.

PROFFERED EVIDENCE - The admissibility or inadmissibility of which is dependent upon the existence or nonexistence of a preliminary fact.
PROMISSORY (NOTE) - A promise in writing to pay a specified sum at an expressed time, or on demand, or at sight, to a named person, or to his order, or bearer.
PROOF - The establishment by evidence of a requisite degree of belief concerning a fact in the mind of the trier of fact or the court.
PROPERTY - Includes both real and personal property.
PROPRIETARY (adj.) - Relating or pertaining to ownership; usually a single owner.
PROSECUTE - To carry on an action or other judicial proceeding; to proceed against a person criminally.
PROVISO - A limitation or condition in a legal instrument.
PROXIMATE - Immediate; nearest
PUBLIC EMPLOYEE - An officer, agent, or employee of a public entity.
PUBLIC ENTITY - Includes a national, state, county, city and county, city, district, public authority, public agency, or any other political subdivision or public corporation, whether foreign or domestic.
PUBLIC OFFICIAL - Includes an official of a political dubdivision of such state or territory and of a municipality.
PUNITIVE - Relating to punishment.

Q

QUASH - To make void.
QUASI - As if; as it were.
QUID PRO QUO - Something for something; the giving of one valuable thing for another.
QUITCLAIM (v.) - To release or relinquish claim or title to, especially in deeds to realty.
QUO WARRANTO - A legal procedure to test an official's right to a public office or the right to hold a franchise, or to hold an office in a domestic corporation.

R

RATIFY - To approve and sanction.
REAL PROPERTY - Includes lands, tenements, and hereditaments.
REALTY - A brief term for real property.
REBUT - To contradict; to refute, especially by evidence and arguments.
RECEIVER - A person who is appointed by the court to receive, and hold in trust property in litigation.
RECIDIVIST - Habitual criminal.
RECIPROCAL - Mutual.
RECOUPMENT - To keep back or get something which is due; also, it is the right of a defendant to have a deduction from the amount of the plaintiff's damages because the plaintiff has not fulfilled his part of the same contract.
RECROSS EXAMINATION - Examination of a witness by a cross-examiner subsequent to a redirect examination of the witness.
REDEEM - To release an estate or article from mortgage or pledge by paying the debt for which it stood as security.
REDIRECT EXAMINATION - Examination of a witness by the direct examiner subsequent to the cross-examination of the witness.
REFEREE - A person to whom a cause pending in a court is referred by the court, to take testimony, hear the parties, and report thereon to the court.

REFERENDUM - A method of submitting an important legislative or administrative matter to a direct vote of the people.
RELEVANT EVIDENCE - Evidence including evidence relevant to the credulity of a witness or hearsay declarant, having any tendency in reason to prove or disprove any disputed fact that is of consequence to the determination of the action.
REMAND - To send a case back to the lower court from which it came, for further proceedings.
REPLEVIN - An action to recover goods or chattels wrongfully taken or detained.
REPLY (REPLICATION) - Generally, a reply is what the plaintiff or other person who has instituted proceedings says in answer to the defendant's case.
RE JUDICATA - A thing judicially acted upon or decided.
RES ADJUDICATA - Doctrine that an issue or dispute litigated and determined in a case between the opposing parties is deemed permanently decided between these parties.
RESCIND (RECISSION) - To avoid or cancel a contract.
RESPONDENT - A defendant in a proceeding in chancery or admiralty; also, the person who contends against the appeal in a case.
RESTITUTION - In equity, it is the restoration of both parties to their original condition (when practicable), upon the rescission of a contract for fraud or similar cause.
RETROACTIVE (RETROSPECTIVE) - Looking back; effective as of a prior time.
REVERSED - A term used by appellate courts to indicate that the decision of the lower court in the case before it has been set aside.
REVOKE - To recall or cancel.
RIPARIAN (RIGHTS) - The rights of a person owning land containing or bordering on a water course or other body of water, such as lakes and rivers.

S

SALE - A contract whereby the ownership of property is transferred from one person to another for a sum of money or for any consideration.
SANCTION - A penalty or punishment provided as a means of enforcing obedience to a law; also, an authorization.
SATISFACTION - The discharge of an obligation by paying a party what is due to him; or what is awarded to him by the judgment of a court or otherwise.
SCIENTER - Knowingly; also, it is used in pleading to denote the defendant's guilty knowledge.
SCINTILLA - A spark; also the least particle.
SECRET OF STATE - Governmental secret relating to the national defense or the international relations of the United States.
SECURITY - Indemnification; the term is applied to an obligation, such as a mortgage or deed of trust, given by a debtor to insure the payment or performance of his debt, by furnishing the creditor with a resource to be used in case of the debtor's failure to fulfill the principal obligation.
SENTENCE - The judgment formally pronounced by the court or judge upon the defendant after his conviction in a criminal prosecution.
SET-OFF - A claim or demand which one party in an action credits against the claim of the opposing party.
SHALL and MAY - "Shall" is mandatory and "may" is permissive.
SITUS - Location.
SOVEREIGN - A person, body or state in which independent and supreme authority is vested.
STARE DECISIS - To follow decided cases.

STATE - "State" means this State, unless applied to the different parts of the United States. In the latter case, it includes any state, district, commonwealth, territory or insular possession of the United States, including the District of Columbia.
STATEMENT - (a) Oral or written verbal expression or (b) nonverbal conduct of a person intended by him as a substitute for oral or written verbal expression.
STATUTE - An act of the legislature. Includes a treaty.
STATUTE OF LIMITATION - A statute limiting the time to bring an action after the right of action has arisen.
STAY - To hold in abeyance an order of a court.
STIPULATION - Any agreement made by opposing attorneys regulating any matter incidental to the proceedings or trial.
SUBORDINATION (AGREEMENT) - An agreement making one's rights inferior to or of a lower rank than another's.
SUBORNATION - The crime of procuring a person to lie or to make false statements to a court.
SUBPOENA - A writ or order directed to a person, and requiring his attendance at a particular time and place to testify as a witness.
SUBPOENA DUCES TECUM - A subpoena used, not only for the purpose of compelling witnesses to attend in court, but also requiring them to bring with them books or documents which may be in their possession, and which may tend to elucidate the subject matter of the trial.
SUBROGATION - The substituting of one for another as a creditor, the new creditor succeeding to the former's rights.
SUBSIDY - A government grant to assist a private enterprise deemed advantageous to the public.
SUI GENERIS - Of the same kind.
SUIT - Any civil proceeding by a person or persons against another or others in a court of justice by which the plaintiff pursues the remedies afforded him by law.
SUMMONS - A notice to a defendant that an action against him has been commenced and requiring him to appear in court and answer the complaint.
SUPRA - Above; this word occurring by itself in a book refers the reader to a previous part of the book.
SURETY - A person who binds himself for the payment of a sum of money, or for the performance of something else, for another.
SURPLUSAGE - Extraneous or unnecessary matter.
SURVIVORSHIP - A term used when a person becomes entitled to property by reason of his having survived another person who had an interest in the property.
SUSPEND SENTENCE - Hold back a sentence pending good behavior of prisoner.
SYLLABUS - A note prefixed to a report, especially a case, giving a brief statement of the court's ruling on different issues of the case.

T

TALESMAN - Person summoned to fill a panel of jurors.
TENANT - One who holds or possesses lands by any kind of right or title; also, one who has the temporary use and occupation of real property owned by another person (landlord), the duration and terms of his tenancy being usually fixed by an instrument called "a lease."
TENDER - An offer of money; an expression of willingness to perform a contract according to its terms.
TERM - When used with reference to a court, it signifies the period of time during which the court holds a session, usually of several weeks or months duration.

TESTAMENTARY - Pertaining to a will or the administration of a will.
TESTATOR (male)
TESTATRIX (female) - One who makes or has made a testament or will.
TESTIFY (TESTIMONY) - To give evidence under oath as a witness.
TO WIT - That is to say; namely.
TORT - Wrong; injury to the person.
TRANSITORY - Passing from place to place.
TRESPASS - Entry into another's ground, illegally.
TRIAL - The examination of a cause, civil or criminal, before a judge who has jurisdiction over it, according to the laws of the land.
TRIER OF FACT - Includes (a) the jury and (b) the court when the court is trying an issue of fact other than one relating to the admissibility of evidence.
TRUST - A right of property, real or personal, held by one party for the benefit of another.
TRUSTEE - One who lawfully holds property in custody for the benefit of another.

U

UNAVAILABLE AS A WITNESS - The declarant is (1) Exempted or precluded on the ground of privilege from testifying concerning the matter to which his statement is relevant; (2) Disqualified from testifying to the matter; (3) Dead or unable to attend or to testify at the hearing because of then existing physical or mental illness or infirmity; (4) Absent from the hearing and the court is unable to compel his attendance by its process; or (5) Absent from the hearing and the proponent of his statement has exercised reasonable diligence but has been unable to procure his attendance by the court's process.
ULTRA VIRES - Acts beyond the scope and power of a corporation, association, etc.
UNILATERAL - One-sided; obligation upon, or act of one party.
USURY - Unlawful interest on a loan.

V

VACATE - To set aside; to move out.
VARIANCE - A discrepancy or disagreement between two instruments or two aspects of the same case, which by law should be consistent.
VENDEE - A purchaser or buyer.
VENDOR - The person who transfers property by sale, particularly real estate; the term "seller" is used more commonly for one who sells personal property.
VENIREMEN - Persons ordered to appear to serve on a jury or composing a panel of jurors.
VENUE - The place at which an action is tried, generally based on locality or judicial district in which an injury occurred or a material fact happened.
VERDICT - The formal decision or finding of a jury.
VERIFY - To confirm or substantiate by oath.
VEST - To accrue to.
VOID - Having no legal force or binding effect.
VOIR DIRE - Preliminary examination of a witness or a juror to test competence, interest, prejudice, etc.

W

WAIVE - To give up a right.
WAIVER - The intentional or voluntary relinquishment of a known right.
WARRANT (WARRANTY) (v.) - To promise that a certain fact or state of facts, in relation to the subject matter, is, or shall be, as it is represented to be.

WARRANT (n.) - A writ issued by a judge, or other competent authority, addressed to a sheriff, or other officer, requiring him to arrest the person therein named, and bring him before the judge or court to answer or be examined regarding the offense with which he is charged.

WRIT - An order or process issued in the name of the sovereign or in the name of a court or judicial officer, commanding the performance or nonperformance of some act.

WRITING - Handwriting, typewriting, printing, photostating, photographing and every other means of recording upon any tangible thing any form of communication or representation, including letters, words, pictures, sounds, or symbols, or combinations thereof.

WRITINGS AND RECORDINGS - Consists of letters, words, or numbers, or their equivalent, set down by handwriting, typewriting, printing, photostating, photographing, magnetic impulse, mechanical or electronic recording, or other form of data compilation.

Y

YEA AND NAY - Yes and no.

YELLOW DOG CONTRACT - A contract by which employer requires employee to sign an instrument promising as condition that he will not join a union during its continuance, and will be discharged if he does join.

Z

ZONING - The division of a city by legislative regulation into districts and the prescription and application in each district of regulations having to do with structural and architectural designs of buildings and of regulations prescribing use to which buildings within designated districts may be put.

www.ingramcontent.com/pod-product-compliance
Lightning Source LLC
Chambersburg PA
CBHW081802300426
44116CB00014B/2215